SCHOOL PHOTOS IN LIQUID TIME

School Photos in Liquid Time

REFRAMING DIFFERENCE

Marianne Hirsch
Leo Spitzer

UNIVERSITY OF WASHINGTON PRESS

Seattle

School Photos in Liquid Time was made possible in part by grants from the Samuel and Althea Stroum Endowed Book Fund and the Capell Family Endowed Book Fund, which supports the publication of books that deepen our understanding of social justice through historical, cultural, and environmental studies.

Printed and bound in the United States of America
Design by Katrina Noble
Composed in NCT Granite, typeface designed by Nathan Zimet
Cover illustration: Marcelo Brodsky, *La Rueca* (The Spinning Wheel), 2017.
(Courtesy of the artist)

24   23   22   21   20   5   4   3   2   1

UNIVERSITY OF WASHINGTON PRESS
uwapress.uw.edu

LIBRARY OF CONGRESS CATALOGING-IN-PUBLICATION DATA

Names: Hirsch, Marianne, 1949- author. | Spitzer, Leo, 1939- author.
Title: School photos in liquid time : reframing difference / Marianne Hirsch, Leo Spitzer.
Description: Seattle : University of Washington Press, [2020] | Series: The Samuel & Althea Stroum lectures in Jewish studies | "A Samuel and Althea Stroum book." | Includes bibliographical references and index. |
Identifiers: LCCN 2019015555 (print) | LCCN 2019019193 (ebook) | ISBN 9780295746555 (ebook) | ISBN 9780295746531 (hardcover : alk. paper) | ISBN 9780295746548 (pbk. : alk. paper)
Subjects: LCSH: School photography—Social aspects. | Children of minorities—Portraits. | Assimilation (Sociology) | Marginality, Social. | Race relations. | Ethnic relations.
Classification: LCC TR818 (ebook) | LCC TR818 .H57 2020 (print) | DDC 779/.25—dc23
LC record available at https://lccn.loc.gov/2019015555

CONTENTS

Plates follow page 132.

ACKNOWLEDGMENTS

> No matter how artful the photographer, no matter how carefully
> posed his subject, the beholder feels an irresistible urge to search
> such a picture for the tiny spark of contingency, of the here and
> now, with which reality has (so to speak) seared the subject, to
> find the inconspicuous spot where in the immediacy of that long-
> forgotten moment the future nests so eloquently that we, looking
> back, may rediscover it.
>
> WALTER BENJAMIN, "A LITTLE HISTORY OF PHOTOGRAPHY"

This book took shape over a number of years by way of multiple conversations between the two of us and with many colleagues—artists, critics,
scholars, and friends who helped us think about school photos as historical
documents of social and political life. If there is an identifiable stimulus for
the start of our project, however, we associate it with a conference titled
"Feeling Photography," organized by Elspeth H. Brown and Thy Phu at the
University of Toronto about a decade ago. Their invitation for us to speak
there, and to consider engaging photography through *feeling* rather than
thinking, paradoxically sent us to the strictly conventional and institutional
genre of school photography. The invitation prompted us both to look at
our own class photos within our family albums and to ask what feelings
these seemingly flat and opaque images might evoke and transmit. Each of
us hoped to find in them what it *felt* like to become the subject of school as
an institution, and of a generational cohort, during turbulent political times.

The rich conversations at this transformative international conference
continued in numerous additional gatherings. An invitation by Noam

Pianko and the University of Washington's Stroum Center for Jewish Studies to deliver the annual Stroum Lectures inspired us to explore a remarkable and moving archive of photos of school children taken in the Jewish ghettos in Nazi-occupied Europe during the Second World War. Placing these images into a deeper historical and connective frame induced us to think about how the history of Jewish assimilation and exclusion, and resistance and refusal, might be linked to that of other groups throughout world. We are grateful for these invitations and many others that helped us expand the shape of this inquiry.

The provocative discussions with students and colleagues in seminars at Princeton University, the University of Chicago, Harvard University, and the Holocaust Education Foundation at Northwestern University have been invaluable, as have questions and responses to talks at Dartmouth College, New York University, the University of Massachusetts Amherst, Heinrich Heine University Düsseldorf, Cornell University, Colby College, Kean University, the University of Ghent, Monash University in Melbourne, the University of Konstanz, and the Catholic University and the Columbia Global Center in Santiago, Chile. We are most grateful to Dirk Hartog, Agnes Lugo-Ortiz, Susan Suleiman, Svetlana Boym, Sarah Cushman, Silvia Spitta, Jo Labanyi, James Young, Susan Winnett, Jonathan Boyarin, Dennis B. Klein, Stef Craps, Mark Baker, Noah Shenker, Aleida and Jan Assmann, and Milena Grass for their incisive suggestions during what for us were motivating visits and residencies.

We also greatly benefited from discussions at the conferences "Framing Lives" at the Australian National University at Canberra, "The Dynamics of Cultural Remembrance" in Utrecht, "Transnational Holocaust Memory" in Leeds, and at meetings of the Modern Language Association and the American Comparative Literature Association. These occasions allowed us to research and write different sections of the book and to think further and deeper about the work that school photos do. We thank Rosanne Kennedy, Ann Rigney, Jay Prosser, Michael Rothberg, and Debarati Sanyal for their invitations and suggestions.

At each point, our thinking and writing has been in dialogue with the work of the brilliant artists we discuss in the book who have reframed and commented on school photos, revealing their rich and multiple dimensions.

We are fortunate and grateful to be able to collaborate on an ongoing basis with Lorie Novak and Mirta Kupferminc. We also want to thank Marcelo Brodsky, Carrie Mae Weems, and Tomoko Sawada for their help and Christian Boltanski, Vik Muniz, Adrian Piper, and Marjane Satrapi for their inspiration. Steven Deo and David Wojnarowicz left images that have touched us deeply.

The Engendering Archives and the Women Mobilizing Memory working groups at Columbia's Center for the Study of Social Difference, as well as the University Seminar on Cultural Memory, have been generative intellectual companions during the years in which this book took shape, and we are grateful to all of their members and especially to their co-conveners, Saidiya Hartman, Jean Howard, Tina Campt, Laura Wexler, Diana Taylor, Ayşe Gül Altinay, Andreas Huyssen, Jenny James, Sonali Thakkar, Alyssa Greene, and Daniella Wurst. Discussions about the work of photography and visual culture with Ariella Azoulay, Susan Meiselas, Patricia Hayes, and Griselda Pollock, in addition to those we have already named, have spurred our thinking at each stage.

The publication of this book is accompanied by an exhibit at Dartmouth's Hood Museum of Art titled "School Photos and Their Afterlives," January–April 2020. We are grateful to the museum, and especially to Juliette Bianco, Katherine Hart, Amelia Kahl, and John Stomberg, for the opportunity to display this material in this context and for their generous professional engagement. Mieke Bal, Banu Karaca, Barbara Kirshenblatt-Gimblett, Işin Önol, and Brian Wallis have thoughtfully consulted on the exhibition conception and design with us, and Deborah Willis has supported both the exhibit and the book with illuminating suggestions and wonderful connections.

Over the course of our school photo project, a number of people have read portions and drafts of this work offering incisive observations, critiques, and specialized knowledge. Jane Coppock, our lifelong friend, was a stimulating interlocutor and constructive critical reader of the entire manuscript. A special debt of gratitude goes to Laura Wexler, who has inspired and accompanied our work on photography since its beginnings, and who provided invigorating support and critique for manuscript revisions. We also benefited from the suggestions of two anonymous readers for the University of Washington Press. Nicole Gervasio's editorial assistance came at a crucial moment. We could not have completed this book without the immensely generous and efficient editorial expertise, once again, of Gail Patten. She also provided vital help in securing images and reproduction rights from innumerable archives across the globe. Our gratitude extends to the many archivists who have so kindly responded to these requests. It has been a great pleasure to work with the University of Washington Press. We thank Larin McLaughlin, Caitlin Tyler-Richards, and their collaborators in every department, who have been patient, generous, responsive, and impeccably professional at every point. Jennifer Comeau's outstanding editing has improved this book immeasurably.

Parts of this book were written with support of fellowships from the intellectually invigorating spaces of the Stellenbosch Institute for Advanced Study in South Africa and the Liguria Study Center of the Bogliasco Foundation in Italy. We are enormously grateful to both institutions for hosting us in such beautiful and generative settings.

During the process of writing this book we have had the chance to think not only about photography but also about schooling—about what schooling means to students and to teachers. Our discussion of every image in the book is inflected by our attention to the children depicted and our commitment to their well-being, as well as by our critical engagement with the institutions that frame them. Many of the children depicted in the images we discuss suffered immeasurable losses, but our readings try to do justice not only to loss but also to the more hopeful futures they were envisioning as they faced the cameras. In Walter Benjamin's resonant terms, we attempted, at each point, "to search . . . [their] picture[s] for the tiny spark of contingency, of the here and now, with which reality has (so to speak) seared the subject, to find the inconspicuous spot where in the immediacy of . . . long-forgotten moment[s] the future nests so eloquently that we, looking back, may rediscover it."

In our own roles as teachers, parents, and grandparents, we have been able to observe from close up the importance of school in every child and young adult's life. Our students, our children, and our grandchildren, and their unstinting enthusiasm for learning, have been invaluable companions, and we thank them for the hope and affirmation they continue to offer us.

The cover image of this book illustrates this future-oriented affirmation. In *La Rueca* (The Spinning Wheel), the artist Marcelo Brodsky reworks a photograph, taken in the Ukrainian town of Kajovka around 1908, of his grandmother, Rosa Mascevitch, and her classmates in a training school for teachers of Russian. Rosa arrived in Argentina in 1914 and lived in the southern city of Bahia Blanca, working in the English General Store and raising her family. Marcelo Brodsky reworks the archival class photo to highlight the young assimilated Jewish women's love of Russian and their fantasy of becoming Pushkin, Dostoevsky, or Tolstoy. Yet he also includes, and in fact names his image after, the spinning wheel that even young intellectual women needed to learn how to use. "The century is beginning," Brodsky imagines the women thinking, and his lively and playful use of color and writing infuses their rather earnest class photo with hope and confidence in new beginnings.

Parts of the introduction and chapters 2 and 4 were previously published in "About School Photos," *Nomadikon* (www.nomadikon.net/contentitem .aspx?ci=162); "Das Nachleben der Schulfotos," in *Sehen-Macht-Wissen: ReSaVoir. Bilder im Spannungsfeld von Kultur, Politik und Erinnerung*, edited by Angelika Bartl, Josch Hoenes, Patricia Mühr, and Kea Wienand (Bielefeld: Transcript, 2011); "School Pictures and Their Afterlives," in *Feeling Photography*, edited by Elspeth Brown and Thy Phu (Durham: Duke University Press, 2014); and "The Afterlife of Class Photos: Schooling, Assimilation, Exclusion," in *Partizipation und Exklusion: Zur Habsburger Prägung von Sprache und Bildung in der Bukowina*, edited by Markus Winkler (Regensburg: Verlag Friedrich Puster, 2016).

SCHOOL PHOTOS IN LIQUID TIME

The word *school* still carried a faint whiff of hope.

YOKO TAWADA

Introduction

I look for my childhood self in two tattered school photographs from the early years of my family's refuge in La Paz, Bolivia, and I see a somber-looking boy amid a group of unsmiling children and adults.

The two photos have captions written by my father in German on the back—"Schule [school] Miraflores 1944" and "Poldi 5 Jahre [Leo, 5 years old], Kindergarten." Both photos were taken outdoors, probably on the same day, in a stone-paved yard in front of a weather-beaten and discolored whitewashed adobe wall, with a scattering of houses and the cloud-heavy Altiplano mountain plateau visible in the background. The building where we lived in an apartment overlooking the school is on the immediate right. The photo depicting a larger assemblage (fig. I.1, top) shows all the day students and teachers in the "Kinderheim"—the "Children's Home" sponsored for Jewish refugee children in La Paz by the American Jewish Joint Distribution Committee in New York; the other one (fig. I.1, bottom) shows only my kindergarten class, our teachers and their aides, and some two dozen preschool infants who attended the institution during their parents' working hours.

Nowadays I recognize only one other child in the photos, the light blond Yoram Warmuth, who is standing next to me and would later become one of my best friends in La Paz, and one adult, the young teacher's assistant Ilse Herz (second from the left in the kindergarten photo), whom I met

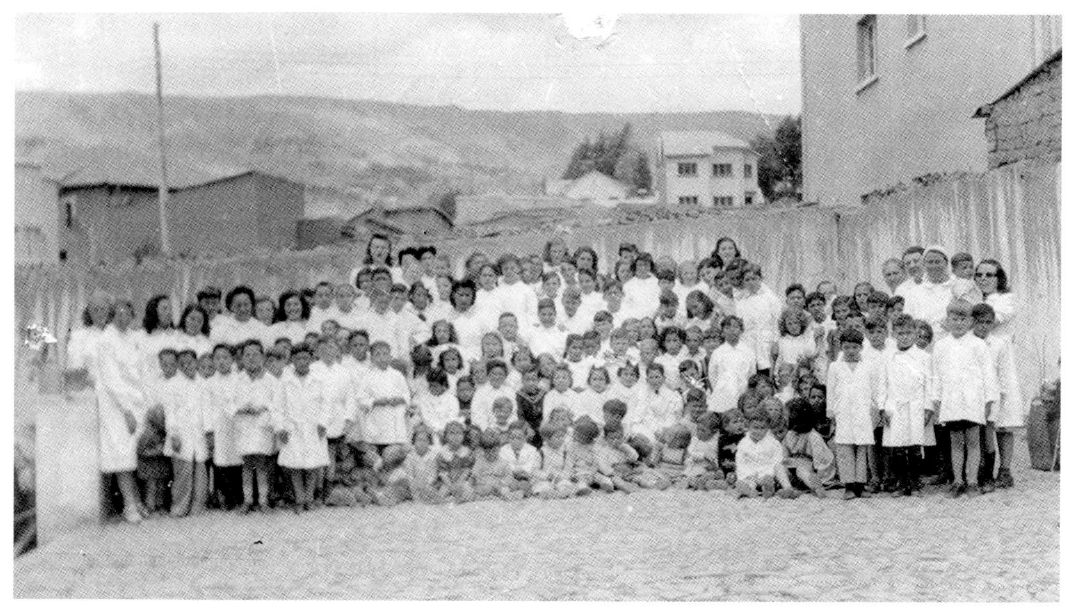

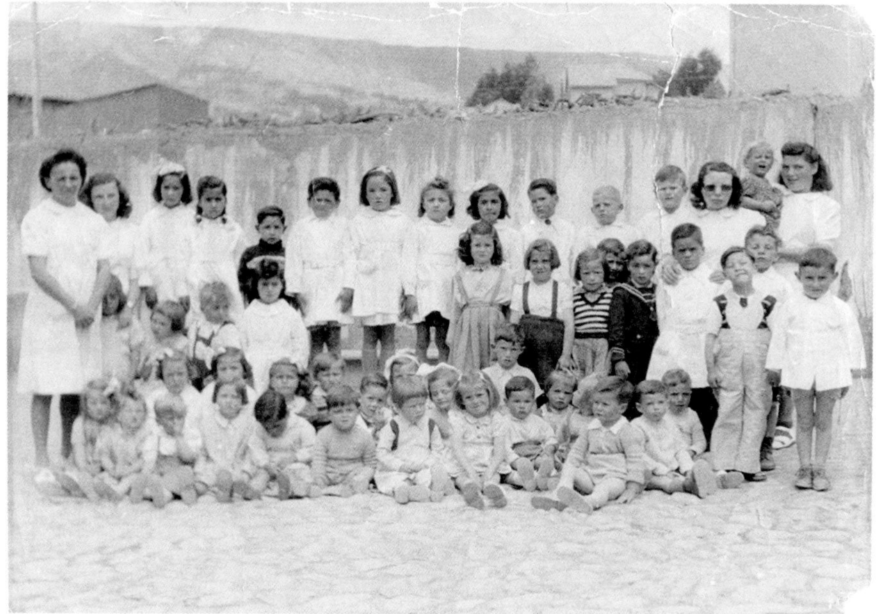

FIGURE I.1. Before Poldi became Leo. My first school photos, at the *Kinderheim* in a cheerless time. La Paz, Bolivia, 1944. I stand first on right, front row (*above*) and fourth from right, top row (*below*). (Spitzer collection)

again almost fifty years later in Ardsley, New York, and interviewed for my book Hotel Bolivia.[1] *I can no longer remember the names of the teacher wearing sunglasses or the stern-looking woman on the far left of the kindergarten picture. But I do recall that my mother later revealed to me that the stern one was the teacher who told my parents that I was a difficult child, perhaps even a slow one, because I was unreceptive to the routines and unmindful of the rules that the Kinderheim's adults tried to establish for us.*

The majority of us in the kindergarten class—as well as our teachers— are wearing white apron coats in the photos, the requisite uniform in Bolivian schools at the time. Unlike in more elite institutions, our uniforms bore no identifying school insignia proudly displaying the school's name and motto. While they served to protect our clothing underneath, their primary purpose was to mask differences among us: the slightly better-off children and those from more impoverished homes were equalized behind the apron coats and their depersonalizing whiteness.

But what is most striking about my school images is the fact that hardly a person in them is smiling. Almost everyone looks solemn, serious, largely cheerless, unhappy. This, by the early 1940s, had nothing to do with photographic technology—with slow film or slow shutter speeds that in earlier decades had made it easier to take photos of serious faces than of those with natural smiles that were harder to sustain. Nor did it reflect an older, more formal portrait convention that encouraged dignity over a grinning frivolity.[2] The cheerlessness in these two photos may well have mirrored the general bleak atmosphere of the Kinderheim—a joyless institution in my memory, whose staff seemed much more concerned with establishing order and maintaining discipline than with our instruction or imaginative potential. And it definitely reflected the general gloom and uncertainty pervading the times—the ongoing world war and the repeated, traumatic confirmations of the horrors that would later be named the Holocaust.

The fact was that all of us in these photos were either recent refugees or (like me) children of recent refugees born in the land that had granted our parents a haven. All the teachers, their assistants, and the older children in the group had fled from Europe only a few years earlier and had directly or indirectly experienced Nazi intimidation and persecution in the homelands from which they were displaced. Every day, news about the war and the fate of relatives and loved ones left behind made its way to Bolivia and fueled our parents' conversations and apprehensions. There was certainly no way that their fears and sorrows could be hidden from us children. In our family, it was during the months that we lived in the Miraflores apartment above the Kinderheim that we received confirmation that my father's half-sister, Gisi, her husband, Leopold, and their youngest daughter, Rosi, had been killed after being transported from Vienna to Riga.

The bleakness in which we children were enveloped thus pierced images even as conventional as our school photographs. And yet, although these photos were taken in a traumatic period of dire uncertainty, the Bolivian Kinderheim images do reveal qualities characterizing school photography more generally. Childhood vulnerability, the social integrationist effects of schooling, the process of creating community and group identity, the promise of a future—all these are reflected within these images. They mark a particular moment of transition for us children, for our parents, and for the place where they were produced.

SCHOOL PHOTOGRAPHY IN TIMES OF EXTREMITY

The conformity of the Bolivian Kinderheim pictures to the genre of school photography may precisely be the motivation for why they were produced and distributed and why they survived in official and family archives. Both images can also be found in the archives of the American Joint Distribution Committee (popularly known as "the Joint"), an organization that supported Jewish refugees during the Second World War and helped fund the Kinderheim as well as numerous other Jewish refugee organizations and activities throughout the world. These images were made for the Joint, but they also became memorial objects for the children and their families. Their reproductions could be sent to relatives dispersed in other parts of the world, and they could be saved in hope that family members, long unheard from, might somehow survive the war and view them. The Kinderheim photos would communicate to all who viewed them that even as the parents' world of origin was being destroyed, the children were safe, healthy, cared for, learning in ordinary circumstances of everyday life, looking to the future.

This message of continuity would also have been highly meaningful for officials of the Joint Distribution Committee, who used them to apprise their organization's donors. The Joint required regular reports about activities they supported, and its officials needed visual materials from places of refuge in order to advertise and gain additional funding for their humanitarian work.

The Kinderheim images, however—serving specific memorial and utilitarian functions relating to the Bolivian refuge but congruent with the photographic camera setup of outdoor school pictures taken elsewhere—also connect historically to images that are more painful to see and more difficult to understand: school photographs, taken around the very same period in the early 1940s, in wartime Europe and the United States. They are images of children who were not able to escape persecution and incarceration but who nevertheless persisted in attending school.

Three of these European and North American photographs (figures I.2–I.4) can illustrate both their kinship with, and their profound difference from, the contemporaneous Bolivian Kinderheim pictures. Like many other school photos, these too show students grouped around one or more authority figures, their teacher or teachers; children assembled outdoors near a building, possibly their school; and pupils engaged in class lessons.

But a closer, more deliberate look at these photos is jarring. In two of them, the children and adults depicted are wearing a Star of David on a lapel—the "Jew Star," as the Nazis derisively renamed it, the emblematic mark of difference and subordination imposed on Jews throughout Nazi-occupied Europe. In the third, we see barracks and barbed wire fences outside the schoolroom window. The incongruity between these disorienting details and the photos' apparent conventionality as school pictures demands both contextualization and explanation.

Like the Kinderheim images, these were produced in circumstances of political extremity. The first two were taken in 1941 and 1942 in Eastern European ghettos that Nazi authorities established for Jews after Germany invaded and defeated Poland. One was taken by a Nazi official who was an amateur photographer. The second was probably a clandestine photo snapped by a member of an underground organization in the Kovno ghetto in Lithuania. And the third was taken in one of the US concentration camps established in 1942 to incarcerate Japanese Americans after the attack on Pearl Harbor and the outbreak of the war in the Pacific.

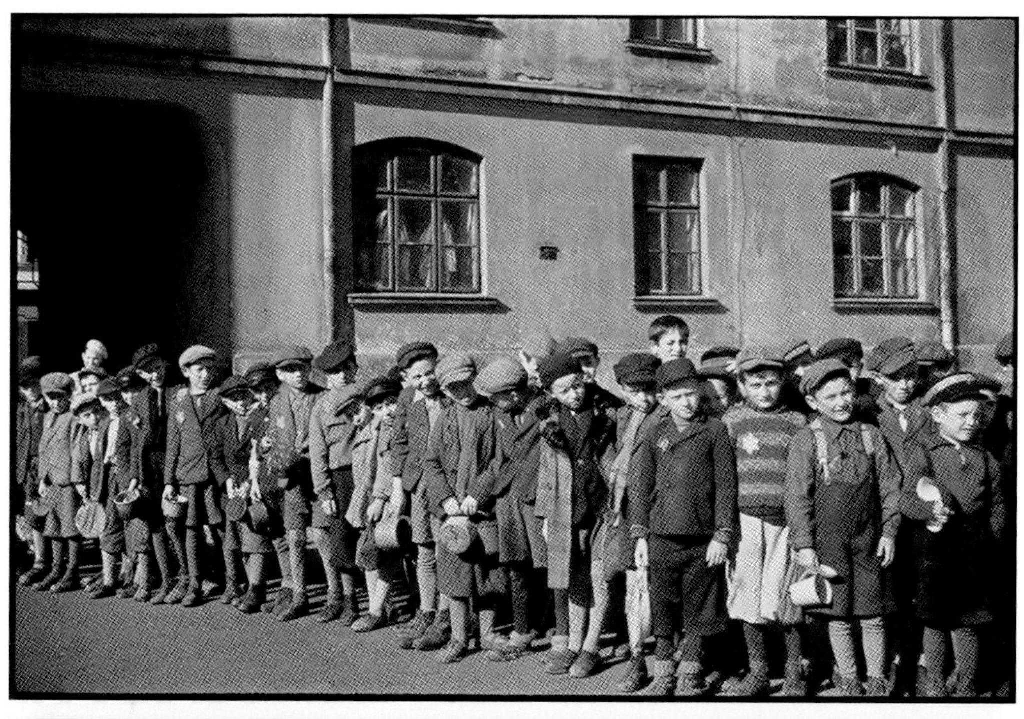

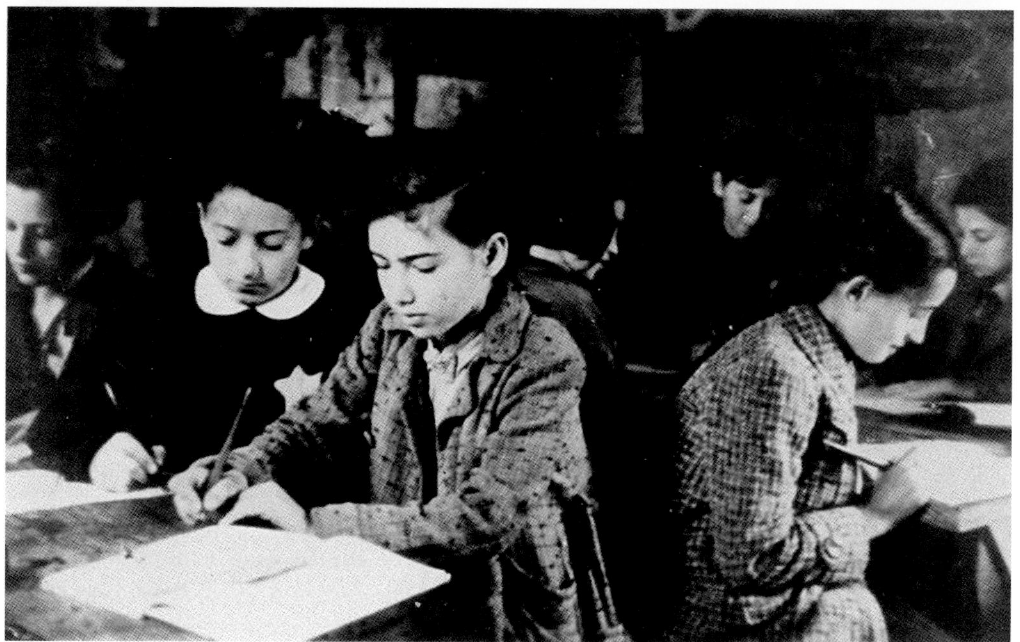

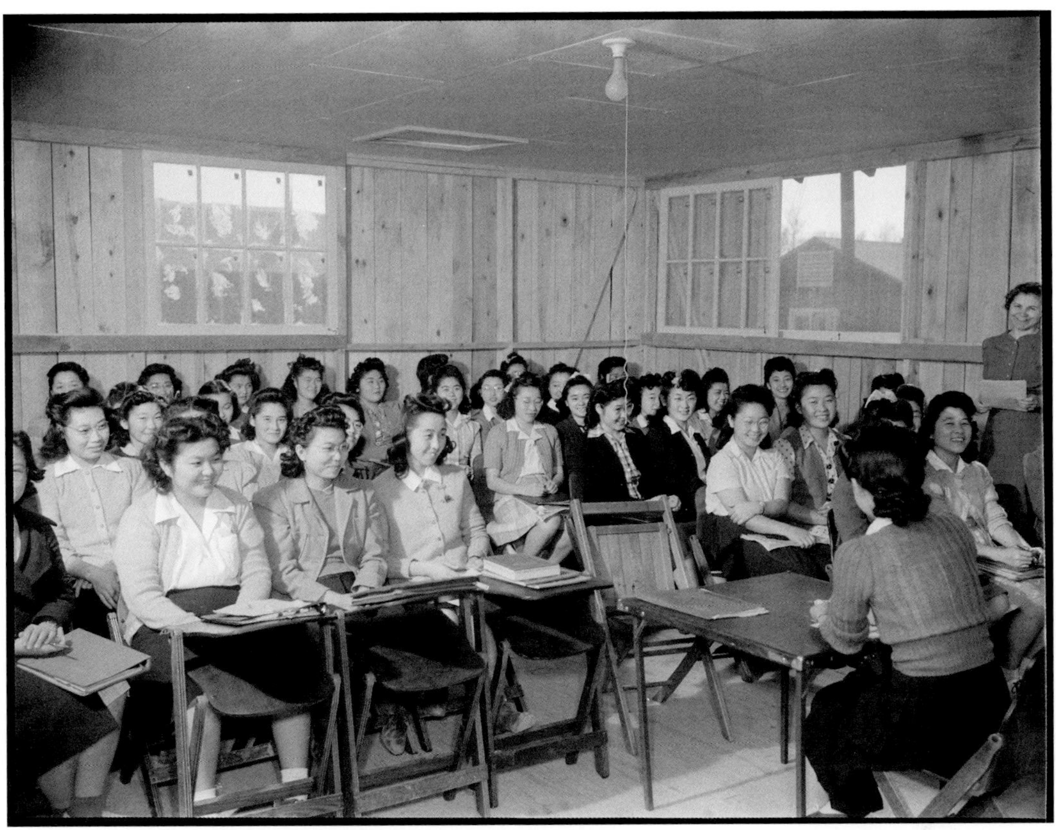

FIGURE 1.2 *(opposite, above).* *Schulausspeisung* (school lunch), Lódz ghetto, Poland, 1941. Photo by Nazi official Walter Genewein. See also plate 9. (Jewish Museum Frankfurt, Photo Archives)

FIGURE 1.3 *(opposite, below).* Clandestine school, Kovno ghetto, Lithuania, 1941–42. Photo possibly by David Chaim Ratner. (United States Holocaust Memorial Museum, courtesy of Eliezer Zilberis)

FIGURE 1.4 *(above).* The girls of Grade 12-A in home economics class, November 25, 1942; Mrs. Mildred Howell, teacher. Rohwer Relocation Center, McGehee, Arkansas. Photo by Tom Parker. (National Archives)

What can help us understand these incongruous images? Why, in circumstances when photography was curtailed by Nazi and US authorities, were they taken and saved? What function did they serve? Who were their envisioned viewers? And how might images taken of school pupils in circumstances of extreme xenophobia and persecution enhance how we understand the parameters of oppression, resistance, and the transmission of cultural memory through photography?

Certainly, it is hard not to read these wartime images through the retrospective lens of our knowledge of what came to be: as photos of young and teenage children looking toward a future that either would be cut short or would be marked by trauma transmitted across generations. And indeed, second-generation French artist Christian Boltanski provides such a reading.

Repeatedly using school photos of Jewish children from the years closely preceding World War II in his artistic work, he has shaped a postcatastrophic, post-Holocaust, postmemorial aesthetic based on the retrospective historical knowledge of catastrophic loss and impending annihilation. Conveying that tragic knowledge, Boltanski's artistic installations in his *Lessons of Darkness* series (for example, fig. I.5), consist of individual faces cropped out of group school photos and enlarged to a point where they lose all resolution. Stripped of their specificity and disaggregated from their class community, these enlarged faces are set into new groupings on walls, or mounted on biscuit boxes, or printed on white sheets. The aggressive incandescent lightbulbs with conspicuously exposed electrical cords with which he illuminates the children's blurred countenances jarringly evoke interrogation lamps, producing what Ernst van Alphen has termed a "Holocaust effect."[3] Boltanski has always maintained that his art is not "about" the Holocaust; it is "after." In this sense, it has helped generate an aftermath aesthetic of loss and mourning in which children's faces become ghostlike projections that haunt the archival photographs from which they have been cropped.[4] Indeed, even if some, or even many, of the children in the original school images survived, they are marked by the death they were not supposed to have evaded.[5] In this regard, Boltanski's installations illustrate Roland Barthes's well-known assertion: "By giving me the absolute past of the pose (aorist), the photograph tells me death in the future."[6]

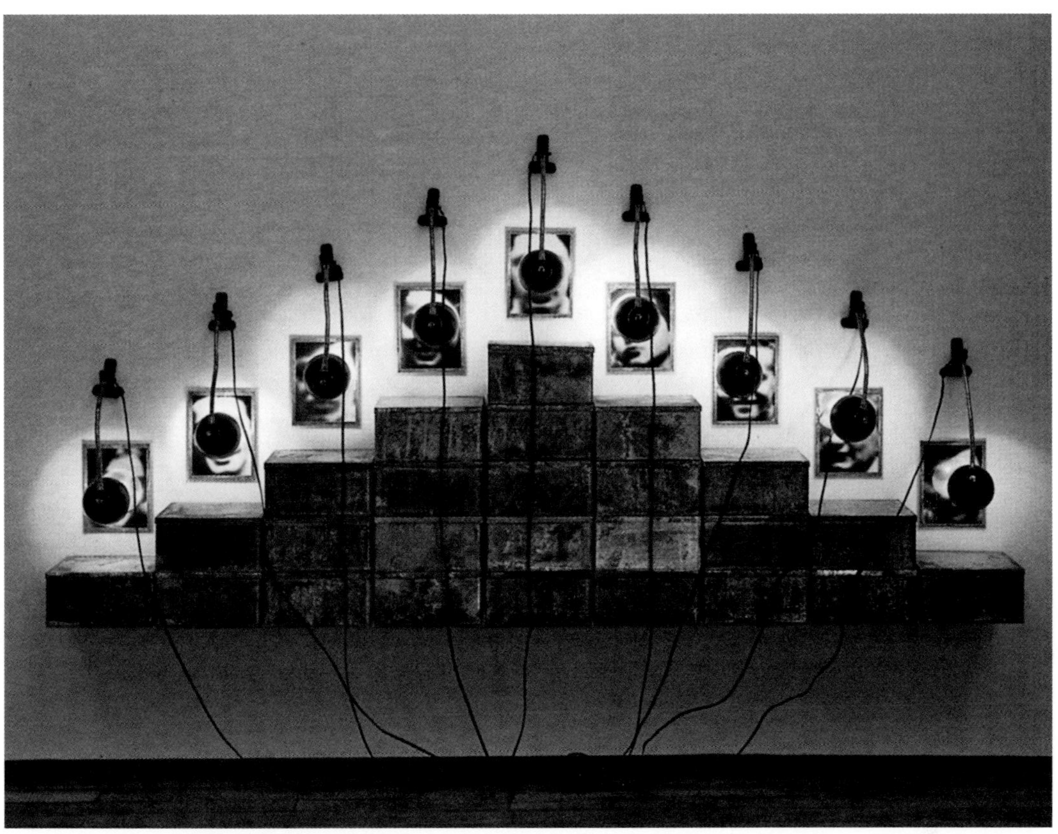

FIGURE I.5. Christian Boltanski, *Autel Chases*, 1988. See also plate 1. (© 2019 Artist Rights Society [ARS] New York / ADAGP, Paris)

Yet what happens if we try to view photographs of schoolchildren in these extreme circumstances differently: not as images of children about to die or doomed to lead traumatized lives but simply as class photos—examples of the largely unremarked genre of school photography itself? Such a reading of school photos in times of extremity—one not limited to memories of one specific history but more broadly comparative and connective—will also enable us to return to Boltanski's installations later in our narrative. Looking at his work again as a reframing not of pictures of child victims but of *school pictures* will enable us to find a less purely elegiac and a more politically forceful intervention. Along with several other contemporary artists who reframe school pictures, Boltanski thus becomes a guide in exploring the genre.

Like all photographs, school photographs do more than document the event of their production. Usually they generate a sense of a future in which they will be looked at—by the photographed subjects and their descendants, and by others interested in the history they tell. They thus serve as memorial objects, measuring time and progress, survival and loss, breaks and continuities. But class pictures taken in times of extremity, like these photos from World War II ghettos and concentration camps, show us that in their future, they can also serve as documents of injustice and accusation—objects to be mobilized for action toward justice and repair.

Images of children who may not survive to look back at them as adults inhabit what we think of as a liquid temporality. The idea of "liquid time," inspired by the artist Jeff Wall's essay "Photography and Liquid Intelligence," derives from the developing process for analog photographs.[7] In a darkroom, where this procedure normally takes place, both the camera's film and the photosensitive paper onto which the film's image has been projected are immersed and developed in a liquid solution. Until they are chemically "fixed" into permanence, they change and transform in subtle and unexpected ways. When Wall wrote his essay in the late 1980s, he wanted to mark the beginnings of the digital turn in photography, which introduced a different technological and temporal regime from the analog one, effecting, as he argues, a "new displacement of water in photography." But Wall also wanted to complicate the pervasive view of photography as an inexorable apparatus and tool of ideological power and domination, embodying a "dry" and thus *unalterable* optical and technological "intelligence." In highlighting the photograph's "liquid intelligence" instead, he revealed its connection to nature and water, and thus the contingencies, affective registers, and possibilities for change of the photographic image-making process.[8]

School pictures are institutional technologies, shaped by an institutional gaze that frames children, making them into subjects of schooling and the state. Like report cards, they measure time dryly, picturing linear progress from one school year to the next. They can be read as evidence of that progress, in the sense that Roland Barthes discusses photographic evidence when he insists that the photograph bears witness to a "ça a été," a "this has been"—"that instant, however brief, in which a real thing happened to be motionless in front of the eye." For Barthes this is the "very essence" of photography.[9] But Barthes also inspires a different, less motionless and more fluid, reading of the photograph's evidentiary qualities when he considers the medium of light as a form of connection between the viewer and the photographed object. The photograph, he muses, is "not a 'copy' of reality, but . . . an emanation of past reality: a magic, not an art."[10]

Stressing water rather than light, Jeff Wall echoes Barthes's invocation of archaic and alchemical traces that shape photography's connection to the past and thus to time. It is here that we derive the notion of photography's "liquid temporality," which school photos, as group images of children, embody and illustrate. Images of schoolchildren show us not only the past in which they were taken but the present and the futures contained in that past, futures that their diverse subjects may have been envisioning.[11] They challenge a conception of time as linear, precisely because they show children's development: some children do not grow forward, grade by grade, in modernity's mandated progressive narrative. As Katherine Bond Stockton has argued, for example, children often "queer" the temporality of what is considered an ordinary life, growing "sideways" rather than "up."[12]

Over time, moreover, we might say that photographs keep developing in unforeseen directions when they are viewed and re-viewed by different people in different presents. In "liquid time" they are not fixed into static permanence; rather, they remain dynamic, unfixed, as they acquire new meanings, in new circumstances. And as they do so, they can also reveal a great deal about their subjects and about their viewers, enabling us to perceive the queerness of the child, as well as the interruptions of kinship, generation, and progress caused by prejudice, persecution, and state violence. Wall poetically suggests this reflexivity when he writes that "in photography, the liquids study us, even from a great distance."[13]

Such a "liquid" and multitemporal reading displaces the retrospective gaze, shadowed by a known and predetermined outcome, that has dominated critical approaches to images of past violence, war, and genocide.[14] Indeed, if we read them in this more open-ended fashion, what do these incongruous wartime images allow us to discover about the textures of life during the Second World War and the Holocaust? What, more broadly, can school pictures taken in troubled times tell us about photography's role in shaping the social institutions of modernity and their practices of social inclusion and exclusion—practices that morph into a violent extreme during the Second World War? Is photography continuing to play a similar role today?

These are some of the questions animating this book. Written in response to, though not exclusively about, the remarkable archive we have assembled of photos taken in World War II ghettos and concentration camps, it is a work of cultural postmemory.[15] *Postmemory*, we have argued, describes the relationship that subsequent generations bear to the personal, collective, and cultural trauma or transformation of those who came before—to events that they "remember" only by means of the stories, images, and behaviors among which they grew up. But these events were transmitted to them so deeply and affectively as to seem to constitute memories in their own right. Postmemory's connection to the past is thus mediated not by recall but by imaginative investment, projection, and creation—by what Robert Jay Lifton has called "formulation" for survivors of catastrophic histories.[16] To grow up with such overwhelming inherited memories is to be shaped, however indirectly, by traumatic fragments of events that defy narrative reconstruction and exceed comprehension. These events happened in the past, but their effects continue in liquid time into the present. This is certainly the case for descendants of World War II survivors.

Group photos, such as school photos, play an important role in postmemorial efforts to reanimate lost communities and to measure the extent of the loss, as well as the determination to resist and continue in the face of present or imminent catastrophe. Descendants' efforts to reconstruct lost lifeworlds often rely on school pictures, if those are available.[17] Significantly, however, none of the photo archives we searched had indexed these incongruous wartime images as school or class photos. Some, especially the Japanese American ones, were cataloged under "wartime relocation," the photographer's name, or "internment camps." Many others were organized under a general category like "ghetto photos," "photos of children," or simply "camps." Many were donated to archives like Yad Vashem or the United States Holocaust

Memorial Museum by persons who survived their devastating wartime experience, or by the descendants of teachers or depicted students. Their labels give information about these donors but, in the case of the Jewish ghettos, they are often of little or no help in providing details about the photographs themselves—especially about those astonishing ones produced clandestinely under severe danger: Who took them? How and when were they developed? How did they survive? How do they resonate with school photos taken elsewhere in different times of extremity? How are we to read them?

These questions are especially relevant now, in the present of this writing, with its own forms of social exclusion and incarceration. School-age children in refugee camps and holding facilities are particularly affected: in an August 2018 report, the United Nations Refugee Agency found that of approximately 7.4 million refugee children of school age, 4 million were currently out of school, and that only 61 percent of refugee children attend primary school—despite the fact that both the 1951 Refugee Convention and the 1989 Convention on the Rights of the Child stipulated that education is a human right.[18] When that right is endangered, as it often is in situations of political conflict and persecution, school photos can be used as claims for educational justice.

In 2018 some Palestinian refugee schools, for example, were closed when the United States withdrew funding for UNRWA, the United Nations Relief and Works Agency for Palestine Refugees in the Near East.[19] UNRWA currently educates about fifty thousand students across the West Bank, many in refugee camps, many belonging to a second or third generation of students born and raised in the camps. UNRWA school closures would leave many of these students without a chance to study. Protests against school closures in these camps and throughout the West Bank have produced powerful visual documents of children claiming their right to schooling.

Conversely, the lack of school photos becomes a telling sign of educational failure. In another current case, although US federal law mandates that children seeking asylum in the United States be educated while detained in shelters and holding facilities, school conditions in these facilities are appalling and programs are severely underfunded. Journalists' access is curtailed, and many of the shelters are rarely seen by members of the public, who are thus unable to assess the availability and quality of education.[20] The lack of school pictures in the US refugee context is counterbalanced by the abundance of photos published by the United Nations of schoolchildren in refugee camps across the globe. The hundreds of school photos of smiling refugee children who are receiving an education do some of the same political work as the historical images we are discussing in this book.

EVERYDAY PHOTOS

Searching for ways to understand the production and survival of these historical photos taken in times of extremity, and their relevance for today, led us to consider closely the utterly conventional genre of school photography—to think about what school pictures *do*. This book addresses these questions textually, theoretically, and historically from a broadly comparative and connective perspective. Focusing in particular on photography's role in advancing ideologies of assimilation and exclusion, it places the history of Jews in conversation with the histories of other minority or persecuted subjects in different imperial and national centers across the globe. It views the images of Jewish children in Nazi ghettos and the Japanese American children incarcerated in US camps in a larger context of school photos taken elsewhere in situations of peril and subordination: native and black children in late nineteenth- and early twentieth-century North America, and African, Asian, and Australian children in the era of European colonial domination.

School photos appear surprisingly early in the development of photography. Pervasive worldwide in communities that enjoyed the means to memorialize their educational institutions, these photographic images have attracted no critical attention. No doubt due to their strict conventions, uniformity, and seriality, they are virtually absent from histories of photography and mostly also ignored as historical sources. Their largely uniform surfaces seem as opaque as their meanings seem obvious.

School photos share many qualities with family and other institutional photographs that play instrumental social roles—images whose meanings need to be unpacked because they seem so transparent. Such images are most frequently categorized and referred to as "vernacular" photographs. In a groundbreaking essay defining vernacular photography in 2000, Geoffrey Batchen uses the term to categorize "ordinary," "everyday," "popular," and "utilitarian" photographs that are left out of art museums and are, in his terms, often "repressed" in histories of photography. Yet, he argues, these images show photography as a popular everyday practice and should be accorded serious critical attention.[21] This early distinction of "vernacular" from "art" photography relies, we believe, on a problematic judgment of the photographer's intention, ambition, or quality. Even if its definition necessarily remains vague, the term *vernacular* is enjoying great critical purchase: it fulfills a need for a more general category into which everyday photos can be grouped. Batchen's essay is credited with authorizing the lively current critical interest in "vernacular" photographic practices, both personal and institutional. Yet his 2000 intervention followed a decade or more of theoretical attention to the ideological uses of photography to categorize and discipline social subjects, by artists who reframe everyday images and by scholars analyzing the social workings of gender, sexuality, race, class, ability, and power. The very development of the field of "visual culture"—a field that views images and image making as performative practices not only recording but shaping everyday life—is intricately tied to everyday, or "vernacular," photographic acts.[22] And yet, school photos have been left out of these conversations entirely.

In this book, we discuss school photos as "everyday" and "instrumental," even as we try to avoid reifying or generalizing anything that might constitute the "everyday" or "ordinary."[23] Eschewing a ready-made general definitional category encompassing a great variety of images serving distinct social and artistic functions enables us to think more about what school photos *do* than about how they might be classified.

This book looks particularly at school photos taken in times of social and political crisis or transformation. Such photos break through the seemingly uniform surfaces of images conforming to strict conventions, compelling us to pause over them—to look and listen more slowly, deeply, and attentively than their uniformity would on first glance invite. Indeed, in Ariella Azoulay's terms, they compel us not just to look but to "watch" them, as though we were watching a moving picture, not a still one, thus considering "dimensions of time and movement."[24] As vehicles of postmemory, photographs demand a scrupulous reading practice, one attentive to the photographer's identity, the historical and political context, the image's institutional framing, and the possibilities of unfixing and reframing its meanings over time. They enjoin us, as retrospective viewers, to address, and to resist, the determinative power of the photographer's gaze in framing children into institutional subjects, and to resist also the seeming inevitability of those institutions' inequalities and social stratifications. Thus reinserted into the contingencies of "liquid time," they bid us to form affective connections with the photographed children themselves, reclaiming their forgotten stories, imagining what they see as they face the camera, sensing their life and their imagined future that persists beyond the constraints of the photographic frame. To do so, we must confront the violence that shapes image archives of social exclusion, discrimination, and persecution and develop ways of looking that do not replicate that violence.[25] And we must develop a reading practice that both exposes photography's institutional and instrumental functions and encounters the images through the eyes of the subjects who are photographed and framed— a reading practice sensitive to institutional constraints and to the possibilities, pleasure, and freedom that children find in the act of learning.

In this book, we combine archival work, historical interpretation, and detailed attention to individual images to explore photography's role in staging social difference and hierarchy in the visual realm. We use individual images emerging from specific historical moments as case studies that might help us understand the connections between different moments in which practices of social assimilation and exclusion have occasioned photographic practices that have helped shape them. Our access to these histories and archives is both personal and scholarly. The book is coauthored, and the two of us appear in it both individually, with our own photographs and our own personal relation to them, and jointly, as writers committed to a scholarly practice that we share as we combine our training in literary and cultural studies and comparative history. If we use the first person singular and images from our own archives, it is to testify to the effects and the emotional experience of being photographed as a subject of school. We hope also to activate our readers' interest in their own class pictures, salvaging them from the anonymity into which they so readily fall and reinserting them into history. The first person, singular and plural, is meant to model a particular kind of embodied and affective reading practice that is historical, contextual, and scholarly. The "we" in these pages thus reflects the two of us as authors, as well as the circle of readers whom we invite to join us in exploring school photos. It is important to point out that our own biographies relate specifically to the Jewish history this book tells, a history of which each of us is a product. But our analysis of the images emerging from this and other histories is based on our research and on a desire to look, watch, and listen to the voices of the children depicted in these photos in the full context of their particular sociocultural circumstances and experiences.

In the chapters that follow, we turn to historical and memorial accounts of schooling's role in the assimilation and exclusion of colonized and racially "othered" populations to understand how class pictures further these processes. Conversely, we also turn to class pictures to disrupt, enlarge, reframe, and complicate those accounts. We thus establish a multifaceted dialogue between photography and history, seeing photographs as historical and memorial documents and sources, to be sure, but seeing them also as historical actors.

Specifically, the following chapters consider a number of late nineteenth- and twentieth-century images and accounts from schools educating Jews in Central Europe as well as from institutions set up to transform colonial subjects in Africa as well as indigenous and African American children in North America. The pervasive genre of school photography and, indeed, the role of photography in different histories of assimilationism invite this comparative/connective approach. At the same time, we are eager not to obscure important differences in the modern histories of imperial and racialized subjects, as well as differences between the chronology and ideology of assimilationism that affected them and in which they participated. To that end, we prefer the notion of "connective" to "comparative" history, precisely to avoid the implication that these histories of assimilation and persecution are easily comparable. Each has its own starting points and specificities. Yet there are clear historical and structural points of connection between them, as imperial and national regimes employ similar tactics to address their heterogeneous populations and to practice social inclusion and exclusion. The exposure and analysis of these connections is a distinctive feature of this book.

It is surprising that as absent as class photos have been from critical and theoretical discussions of everyday photography, they have served as fertile ground for visual artists from around the world. Artists as varied as Christian Boltanski, Carrie Mae Weems, Lorie Novak, Steven Deo, Vik Muniz, Marcelo Brodsky, Marjane Satrapi, Tomoko Sawada, Mirta Kupferminc, David Wojnarowicz, Adrian Piper, and others have, in their own creative ways, re-viewed and reframed school photographs, thus revealing their liquid "intelligence" and temporality. They have reframed utterly conventional pictures in a variety of media—photography, video, painting, comics, and installations. Many of them have come to these images in order to explore personal memory and postmemory, loss and longing; others, to critique transformative ideologies of education in specific sociopolitical circumstances, including colonialism, postslavery, cultural chauvinism, and military dictatorship; still others, to examine and enlarge photography's ideological and emotional work in daily life; and others, simply to work with rich familial and institutional archives. Specifically, the artists we discuss in this book explore and critique how educational institutions in different societies use photography to confront social difference by attempting to minimize it, to disguise it, or, conversely, to maximize it. Reflecting on the afterlives of school photos, their artistic work aids us in making visible the powerful and problematic social and political role of everyday instrumental photographs and photographic archives.

By enlarging the tightly cropped frames and opening up the conventionality of this everyday photographic genre, these artists enable us to access some of the affective resonances of seemingly opaque images. As they reveal the before and the aftermath school pictures already contain, they confirm that, as Ariella Azoulay puts it, "the event of photography is never over."[26] In addition, through their reframings, they tend to practice a particularly irreverent gaze in relation to the archival pictures themselves, one that Gabrielle Moser has usefully called a "disobedient gaze." Looking at colonial photographic archives and how to discuss and to mobilize them, Moser considers archival absences or, as Ann Laura Stoler calls them, "historical negatives."[27] To reveal possible spaces of resistance and critique within institutional, and specifically colonial, archives, Moser suggests adopting a "disobedient gaze" and "developing" latent contents contained within archival images.

Obedience and disobedience are fundamental to the experiences of schooling and of being photographed in school. Reframing school photos, the artists we discuss introduce a note of irreverence that weakens the institutional control of images, distributing that control among the various subjects involved in producing them. They invite a more persistent look at institutional implication in social practices of inclusion and exclusion. Thinking about school photographs in "liquid time" and seeing them through contemporary artists' "disobedient gaze" provokes us to see, feel, and hear them from different vantage points across different moments in time. The theoretical insights we can glean from these artists' work enables us to develop tools to explore what cultural and social work school photos do. Thus we can also find in them alternative pasts, presents, and also futures—futures latent but not yet realized in the present of the photographic event.

TWO: WHY SCHOOL PHOTOS?

I have two pictures of my first day of school, both taken in front of the hedge of the house next door to ours. We lived on Drumea Rădulescu, a dead-end street in a peripheral area of Bucharest. It was September 1956 and I was about to turn seven. In one of the two photos (fig. I.6), I am facing the camera, my body slightly turned to show off the school bag I am carrying on my back, my arms holding on to the straps across my shoulders—a new gesture that would become a daily practice. My hair is held back by a hair band; I am wearing white knee socks, a short gray skirt, and a navy jacket, with a belt and buckle (the photo is black and white so I am identifying the colors from memory). I remember this event—having my picture taken to mark the first day of school—and I remember practicing, quite consciously, the identity of the pupil, an identity I was eager to assume.

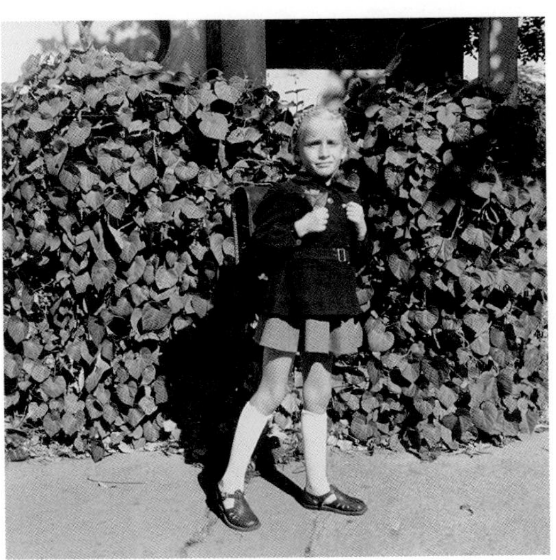

FIGURE I.6. Marianne, on the first day of school, but not looking happy. Bucharest, Romania, 1956. (Hirsch collection)

But where is that excitement in the photo? Why do I look so unhappy? My face is almost a grimace: am I sad to be leaving home and my mother, or am I mimicking sadness for the camera—or for her? Or merely squinting into the sun? My father usually took the photos in our family; would he have been home as I was leaving for school? Unlikely. Except on Sundays, he left for work very early, around seven in the morning. Maybe this isn't even the first day; maybe it's a performance of the first day for posterity, taken by him on a Sunday before or after the event.

In the second photo (if this is the right order) the (earlier?) show of recalcitrance seems to have given way to quiet acquiescence: the image is taken in profile, I am bowing my head, eyes cast down, carrying my school bag and, in my right hand, a little flower bouquet to mark the day's importance (fig. I.7). While in the other photo I was turned sideways, with my body twisting back toward home, here I am facing the direction of the streetcar that will take me across town to the Școala Germană, or Deutsche Schule—the German-language school to which my parents (German-speaking Jews from the former Austrian-ruled province of Bukowina) had decided to send me. I am setting off; I will be a good student, a good girl.[28]

I certainly play the part of the good girl in my official first-grade class photo as I sit in the middle of the first row, smiling perhaps too sweetly off to the right (fig. I.8). The photographer or an assistant standing to the left of the camera must have been trying to amuse us because most of us are grinning, even giggling. Even our teacher, Frau Singer, is smiling brightly, if somewhat self-consciously. Between the first day of school and the day this picture was taken, I seem indeed to have become a pupil, integrated into my class, I-C, of the German-language school in Bucharest. I'm not wearing the uniform that some of the girls have on—a long-sleeve gingham dress, white button-on collar, and dark blue

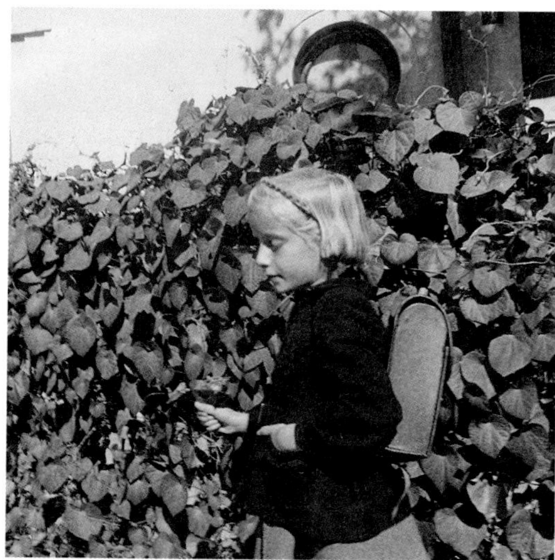

FIGURE I.7. A good girl on the way to the *Școala Germană* (the German School), Bucharest, 1956. (Hirsch collection)

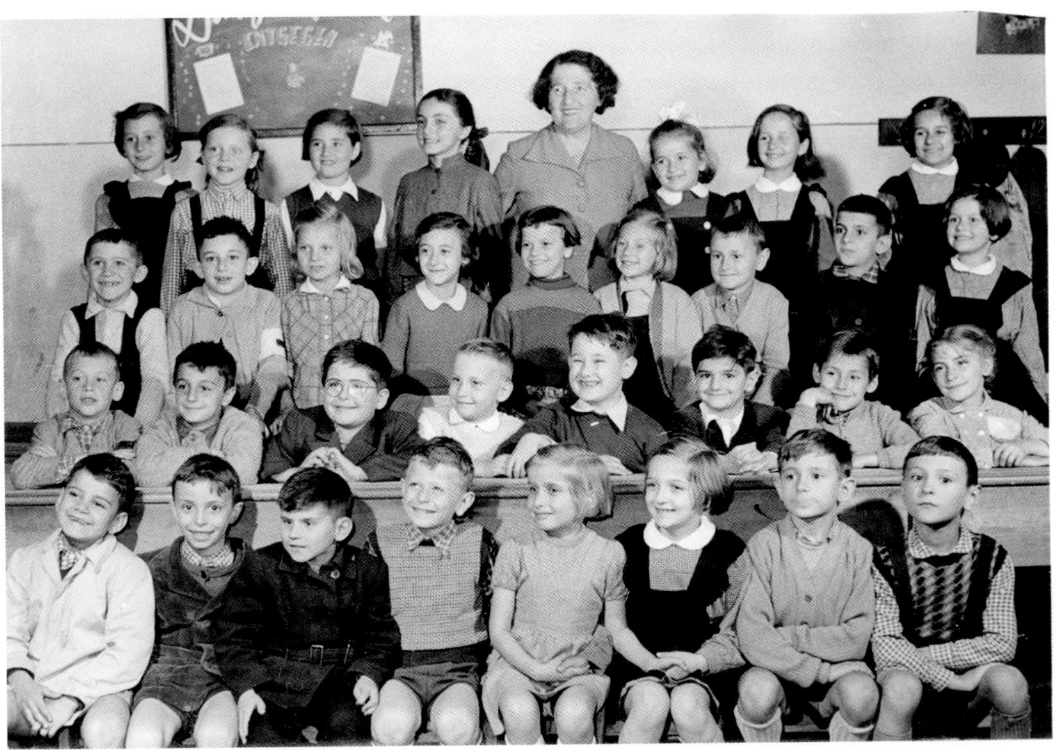

FIGURE I.8. Marianne, now a first grader, *Class IC, Şcoala Germană,* 1956. (Hirsch collection)

apron—but I know how to laugh at the same jokes that amuse the others. And yet the picture also shows a distinctive gesture of differentiation: unlike the other children, who sit with arms close by their sides or leaning on the tables, I cross arms with a little girl sitting next to me whose smile matches my own.

When, nowadays, I peruse others of my class photos, I notice that I made it a habit to touch or hold hands or cross arms with a "best friend." In this first-grade picture, however, Donca Vianu and I are not the only ones holding hands: the boys behind us, Tibi and Mihai, have also linked arms in a gesture of closeness and camaraderie.

Although my arms are linked with Donca's in the photo, my actual "best friend" in first grade was Gaby Langada. She is not in the picture *because, to our chagrin, she was placed in section A and not section C. I recognize and remember a number of the other girls—Gaby Lehrer, in the last row next to the teacher; Thea, last row next to Gaby; Roxana, third row extreme right; Zenaida, second row right. Looking back, I sense how different we all were from one another, and how hard I tried to find commonality with one or two, or more, of my classmates, and how much I wanted to be accepted as part of the group. I remember, viscerally, the poor kids in the class, those who wore the same clothes every day and probably could not afford the uniform until it was mandated. I remember, particularly, the "bad boys," troublemakers who terrorized us—Dan, first row far left, who threw a piece of broken desk across the room in second grade, making a big hole in another boy's forehead; Ion, above him, a bully who teased the girls by pulling our hair. Next to Ion, another troublemaker (whose name I've forgotten), who distracted the class by making faces and fighting with the other boys. Their wildness and our vulnerability as girls (certainly encouraged by attitudes our teachers loudly projected) might account for the break in decorum, the spontaneous, and no doubt unconscious, gesture of friendship that my little friend and I perform, creating a safer twosome. Or might it perhaps reflect an instinct to resist group uniformity—our move to distinguish ourselves from the collective class grouping, and to gather strength for that refusal by performing it together?*

Hands touching—I look at them now and feel Donca's hand on my hand, which suddenly becomes small and limp, waiting to be held. I touch the skin of the photograph, asking it to let me into its space. For a brief moment I'm inside the photo, looking out, holding on to Donca (fig. I.9).

The heterogeneous assemblage that was this class, I realized much later, was an improbable product of the 1950s in Romania's capital, though the

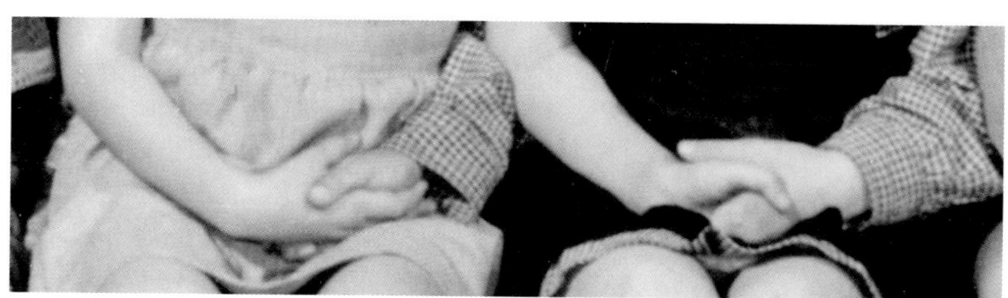

FIGURE I.9. Hands touching. (Hirsch collection)

children's ethnic, religious, and political diversity remain occluded in this conventional class photo. During 1950s communism, Romanian authorities sanctioned separate language schools for its minority populations. Although a large number of Romania's sizeable ethnic German community had been "repatriated" by the Soviets, with Romanian assent, immediately after the Second World War, the students in the Şcoala Germană did include a significant number of children of ethnic German descent, children whose parents' wartime history was a source of lively speculation in my Jewish home. There were also German-speaking Jewish children like me from the formerly Austro-Habsburg Bukowina, a region that had been incorporated into greater Romania after 1918. There were Romanian-speaking Jewish and half-Jewish children whose parents wanted to offer them a German-language education with an eye to eventually fleeing or emigrating from Romanian communism. The majority of the children, however, were Romanians of Orthodox faith who spoke just enough rudimentary German to pass an entrance exam. Like some of the Jewish children, they were sent to that school out of parental ambition or family plans to escape Eastern European communism to the West. I have no doubt that like some of our teachers, a few were children of Nazi collaborators or sympathizers during the war, who had learned German and wanted to transmit this culture, and all that came with it, to their children. Distinguishing among these groups and their politics and prejudices was, for a lot of us children, part of the subliminal lessons we began to master early on. And yet the photograph masks these differences, both showing and helping enact schooling's assimilative power. The joke producing a momentary smile or laugh on our faces can barely contain the tensions and contradictions teeming among us for the moment it took to press the shutter and to frame us into a static, seemingly coherent, collective.

I have a fourth picture from that first year, one taken on the last school day in June. It shows me at home again, this time in a leafy section of the backyard. My head is bowed and I am displaying a book for the camera: it is my prize for being "first" in the class, a large picture book titled Der Mohnkuchen ("The Poppy Seed Cake"). I am still a pupil, I have completed the first grade with academic distinction, and I have managed to stand out—alone this time—from the group depicted in the class photo. As I look at this picture, I notice what is reflected within it—the pride of my father's photographic gaze, mirrored by my own. I have learned, yet again, how to please him.

INSTITUTIONS OF CHILDHOOD

In the family and in school, photos are taken to mark milestone moments of transition. This Hirsch family album is utterly conventional in this regard, and Marianne's four first-grade pictures measure the range of moments that might have been deemed worth archiving in the age of analog photography. By recording the first year of school photographically, they show the transformation from the individual and familial subject to the subject of official schooling, from the domestic to one of the first of numerous public institutions into which children are interpolated. Thus, it also shows the shift from the familial photographic gaze to the institutional school gaze, performed by the school photographer. Indeed, the first-grade class photo (fig. I.8) marks all the children as members of a lateral collectivity outside of the family. The children join a cohort and a generation sharing a communal and a larger national environment and historical moment. While the proud paternal gaze of the prize image enhances individual accomplishment, the class photo deindividualizes the children, projecting similarity.

Family photos and albums have, despite their conventionality and uniformity, elicited a significant critical literature in the last decades, shaping a discourse about everyday photographic practices, about their roles and ideologies, their gazes and looks, and the work they perform in our individual and social lives.[29] School photos, on the other hand, have tended to sit in private albums and public institutional archives without attracting a great deal of critical attention.

WHAT DO SCHOOL PHOTOS DO?

Typically taken by commercial photographers with little interest in deviating from formulaic representations, school photographs everywhere share many features. Most often they depict a group of students standing or sitting on benches or by their desks (or sitting and standing outdoors, in rows, by the school building), facing forward, and looking at the photographer. At other times, school photos also show scenes of instruction, characteristically posed and set up for the camera. The photographer and the camera setup are instrumental in arranging the assemblage, which is often focused around one or more teachers whose presence, like the photographer's, serves as a disciplining force enjoining the children to assume postures and gazes that demonstrate their acquiescence to an imposed group identity.

In this regard, of course, the specific institutional and larger national matrix in which a school—and, by extension, every school class—is embedded plays a key ideological role. Accredited by the municipality, state, or nation, schools are the institutions that teach children to read and write and that provide them with elements of a national literary and scientific culture and, especially, of its versions of history.

They are also the sites that instruct students in rules of acceptable behavior and morality, tutor them in civic responsibility, and instill respect for authority and the established economic order.[30] In addition, schools impart pedagogies of social life: they can provide useful lessons about social hierarchies marking differences in race, class, gender, religion, ethnicity, and political direction. They trace trajectories of failure and success, blockage and advancement, and they evoke factors that shape these in given communities. While other institutions and ideological state apparatuses—the family, the church, the law, the media, and the arts—may aid, or impede, schools in ideological and civic inculcation, schools are primary agencies in shaping and reinforcing values, outlooks, beliefs, and myths that constitute citizenship in the society where they are located.[31] Inasmuch as they are accredited by the state or municipality or by official communal institutions, even private schools dedicated to educating economically privileged children or children of particular religious, ethnic, or language groups must conform to this general ideological role.

Like school report cards and diplomas, school photos can serve as a form of certification available to everyone portrayed—a confirmation of grade level and grade ascendancy, and of participation in a teleological trajectory of socialization that defines group and national belonging and citizenship. As schools are social and political agents of communal life, institution-sponsored images provide visual evidence of a commonality among the children in a class, of the attempt to minimize or erase the differences that shape social life both outside and inside the school. They reinforce forms of conformity and standardization already made evident in the mandated wearing of school uniforms or in regulated dress and hair codes. The photographs' conventions tend to obscure differences among the children—in religion, ethnicity, sociability, creativity, and intelligence; between compliant and rebellious ones; between gender-conforming and queer children.

And yet this visual homogeneity cannot entirely disguise divergences between the "formal curriculum"—the planned lessons, knowledge, and skills taught by educators—and what educational theorists call the "hidden curriculum," the unspoken but implicitly communicated academic, social, economic, and cultural messages conveyed at school.[32] These messages convey to each child their own and others' place in their community's social stratification, what Allan Sekula, in relation to portrait photography, calls the "shadow archive":

> *Every portrait implicitly took its place within a social and moral hierarchy. The* private *moment of sentimental education, the look at-the-frozen-gaze-of-the-loved-one, was shadowed by two other more* public *looks: a look up, at one's "betters," and a look down, at one's social "inferiors." . . . We can speak then of a generalized, inclusive* archive, a shadow archive *that encompasses an entire social terrain while positioning individuals within that terrain.*[33]

School photos thus document school life and reflect the children's understanding of themselves as subjects of schooling back to those looking at them, both at the time of their taking and later. More than archival sources, they are historical actors in their own right. As technologies of modernity, they both record and actualize the processes that support institutional interpellation and integration, no matter how discernible or visibly textured these processes are by marks of difference that define the "social terrain" and its hierarchies.

THE MAKING OF A CLASS

Nowhere is this role of photography as an instrument creating the school pupil more clearly elucidated than in artist Vik Muniz's *The Class* (fig. I.10), from his 2013–2014 *Album* project—a project in which he remakes and com-

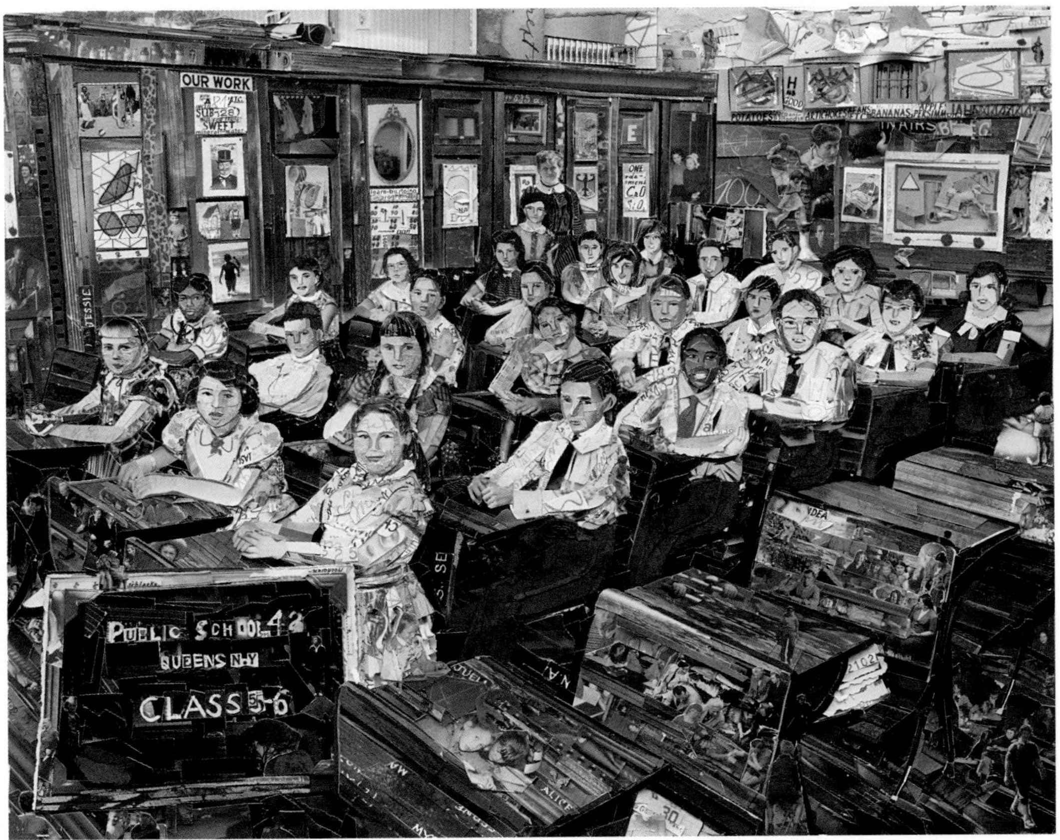

FIGURE I.10. Vik Muniz, *The Class,* collage from the *Album, 2014 series*. See also plate 3. (© Vik Muniz, VAGA at Artists Rights Society [ARS], NY)

ments on several different genres of everyday photography, ranging from wedding and family pictures to tourist photos. In this particular image, we see fifth- and sixth-grade children photographed from the side in a Queens, New York, public elementary school classroom.

The children, all sporting smiles or attentive looks, are sitting at their school desks, arms quietly resting on top, and are turned to face the photographer. The teacher stands in the background with one student next to her. The room's walls are densely decorated with posters, photographs, drawings, and slogans labeled "Our Work." From a distance, the picture looks conventional, formulaic.

On closer look, we see more. We discover that this is a minimally integrated classroom, as two of the children appear to be African American. Their visible presence, as well as the children's clothing styles (round collars and puff sleeves, for example), indicate that this image might date from a period following closely on the 1954 *Brown v. Board of Education* Supreme Court ruling that mandated racially integrated public schooling throughout the United States. In enfolding this diverse group into a unit, the photograph becomes a technology that manages difference and actualizes a fledgling process of integration.

But on even closer look, something quite startling becomes apparent as well. The children's faces and bodies, the desks they are sitting on, and the objects, walls, and floors of the classroom are all composed of cut-up and reassembled photographs. Some of these, possibly the backs of prints, have writing on them in blue and red pen.

Muniz is known for composing his images using materials matching their content, whether string, chocolate, or garbage.[34] He constructed his *Album* project out of found photos of many different kinds and from different periods that he collected over a number of years, cut up, rephotographed, and printed. He subsequently destroyed the original collages, leaving only photos of cut-up photos. Texturing the classroom space and the schoolchildren's bodies, these scraps of found photographs underscore the materiality and the constructed quality of the photographic image more generally. They also point to the multiple circulation and reproduction of everyday photographic images and the relative unimportance of an "original." Everyday photos refer to other everyday photos, conforming to, repeating, or contesting strict generic conventions.

At the same time, this composition is more than an expression of post-modern self-reflexivity, more than a break in illusion or a comment on mediation. It is a telling performance of a "disobedient gaze." Although these children appear to be students, members of class 5-6 in the Queens New York Public School 42 (which indeed exists), they are actually two-dimensional constructed paper figures.

As such, Muniz's image reveals a great deal more beyond its surface, however textured. The photo fragments making up the desks, walls, and objects in the classroom bring additional children's faces and bodies into the frame. These children act as ghosts of the classroom's past, standing for those who might have occupied these desks in previous years. In addition, there are images of adults, of families on vacation, working, sitting, or walking—all that pupils bring to school with them that gets bracketed out of the pedagogies of school lessons. Muniz's recomposition mimics the process, and the violence, by which institutions absorb, integrate, homogenize, and transform their subjects into "material." It thus illustrates how school and its technologies make citizens, literally disintegrating, reshaping, inscribing, and numbering them. These children become subjects of school by simultaneously and literally becoming the subjects of school pictures.

The recursive process of creating a photograph out of photographs viscerally exposes the ways in which photography serves the "ideological state apparatuses" of modernity, materializing their assimilative structures and generating identical subjects as though from a printer. The technique of collage underscores this construction's provisional nature, however—its contingency and its layered quality. In Muniz's *The Class*, the students, like all school pupils, are in construction, portrayed during the process of creating themselves and being created as citizens and subjects of school in liquid time. Like the classroom objects, children also are being shaped and used, unmade and remade by schooling and its pedagogies of citizenship. In this trajectory, much has to be destroyed in order to be re-created. Through the perspective of collage, schooling is a venture as much of unlearning as of learning, of learning by unlearning.

As though defying the image's blatant artifice, however, we find that the children's faces in *The Class* draw us into its flat space, widening and deepening it with what cannot be fully homogenized or erased—individual expression, gesture, and affect. The opening they create is part of the photograph's very materiality: it resides in the innumerable faces and objects that attract our attention from every direction, drawing us in, only to defy us the minute we recognize their artifice. The affective register that emerges from between the paper scraps and their assemblage provides a site of resistance to the ideology of schooling Muniz's photograph exposes, enabling us as viewers to confront its homogenizing process with a "disobedient gaze" that yields additional forms of knowledge and engagement.

The space and time that open up in Muniz's image surpass the confines of the institutional gaze and linear temporality structuring school photographs. They elicit a very different kind of reading—one more akin to Roland Barthes's notion of the piercing insight of the "punctum" than what he termed the historical "studium" and the ideological critiques it occasions.[35] They thus reveal the more complex field of looks and gazes that emerges when we examine school images not from the institutional viewpoint of the photographer and the camera's single-point lens but from the perspective of the image's subjects—the children who are being photographed—and its viewers, whether at the time the photographs were taken or later. These perspectives open additional dimensions of affect, meaning, and desire.

School photos, like all photographs, are able to record contradictions that the conventionality and uniformity of poses, middle-distance camera angles, and institutional sanctions would seem to exclude. Certainly, every group image, assembling diverse individuals, inscribes a greater range of gestures and meanings than the photographer would have intended to record or the event of the image would have accommodated. These excesses—often subversive and resistant—are part of the multifaceted pedagogies of sameness and difference that school photographs represent. And it is this multiplicity of meanings, what Ariella Azoulay calls the "heterogeneous knowledge" of photographs, that makes them such valuable documents of social, political, and civic life.[36] Thus, while the camera gaze is institutionally sponsored and sanctioned, the subjects and viewers introduce a set of looks that modulate and interrupt that gaze's determinative power.

Shaped by diverse individual looks, school photographs reflect what Azoulay has called a "civil gaze" that, in her terms, delineates a "shared space of the governed."[37] As the subjects both of schooling and of photography, children and their parents can contest the images' sovereign institutional control and reclaim the democratic potentials of this participatory technology. In so doing, they reinscribe heterogeneous perspectives and means of opposition and refusal. Group photos, more than other kinds of images, illustrate "photography as a phenomenon of plurality, deterritorialization and decentralization."[38] They are products and instruments of sovereign power and subjugation, to be sure, but at the same time they are vehicles of critique and possibility, eliciting a "civil imagination" that can recognize the performances of citizenship.

Exhibiting the assimilative, integrating process of schooling, school photos help us realize when and how that integration erases individual and group differences excessively, or when and how it fails, impairing citizenship. As a rephotographed collage, *The Class* not only performs heterogeneity and multiplicity but decenters, to the point of eliminating, the camera's instrumental role, its power and centrality. Each of the photo scraps within Muniz's image was the product of a different camera gaze and a different photographic event, and their multiplication erases the authority of any single one of them. By way of this decentralization, Muniz coaches us to deploy a civil gaze that, in Azoulay's definition, "does not seek to control the visible, but neither can it bear another's control over the visible."[39]

"WEAR THIS!"

Marjane Satrapi's 2000 graphic memoir *Persepolis* begins with a drawn class photo (fig. I.11) depicting an induction into schooling and national belonging that illustrates well the conflict between the institutional and the civil gaze, as well as between collectivity and individuality.[40]

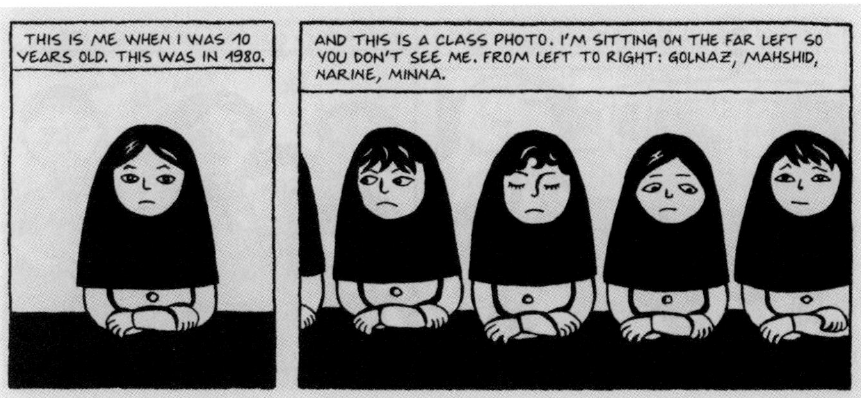

FIGURE I.11. *"You don't see me."* Graphic memoir excerpt from *Persepolis: The Story of a Childhood* by Marjane Satrapi, translation copyright © 2003 by L'Association, Paris, France. (Used by permission of Pantheon Books, an imprint of the Knopf Doubleday Publishing Group, a division of Penguin Random House LLC. All rights reserved.)

"This is me when I was ten years old," says Marji in the graphic memoir's first frame—a simply drawn little girl wearing the veil and looking serious, if not glum. The present tense and the next frame confirm that we are looking at the drawings of two photographs, a "portrait" and a "class photo" through which Marji introduces herself. She is not visible in the class photo: all we can see is part of her left arm and the right hand that crosses over it, as she assumes a pose identical to that of the other four girls. "You don't see me," she tells us as she names the other four from left to right. All five wear a required black veil and all look equally distressed, although, with a few lines, Satrapi is able to convey physiognomic differences and a range of facial expressions.

Why use a class photo by way of introduction to this memoir? And why is Marji invisible within it? Satrapi's opening frames tell us a great deal about this genre of everyday photography that, along with the visual structure of comix, underscores the ideological transformation effected by the Iranian Islamist Revolution, which interrupted Satrapi's childhood and provoked her graphic memoir. The rest of *Persepolis* plays out the uneasy and sometimes violent oscillation between a "me" that can be visually captured in an image and the evasive "you don't see me"—the rebellious memoirist's flight into the gutter between the institutional frames that visibly create compliant subjects of a totalitarian religious state and reinforce its gender repression and hierarchy.

In the large double frame at the bottom of Satrapi's first page (fig. I.12), we see the girls' rebellion against the imposition of the veil—a rebellion that forms the backdrop against which the acquiescence registered in the class photo must be read.

"We didn't really like to wear the veil," the narrator tells us, and individual children, wearing uniforms but sporting different hairstyles, gestures, and facial expressions, run around the schoolyard playing hide and seek, jump rope, and even "execution" with the piece of black fabric. The school building with its foreboding black windows remains visible and the games occur in a space external to it, just as in the frame above, girls can be unruly outside the school walls but must comply with the teacher, seen in the foreground, inside. As these frames from *Persepolis* show, the assimilating pull toward sameness in setting up and posing in class photos minimizes the possibili-

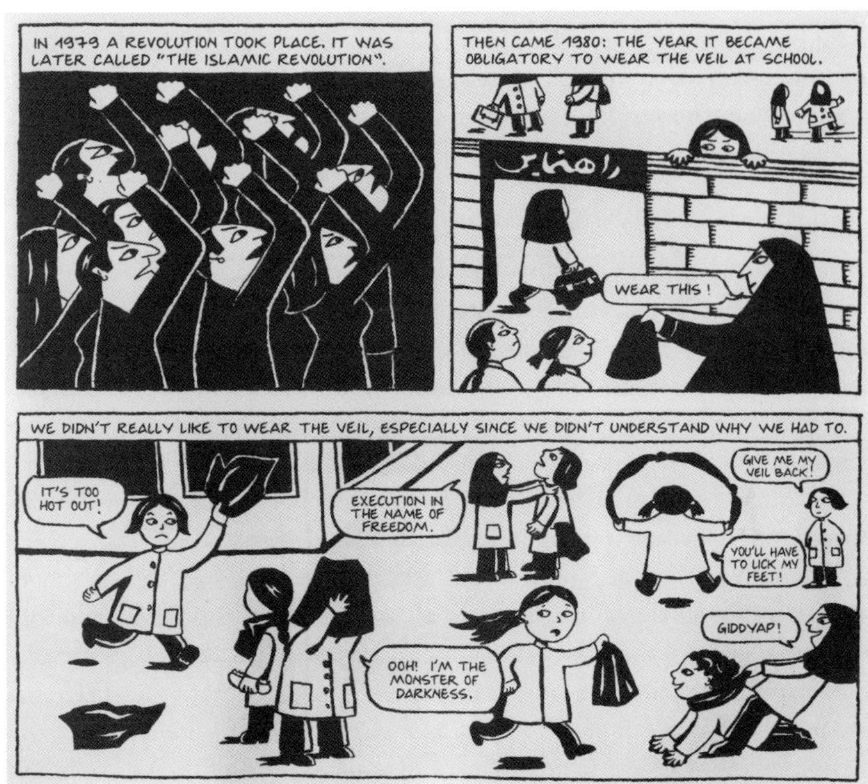

FIGURE I.12. *"We didn't really like to wear the veil."* Graphic memoir excerpt from *Persepolis: The Story of a Childhood* by Marjane Satrapi, translation copyright © 2003 by L'Association, Paris, France. (Used by permission of Pantheon Books, an imprint of the Knopf Doubleday Publishing Group, a division of Penguin Random House LLC. All rights reserved.)

ties of subversion, something that is true even within pictures taken in more democratic political settings. Children may try to fool around before or even while the photos are being taken, but the class photos that survive are no doubt the ones that record the most uniform look on all the faces. In Satrapi's image, only the eyes move.

Marji's disappearance and refusal, her flight from the image, provokes viewers to disaggregate these group photos and to introduce fissures that highlight the individual child as a willing or unwilling institutional subject. Class photos, even under politically less extreme circumstances, dramatize precisely the individual child's struggle between singularity and ideological interpellation, as well as the violence of the deliberate desubjectification produced by schooling and underscored by school photography's constricting institutional frames.

TECHNOLOGIES OF (UN)BELONGING

If we read class photos as a subset of the more encompassing genre of group portraits—of paintings and photographs of guilds, army units, clubs, unions, and youth groups, for example—we can perhaps speculate more widely on the contradictory resonances they might evoke in and among group members and within the communities to which they belong. Doing this, we might see them in the terms introduced by art historian Aby Warburg, who, in his "Mnemosyne Atlas," mapped a large set of "pre-established expressive forms" that carry and transmit affect across time, constituting a transgenerational memorial repertoire in visual form.[41] What kinds of affect do school photos carry and transmit over time and space? What, in art historian Jill Bennett's terms, is their "emotional life?"[42]

In considering this question, it is important to remember the emotional pedagogies that are inherent in schooling, however implicitly. States use school to bind students to group and national belonging, through civic and historical education but also through spoken and unspoken lessons in group and communal allegiance and patriotism. Photographs underscore this binding through optical forms of allegiance. This focus on civic belonging is part of the "organization of feeling" imparted by schools' "hidden curricula."[43] School photos carry the feelings and affects of schooling, social conformity, and belonging, eliciting both attachment and resistance in their viewers.

By bringing into focus the subordination of individuality to group membership and incorporation into a social and civic assemblage, school pictures viscerally convey the desire, but often also the reluctance, to belong to the group. And indeed, this tension between individuality and transindividual anonymity, between assimilation to the group and subversion and resistance, is an important characteristic of the emotional life of class photos.

Unlike portraits, which, in Hans-Georg Gadamer's terms, produce an "increase of being," a "surplus" that consolidates the uniqueness of the individual subject that is being depicted, class photos tend to negate that uniqueness and, in that sense, become "antiportraits" structured by the school's institutional gaze, a gaze that operates by way of the camera lens and its work of mechanical reproduction.[44]

Tomoko Sawada's digitally produced images in her 2006 series *School Days* are such antiportraits. The project speaks to the emotional education practiced in school and offers a vivid commentary on the conformity imposed by Japanese schools. Each of Sawada's ten images (see, for example, fig. I.13) displays around forty students and a teacher sitting in front of a backdrop conventional to Japanese class photos. The girls are dressed in identical uniforms within each image, though the uniforms vary across images.

All of the faces in these school photos, however, including the teacher's, belong to the artist herself. Introducing slight variations in gesture and hairstyles, she performs the part of 410 schoolgirls and teachers. And yet throughout these variations, affect is missing or unreadable. The faces are made to seem different, but they remain equally expressionless, blank.

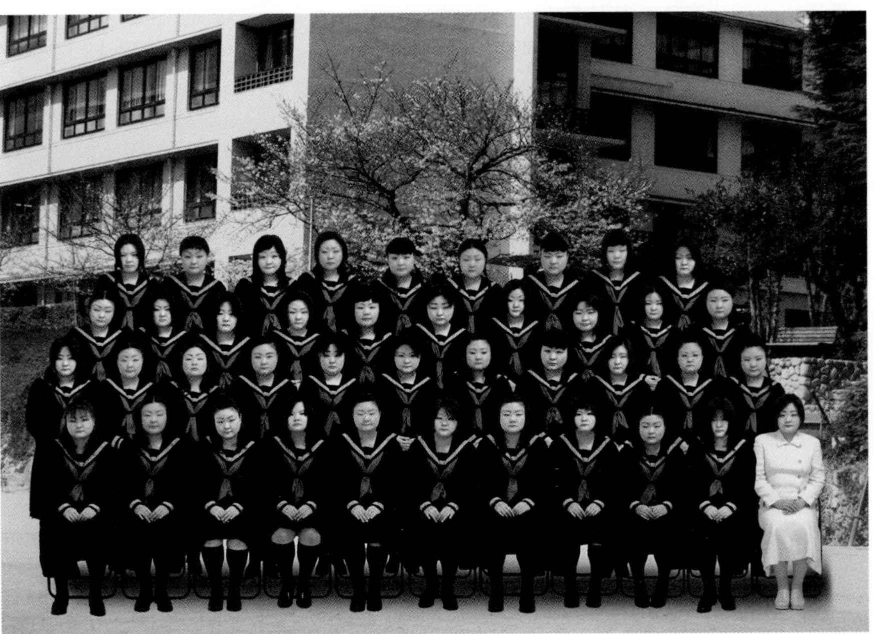

FIGURE I.13. Tomoko Sawada, *School Days #1*. 2006. See also plate 4. (© Tomoko Sawada, courtesy of the artist)

Forty students and the teacher in each image are actually just one. Staging enforced conformity through her use of digital multiplication, Sawada performs and plays with the rituals of school photography. Even amid strict parameters of social control she enables a distinct individuality in each one of the bodies and faces.

HANDS

Striking in Sawada's *School Days* is the absolute stillness of the girls' bodies and, especially, their hands. The seated girls in the first row have their hands folded on their laps, as does the seated teacher. The most conspicuous elements of class pictures more generally are the children's faces, but their hands are almost always as prominently featured as they usually are in painted or photographic portraits. In school photos, hands are often folded on laps or desks in ways that seem choreographed by the photographer to communicate compliance, quiescence, a pause from activity that constitutes the time of the photographic event. In Marjane Satrapi's comix frames, the faces show different expressions, but Satrapi draws the girls' hands identically.

Folded hands help give the image its overall uniformity. But they also signal the children's responsiveness to authority, their quiet stasis during the event of the image when, presumably, they were told to "keep still." In *Listening to Images*, Tina Campt distinguishes between stillness and stasis. Stillness, she argues, is motionlessness, but stasis is a "tension produced by holding a complex set of forces in suspension" and also an "unvisible motion held in tense suspension of temporary equilibrium; e.g. vibration."[45] This definition of stasis enables us to see the predominance of folded hands not as quiescent but as holding the many tensions structuring the class and the inclusion of each individual child within the picture. By adding vibration, Campt theorizes sound and listening as dimensions of photographic images. Certainly, the momentary quiet of a class photograph just barely holds the commotion preceding and following it at bay. We can hear that commotion in the bottom frames of Satrapi's first page. We cannot hear anything in Sawada's digital constructions.

But, as in Marianne's first-grade photo, folded and interlacing hands also signal the desire to touch and to be touched—or not to be. They signal connection between the children, however desired or rejected. With their prominent focus on hands, school photos highlight photography's *haptic* (from the Greek *haptein*, to touch) qualities, which supplement and enhance vision by embodying it.[46] These images invite us not only to look but also to relate to them and their subjects through the medium of touch. Touch connects us to images in their materiality. For historical photographs, their sometimes cracked, scratched, or damaged surfaces and frames remind us of the conditions of their production and survival.

But for viewers looking at hands touching in the picture, the image's skin does more—it becomes a space of connection across time and space. In Elizabeth Abel's eloquent terms, the image's skin can be envisaged as a shared space, "a mediating zone" in which we can encounter and share the vulnerability of the subjects depicted—in this case, of children who often elicit a protective reaction from adult viewers who identify with their images by way of a vision of their own child selves. Looking specifically at protest images from the Jim Crow era, Abel makes clear, however, that there are limits to this connective way of looking. She asserts that "the photograph's potential as a milieu of racial crossing does not enter this zone of mutual vulnerability."[47] This ambivalent desire for, or aversion to, touching and being touched can help deepen our exploration of photos addressing social difference in particular. Touch based on mutual vulnerability becomes violence when power and prejudice intervene.

The hands in these images also enjoin us to develop and to reflect on the multisensory dimensions of our own practices of looking at school photos. In Laura Marks's terms, "haptic visuality continues to inform an understanding of vision as embodied and material," but Marks also develops a form of visual engagement that "move[s] along the surface of the object, rather than attempting to penetrate or 'interpret' it, as criticism is usually supposed to do."[48] This form of vision, which aims to touch while at the same time holding back, refusing identification, respecting privacy and otherness, offers a useful approach to images of vulnerable subjects in the face of social and political violence.

THIS KID

We see this vulnerability in David Wojnarowicz's (1990) *Untitled (One Day This Kid . . .)* (fig. I.14), an image where the conformity mandated by civil institutions and represented in school photos appears as potentially lethal. Wojnarowicz's photostat is based on a school portrait of the artist as a young boy. He appears alone, isolated from his peers, and that isolation is exacerbated by the heavy text printed on the very skin of the image overwhelming his vulnerable, smiling face. The text points forward toward a future in which "this kid" will face the violence and annihilation to which gay children are subject in a deeply homophobic society, a violence that, the text tells us, they internalize and turn against themselves. Civil, medical, political, and legal institutions conspire to annihilate children who do not conform to normative heterosexual desire and life. In writing about himself in the third person, Wojnarowicz stands on the outside, looking at the picture of "this kid," who, without knowing it yet, is looking to a future of further isolation, persecution, and potentially murder. "This kid" is isolated even from his own future self, the artist who is making the image. Liquid time does not save "this kid" from preordained death. But at the end of Wojnarowicz's text, we sense something else—the "desire to place his naked body on the naked body of another boy." The desire to touch and be touched. A craving that no institution, however disciplining and violent, can annihilate. A desire that haptic looking can perceive with a noninvasive look.

Satrapi and Sawada denounce an imposed conformity; Wojnarowicz shows its lethal consequences. He shows how fragile the community of schooling is for children who, because they do not conform to circumscribed social norms, are socially ostracized and "othered."

And yet despite the disciplinary constraints that they impose on children, school photos, and their conformity, uniformity, and "normality," can, at some historical moments, come to appear desirable. They can be so for individuals and groups not economically affluent enough to engage in school photography. And they can also be so at moments when citizenship is impaired or denied, and when some social groups within the body politic are singled out to be prejudicially judged and excluded. In such circumstances, school photos reflect not just coercion to conform but the reassurance of community. When school pictures erase individuality and difference, the integration they perform can be unwanted, extreme, or violent. When they allow social differences among the children to come into visibility, they can be vehicles of prejudice and exclusion. But at the same time, they can also

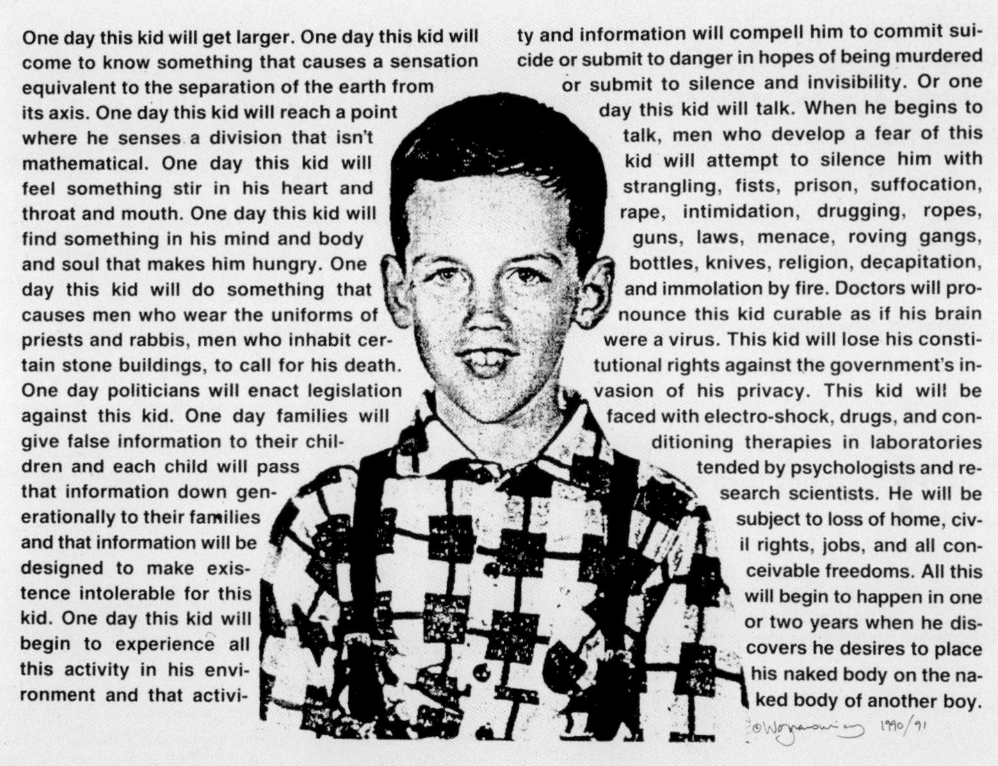

FIGURE I.14. David Wojnarowicz, *Untitled (One Day This Kid . . .)*. 1990–91/2018. Seriagraph on archival paper, 26¾ × 36 in. (Courtesy of the Estate of David Wojnarowicz and P·P·O·W, New York)

show what is lost along with the commonality and community that schools can offer. Doing so, they can be instruments of social critique, of memory and of reclamation.

This is certainly the case for the school photos from the ghettos and concentration camps during the Second World War. Moving back through the history of photography and schooling as mutually intertwined social technologies of assimilation and integration in different imperial and national settings, this book returns to the images from ghettos and camps to trace how assimilationism fails, leading to separation, exclusion, and genocide.

But it also traces how school can become a site of community, commonality, and hope that persists and thrives even at extreme moments of vulnerability and danger. As Yoko Tawada writes, in those moments, "the word *school* still carried a whiff of hope."[49]

In what follows, we explore different practices of responding to school photos as media of social cohesion and difference. We read them historically, but we also look, watch, and touch them, as we listen to their sounds and vibrations. We attempt to recover the voices of children themselves, in their memoirs of school, so as to balance the authority of voices that speak to, about, and for schoolchildren. School photos, in the moments of political crisis in which we encounter them in this book, can help produce photographic reading practices that exceed and deepen their own surfaces and frames. By elaborating such practices, we hope to reframe them as archives of possibility.

Pictures do lie!

PETER GAY

1

Imperial Frames

DAGUERREOTYPES

An untitled daguerreotype (fig. 1.1) is perhaps the oldest surviving class photograph in the United States, possibly the world. Housed in the Princeton University Archives and set in a now slightly blemished frame and gilt mat, it shows a sober assemblage of formally dressed men, probably members of the College of New Jersey Class of 1843 and a few of their teachers.[1] Depicting a group of students who jointly belong to a particular university class and who share a graduation year in common, the image adheres to conventions of group portraiture commonly employed in paintings of guilds, army units, or clubs. It presents viewers with a photographic portrait of an institutional group in which individual personalities and differences are subsumed within a collective assemblage. It highlights standardized clothing, conformity of appearance and posture, and a camera-facing multirow lineup—group features probably arranged by the photographer to serve institutional wishes, and enforced by the students' most immediate institutional disciplining powers, the teachers.

The practice of photographing school classes and student groups was established during photography's earliest years, as evidenced by the many surviving daguerreotypes of school groups made in the 1850s in the United States. The portrait of students from the Emerson School for Girls in Boston in the early 1850s (fig. 1.2) is especially noteworthy for its excellence as a school photo employing the daguerreotype technology.

Made by photographers hired by the institution, these and other daguerreotypes of school assemblages certify the constitution of a class or grade of students at a particular moment in time. As daguerreotypes, however, they are restricted by the constraints of the medium in which they were created. All were produced on mirror-like reflective polished silver—material easily tarnished in open light and air. They could not, and cannot, be displayed unshielded for very long without sustaining corrosive damage and are thus viewable only in a light-controlled space. Each is a *singular* photographic product—a one-of-a-kind image that cannot be replicated and shared. Daguerreotypes are dedicated to the needs of the institution that commissioned their making, and to that institution's vision and recording of its own history, rather than to the personal and collective memories of the students in the images or those of their families.

The culture of photographic images, however, changed dramatically in the early 1850s. The development of the collodion/albumen glass-plate process, large-format printing, sharp detail, tonal variation, and, most revolutionary of all, image reproducibility made photographic technology more broadly accessible.[2] These technological innovations were profoundly influential in the taking and dissemination of school photos. Very quickly, class photos of children and young adults were recognized as desirable reproducible objects. Professional photographers, perceiving their potentially more widespread commercial appeal, began to promote and feature them within their repertoire of offerings. School photos could

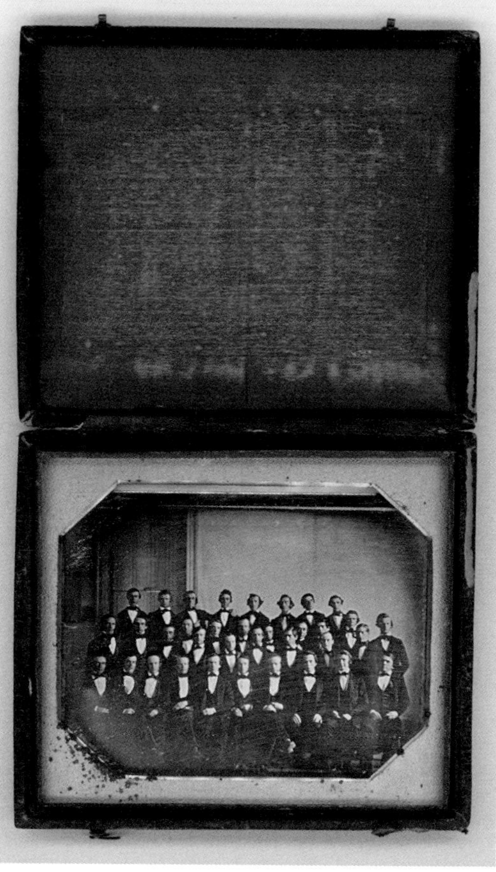

FIGURE 1.1. Group portrait of thirty-five men, thought to be members of the College of New Jersey Class of 1843 with some faculty. Quarter plate daguerreotype. Photo possibly by George Prosch. (Princeton University Archives)

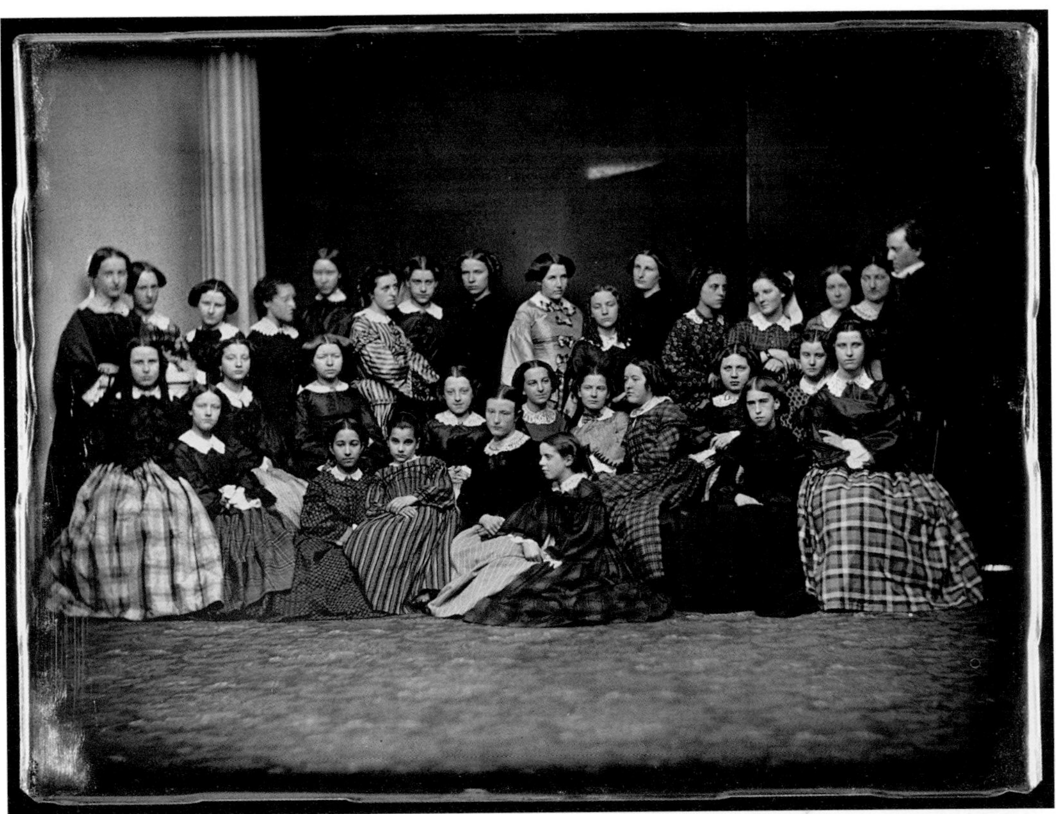

FIGURE 1.2. Class portrait of the Emerson School for Girls, Boston, ca. 1850. George Barrell Emerson (1797–1881), a staunch advocate of women's education, founded his own school in response to the gender segregation of the English Classical School, where he had been headmaster. Daguerrotype by Albert Sands Southworth. (Metropolitan Museum of Art. Gift of I. N. Phelps Stokes, Edward S. Hawes, Alice Mary Hawes, and Marion Augusta Hawes, 1937. Image copyright © The Metropolitan Museum of Art. Image source: Art Resource, NY.)

now be sold and archived not only for exhibition as sources of institutional history and pride but also as mementos of individual and group achievement for all portrayed students and for their families.

The institutional gaze shaping school pictures adhered to them through these technical and social transformations, displacing individuality ever more definitively with a broader, more homogeneous, group identity.

Nevertheless, Frederick Douglass, who escaped from slavery and became a prominent abolitionist, social reformer, orator, and writer, saw photographic reproducibility as a means of individuation and an instrument of liberation. Said to be the most photographed man of the nineteenth century, he was exceedingly deliberate about his visual image. In his famous 1850s speeches about photography—speeches given even as the medium was in the process of being developed—Douglass stresses the democratic potentials of this new technology through which "the humblest servant girl can now see a likeness of herself, such as the wealth of kings itself could not purchase fifty years ago."[3] For Douglass, photographic reproducibility enables the possibility of a broad-based, more egalitarian production of individual and group images—a possibility of representation unique to humans. As he sees it, in the aftermath of slavery, the capacity to create images is a condition of freedom, one able to help reorient the United States' vision of progress and a free, democratic future. In an illuminating close reading of the two versions of Douglass's speech, Laura Wexler argues that Douglass set up his own numerous photographic studio portraits to cast himself as a "revenant" from the social death of slavery.[4]

Indeed, later technical developments, such as the Kodak Brownie camera's invention in the late 1880s and popularization in the twentieth century, enabled many families and children—for the most part, those rising economically into the middle class and able to afford to take and develop photographs—to become image makers themselves. Though they would not generally take class or large group photos, they could reimagine institutional framings, creating more intimate, and thus more resistant, representations of school and class, as well as of civil life. Like Douglass, they could use the evidentiary truth value attributed to photography to create positive self-images that would contest prejudicial or demeaning representations of certain individuals and social groups.

In contrast to this view of photography's democratic potential, Walter Benjamin discusses the loss of authenticity and what he terms "aura" as a by-product of a work of art's reproducibility. While the portrait "was the focal point of early photography," he argues in his classic 1935 essay "The Work of Art in the Age of Mechanical Reproduction," mechanically reproducible photographs become instrumental: they serve as "standard evidence for historical occurrences and acquire a hidden political significance."[5] Reproducibility, combined with instrumentality, inaugurates the modern subject, one who lacks the aura of individuality, fading into the undifferentiated masses. The modern subject, Benjamin suggests, is the subject of mechanical surveillance and close examination. His (or her) actions and movements can be more clearly discernible to the mechanical camera gaze than to the human eye: "The camera introduces us to unconscious optics as does psychoanalysis to unconscious impulses."[6] One might then add that the camera, as an instrument of state institutions and their determinative surveillance, has the potential to influence, shape, and transform the objects of its gaze. These differing views of photography's role in shaping social subjects are especially relevant to the work of school photos throughout the history of public education.

HIERARCHY, DIFFERENCE, SCHOOLING, AND PHOTOGRAPHY

Technical innovations in photography in the second half of the nineteenth century coincided with the development and growth of public education in the United States and in Western Europe, and with efforts to train populations for the economic, social, and political demands of a rapidly expanding capitalist world. But they also coincided with two related, and extremely consequential, nineteenth- and twentieth-century sociopolitical processes undertaken by civil and imperial authorities throughout Europe and the Euro-American worlds.

The first process attempted to realize the political desire (*need* is perhaps the more accurate term) on the part of imperial authorities in pre–World War I Europe to integrate far-flung and culturally diverse subjects and colonized people into more effectively consolidated, centralized, and hence controllable imperial states. The second process expressed a vigorous intent by dominant, white, political, civil, and religious/missionary authorities to transform colonized and subordinated groups into culturally similar versions of themselves so that those groups might effectively serve the imperial mission.

Both of these processes, involving cultural transformation and social and political integration, were ideologically assimilationist. Both challenged the late-nineteenth-century growth and increasing dominance of a new Euro-American pseudoscientific racism that maintained that subordinated, racialized "others" were biologically/genetically—and thus unalterably—inferior to Euro-American whites. But while not explicitly racist in a biological/genetic sense, the assimilationist changes these civil and imperial agencies attempted to engineer in Jews, black and Native Americans, and colonized people in Africa and Australasia were based on a racially coded *cultural chauvinism* that rested on racialized notions about the contrast between what dominant whites termed "savagery" and "civilization," "heathendom" and "Christianity." Accordingly, in their own descriptive terms, "primitive," "barbaric," "backward" ways of living, thinking, and worshiping—which they considered culturally induced, not biologically inherent, but associated with "less enlightened" or "less evolved" nonwhite and non-Christian people—needed to be erased and replaced by what they firmly regarded as superior, white, Euro-American and Christian ones.[7] If this eradication and substitution was not achievable within the older generations through so-called civilized education, hard work, and disciplined control, then it had to be carried out within their children and grandchildren.

"The kind of education they are in need of is one that will habituate them to the customs and advantages of a civilized life . . . and . . . cause them to look with feelings of repugnance on their native state," stressed George Wilson, a commentator on Indian affairs, in an 1882 *Atlantic Monthly* article about the education of Indians in the United States.[8] "Kill the Indian, and Save the Man," concurred Captain Richard Henry Pratt, the founding superintendent of the Carlisle Indian School, in a publicly presented and much-quoted lecture in which he argued for Indian youths' "disciplined" assimilation into "civilized" Anglo-America. "It is a great mistake to think that the Indian is born an inevitable savage," he noted:

> *He is born a blank, like the rest of us. Left in the surroundings of savagery, he grows to possess a savage language, superstition, and life. We, left in the surroundings of civilization, grow to possess a civilized language, life, and purpose. Transfer the infant white to the savage surroundings, he will grow to possess a savage language, superstition, and habit. Transfer the savage-born infant to the surroundings of civilization, and he will grow to possess a civilized language and habit.[9]*

State-certified schooling came to play a key role in furthering these culturally assimilationist goals in Euro-American imperial realms. It did so through two structurally divergent approaches. The first, *integrated education,* incorporated students from different ethnic, national, and religious backgrounds, including children affiliated with dominant groups, in joint classrooms. The second, *segregated education,* predominantly used with colonized and minority or subordinated populations, could serve similar transformative goals by educating them apart from Christian whites. Both integrated and segregated education, however, shared a common purpose: to induce students to become loyal supporters, if not agents, of the ruling state. And they were to be induced to do so without challenging hierarchies that maintained white Euro-American social and economic supremacy.

Photography, especially school photography, became a central technology to visually publicize and certify the assimilationist project's institutional efficacy and cultural erasures. School photos assumed this institutional function both in integrated schools in Europe and in segregated schools in colonial Africa, Asia, Australia, Canada, and the United States. In both cases, class photos probed the visibility, and thus also the invisibility, of social differences, especially racialized differences. As Coco Fusco writes, "Rather than *recording* the existence of race, photography *produced* race as a visualizable fact."[10] We might specify that school photos schooled students and communities to "see," and thus to reify, difference as racialized.

And yet, as group images depicting multiple persons with different individual histories, psychologies, and attitudes, school photos also became remarkably informative documents. Within them, the variegated textures of assimilationism and induced cultural change could be investigated both from the perspective of the institutions perpetrating them, and from that of their subjects. By eliciting a "civil gaze" that connected photographed subjects and their viewers as members of a shared citizenry, they could indicate not only how assimilationism fostered social cohabitation among different groups, but also how such cohabitation might turn into oppression, persecution, and radical separation. Indeed, it is through the "civil gaze" they prompt that school photos become privileged objects in a study of the contradictions and mutabilities that structure the process of assimilation. In this sense, each photo can be studied as a snapshot of a *moment* in this process that reveals its pushes and pulls, assents and dissents, gains and losses. It can thus disclose what Sara Blair has so usefully characterized as the "temporal instability" of modernity's assimilationist pull and "radically unstable historicity." It can reveal the multiple coexisting temporalities defining a process whose trajectory can shift direction at a moment's notice.[11]

CIVIL FRAMES

A relatively conventional school photograph of an integrated class (fig. 1.3) can illustrate assimilation as a mutable and contradictory process within an imperial frame. Dated "circa 1900," it shows an all-boys class with its teacher. The photo was taken at a municipal public elementary school in Czernowitz, at that time capital of Bukowina, the easternmost province of the Austrian-ruled Habsburg Empire. Jews, a large minority of Czenowitz's multicultural population, lived there with Christians of Ukrainian, Romanian, Polish, Austrian, and German ethnic backgrounds.

The photo, posted on czernowitz.ehpes.com (a website devoted to the history of Jews in this city and the Bukowina province), identifies only one student in the group, Adolf Blond, Jewish, born in October 1892, standing in the back row, extreme right. We are told little else about Adolf Blond on the image page but do learn elsewhere on this website that years later, as an adult, he would survive nine months' imprisonment in Buchenwald, one of the first and largest concentration camps on German soil. We are also told that not long after his pre–World War II release to Vienna in February 1939, Blond managed to get away from Central Europe and emigrate to England. But the site has no information about any of the Christian children who are portrayed in the photograph with Blond, or about other Jewish boys who are undoubtedly also members of this class. Nor do we learn anything about their teacher.[12]

By the time Blond's school photograph was made around 1900, the emancipation of Jews and their adoption of cultural standards fashioned by the German language and lifeways—their cultural infusion by what the Jewish writer Karl Emil Franzos described as "the mediating spirit of *Deutschtum* [Germanness]"—had been ongoing in Habsburg lands for more than a century. Jewish children had already been enrolled, educated, and ideologically

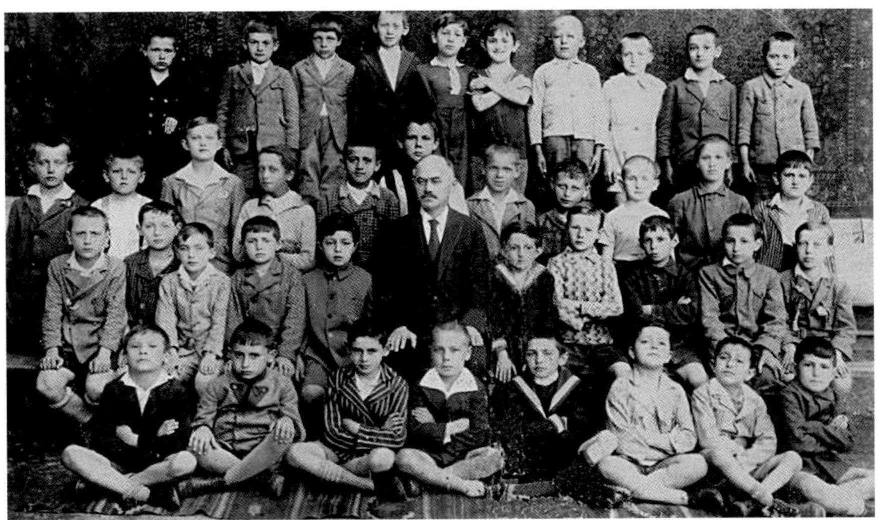

FIGURE 1.3. A class photo in an unidentified municipal elementary school in Czernowitz, Bukowina, Austro-Habsburg Empire, ca. 1900. Photos of integrated classes in Habsburg Europe could conceal ethnic and religious differences. (Blond family archive, courtesy of Arthur Rindner and ehpes website)

inculcated in ethnically mixed schools for decades.[13] The process, therefore, by which a Jewish child would have ended up in an ethnically integrated, state-certified, municipal elementary school classroom such as the one depicted remains outside of the picture's frame. The emancipatory and assimilationist transformation in which Central and Eastern European Jews had been involved, and the long trajectory of cultural, political, and economic change of which Blond and the other Jewish children are products, occurred before photography was popularized. The all-Jewish religious elementary schools (*hadarim*) and Talmudic academies (*yeshivot*) that Blond's grandfather and great-grandfather would have attended fifty to one hundred years earlier in a village or town in the nearby rural regions were not represented in this modern medium.

It is important to highlight that the photo's concealment of the children's ethnic backgrounds, and the multigenerational cultural changes that brought them into this classroom, applied not only to Jewish but to *all* children in the image. Changes of many kinds among Ukrainians, Poles, Romanians, and ethnic Germans in this region of Europe—from peasant agriculture to urban life, from handcraft to factory production, commerce, and professional work—had affected everyone represented, directly or indirectly. In this respect, the Czernowitz photo of Adolf Blond and his class is only one of hundreds of similarly posed class photos of children in public and private state-certified schools taken throughout Europe between the last decades of the nineteenth century and the 1930s. Especially in the west-central and eastern regions that had been under Habsburg, German, and Czarist Imperial rule before World War I, school photos that, like Adolf Blond's, minimize ethnic differences and highlight semblance and commonality among diverse students reflected a photographic response to a long-present (but ultimately not achievable) integrative political goal.

In the Austro-centered Habsburg realm, for example, this integrative goal had a long history. In the late eighteenth century, Emperor Joseph II's noted Patent of Toleration (1781) and Edict of Tolerance (1782) were conceived as two in a series of reform measures that would transform the Empire into a unified and centralized entity by eliminating local ethnic particularisms and the barriers created by estates, corporations, and denominations. Thus, in exchange for the allegiance of Calvinists, Lutherans, and Serbian Orthodox to the Catholic Habsburgs' imperial authority, the Patent of Toleration granted religious freedom in the Empire to adherents of these faiths. The Edict of Tolerance, promulgated a year later and more particularized, extended religious freedom to Jews. In order to bring about their fuller incorporation into the imperial state, it relieved Jews of the obligation to wear the special emblems and distinctive dress that had differentiated and marked them specifically as racialized others, prescribed secular education in German for their children, and compelled Christian schools and institutions of higher learning to admit Jewish pupils. Jews were also permitted to become artisans, enter the free professions, and open factories. Although maintaining restrictions on their freedom to settle where they liked, to own land, and to choose certain vocations, the reforms recognized Jews' right to become naturalized subjects by offering them hope for fuller citizenship privileges and greater equality in the future.[14] Embrace of secular integrated schooling therefore became a powerful incentive for those desiring the benefits of citizenship.

Central European rulers and imperial authorities grasped that children were a key to the long-term success of their assimilative political objective.

Schools, they realized, could serve as prime instruments in forming national subjects within a centralized state—places where a state language could be taught and where civic virtue, love of fatherland, obedience to the law, and the values, ideology, and behavioral expectations of the sovereign culture and its established order could be systematically presented and reinforced. On the basis of this insight, they began to take control of popular education and the pedagogical curriculum. Challenging local, religious, and communal institutions, they mandated state certification of schools, commanded the validation of grade achievement and graduation, and set legal requirements for the age of school admission and length of obligatory attendance.[15]

But as Europe, North America, and subsequently other regions of the world transformed from an agrarian and mercantile capitalist economy to an industrial capitalist social order over the nineteenth century, schools and the educational process took on additional importance. As Mary Jo Maynes indicates in her social history *Schooling in Western Europe*: "The emergent capitalist order demanded a new kind of labor force, indeed, a new human psyche. Schools, along with a variety of other institutions, could help to create it."[16]

The integrative, assimilationist function of schooling, which came to serve the political needs of European monarchs and their allies, was thus supplemented with a second one: the use of education "to make the people love their lot" and "assure that each individual [receiving it] . . . [acquired] the skills and the frame of mind appropriate to his or her station in life."[17] Schools, in other words, were tasked with creating *compliant subjects* within the emerging stratified bourgeois industrial capitalist world order.

This order relied on a strict classification based on gender and socioeconomic class. In Austria, for example, the nineteenth- and early twentieth-century working classes received no more than primary school education until age fourteen. Secondary schools were tracked between the technical *Realschulen* and the *Gymnasien* that taught Greek, Latin, and other humanistic subjects and offered access to university education. Girls had ready access only to primary schools, though private girls' lyceums were formed for the elite. It was not until after the First World War that girls were granted public secondary education.

In some crucial respects, the centralizing reform measures induced, top down, by Joseph II and other imperial governmental authorities converged with contemporary emancipatory and transformational demands by liberal thinkers and activists. Inspired by the Enlightenment's rational ideas, the latter toiled to improve the life conditions of socially subordinated groups, working actively to incorporate them with greater freedoms into the dominant societies. Their goals were wide-ranging: they worked to bring about the liberation of slaves in Europe and the Americas, the emancipation of the Catholic minority in the United Kingdom and of Jews in Western and Central Europe, and the elimination of serfdom throughout Eastern Europe. Some even advocated women's liberation. But liberal reformers were no less culturally chauvinistic than the imperial rulers. They also expected—indeed, demanded—that members of emancipated populations adapt and conform to the emancipators' values, outlooks, and lifeways. Before they could hope for incorporation into and civil acceptance in the sovereign world, emancipated subjects had to be culturally modified and transformed—in reformers' terms, "uplifted," "bettered," or "improved" from a previously "debased" character and existence. The reformers believed that culturally induced ways of living, thinking, and worshiping that they considered "primitive," "barbaric," and "backward" needed to be erased and replaced.

Name reform, language change, and modification in dress and appearance—three aspects of personal identity—were central in the transformations demanded of subordinated subjects, not unlike practices of cultural chauvinism in the British Empire and the United States. To make Jews conform more closely and to register them more effectively, for example, Habsburg officials mandated that they adopt a German surname. Jews throughout the Germanic lands were also induced to replace what some ridiculed as their "laughable jargon," Yiddish (*Judendeutsch*), with German and were prompted to change their external appearance. *Sich Deutsch kleiden*—to dress in German style—was presented and encouraged as the model of "acceptable" attire in society, the preferable alternative to traditional Jewish clothing, traditional head and hair coverings, and general outward presentation.[18] As photography spread, these cultural and material transformations could be optically reinforced.

It is important to emphasize that the changes induced by cultural assimilation were not intended to bring about social equality or eliminate power differences among the rulers and the ruled. Nonetheless, despite their reformist rather than revolutionary intent, significant countercurrents always affected the dynamics of the assimilationist process. On the one hand, officials and citizens unsympathetic to emancipation and assimilation created reactionary and often racist blockages. On the other hand, old-order religious and political authorities rightly perceived that these changes challenged their traditional communities. In the Habsburg-ruled Galicia and Bukowina provinces, for instance, Orthodox and Hassidic Jews resisted the prescribed secular education of Jewish youth, as well as the centralizing imperial policies that limited Jewish communal organizations' autonomy. Many younger Jews, however, especially those in cities like Vienna, Prague, Czernowitz, or Lemberg who were most exposed to Austro-German cultural influences through schooling, increasingly took advantage of the opportunities offered by the newly granted emancipatory rights. Throughout the second half of the nineteenth century, these urban Jews who were "Germanized" in language and culture increasingly moved into the bourgeoisie. They came to view themselves as representatives of the Austro-German *Kulturreich* and as agents of the Austro-Habsburg imperial mission in the East.[19] Their school photos from the early twentieth century reflect and reinforce this sense of incorporation.

The album and exhibit *And I Still See Their Faces: Images of Polish Jews*, displayed by Golda Tencer and the Shalom Foundation in 1998, was compiled during the 1990s from Poles who possessed pictures of Jewish neighbors, classmates, and friends in their personal or family archives. Many of the images are accompanied by accounts of their prewar histories. Not surprisingly, class photos from the 1910s to the late 1940s are heavily represented. Like the images from elsewhere in imperial Central and Eastern Europe, they show integrated classrooms that include Jewish children alongside Christian ones. A 1927 image from Urzedów, donated by Sofia Sobeł, shows a large group of public school second graders seated or leaning on the ground of what looks like a courtyard with wooden barrels and crates (fig. 1.4). The centrally placed teacher looks extremely serious, but the children look friendly and attentive, and some even smile shyly. Sofia Sobeł recalls that "in Urzedów we went to school together. Almost all of the Jews lived on the market square, where they had stores. I lived close by . . . so I hung around with them. . . . When the Germans came and the Jews had to go into hiding,

Lejzur's son came a few times for hot tea. We would cry to think how cold they were."[20] In an image from Oświęcim (Auschwitz) taken two or three years before the end of World War I, the Jewish girls and one teacher were marked with a red-ink *x*, presumably by the photo's donor, in order to point to their difference from the Christian children and teachers: "Among the pupils are four Jewish girls," the donor writes. "The teacher who is standing lower and closer to the girls, is also Jewish." On the reverse side, the same, or perhaps a different writer added: "[taken] in the time of Franz Habsburg [*sic*]."[21] This inclusion of Jewish subjects in the schools, and in the school photos, merits the photo's presence in Tencer's memorial collection. But the invisibility of a form of social difference that would become increasingly racialized and lethal marks that inclusion with retrospective irony.

In another photo from the late 1910s (fig. 1.5), Marianne's aunt Friederike Gottfried is standing in the back row, second from left, surrounded by classmates from other ethnic groups in the recently Romanianized city of Cernăuți, as Czernowitz was renamed after the First World War and the fall of the

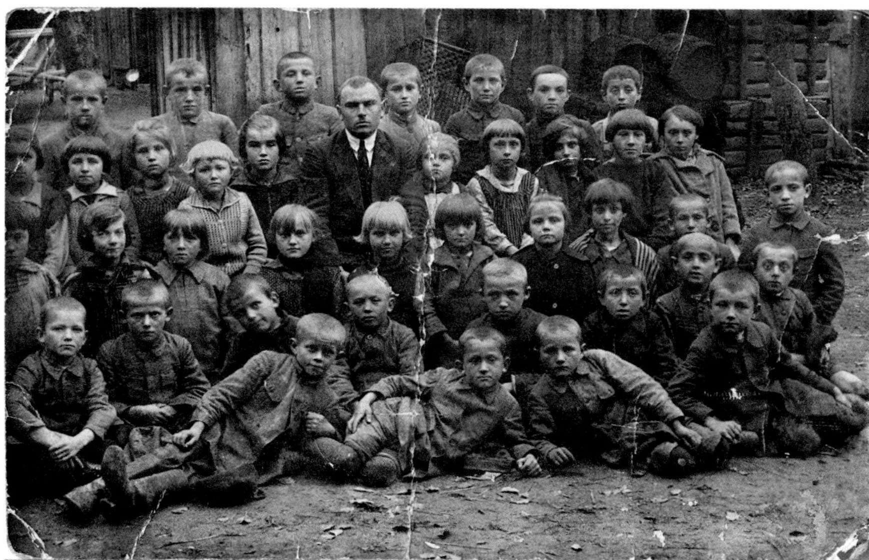

FIGURE 1.4. October 27, 1927. "There are quite a few Jewish children here . . ." Second grade of the public school in Urzedów, Poland. The photo is included in Golda Tencer, ed., *And I Still See Their Faces*, 1998. (Courtesy of Ms. Golda's Tencer-Szurmiej, Shalom Foundation, Poland)

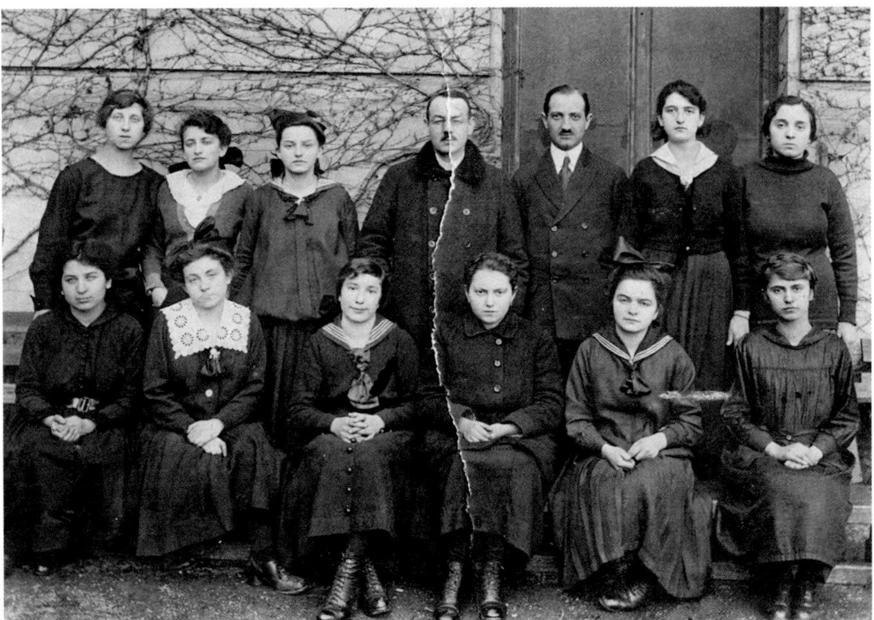

FIGURE 1.5. Friederike Gottfried (back row, second from left) attending the private, ethnically mixed Girls Lyceum in Cernăuți, Bukowina, ca. 1919, shortly after the fall of the Austro-Hungarian Empire and the implementation of a nationalist, increasingly anti-Semitic, policy of Romanianization. (Hirsch collection)

Habsburg empire. All the young women here have donned modern cosmopolitan European uniforms and have learned to assume "proper" postures: folding their hands, holding themselves upright, and keeping their legs together, they assent to the school's corporeal discipline, enforced by the centrally standing male teachers and reinforced by the photographer and his camera.

Like so many others from this period, this photograph is a testament to a moment of civil integration and a sign of modernity. The women's compliance would indeed bring them the rewards of an excellent education. Friederike and others in this class went on to receive PhDs and to work as teachers and scientists during the 1920s. But by the 1930s, Friederike and her classmates, as Jews, began to be excluded from the professions. In order to teach French and German, she formed her own private school for Jewish girls, acquiring her pupils from increasingly anti-Semitic integrated public schools.

As in Europe, photography entered sites of Euro-American imperial involvement very soon after the medium's development in the early decades of the nineteenth century. As photographs of missionary and imperial school classes devoted entirely to African students attest, it quickly became the primary visual channel for disseminating and certifying assimilationist ideologies throughout the Euro-American imperial world.

Starting in the 1830s, French, British, and American daguerreotypists traveled to Africa, the Mideast, South America, India, and Australia, intending to satisfy some of the European and American public's interest in viewing "real"—not hand-painted—images of what, in the popular imaginary, were exotic peoples and far-away lands, portrayed in accounts by returning explorers, merchants, and soldiers. But photography also took root in many of the very places to which the medium was brought. By the early 1840s the daguerreotype process had been introduced in all of the West, South, and East African port towns where ships heading to India or Australia would stop. Ten years later, with the invention and rapid spread of the technology permitting low-cost, high-quality, replicable photo images on albumen paper, photography's popularity in many of these places grew immensely. This was especially true among local inhabitants who were most directly associated with European-linked commercial, educational, and religious institutions—members of what many in Europe and the imperial areas came to consider the "colonial elite." The coastal towns became homes to photographic studios, in large part owned and serviced by local photographers who had successfully acquired equipment, technical knowledge, and an understanding of the latest photographic styles from European mentors with whom they had apprenticed or worked as assistants.[22] These studios offered a wide variety of services: individual and family studio portraits, landscape pictures, and photos of urban everyday life, as well as exoticized pictures of "native types" in "native garb." All these images were intended to be purchased by both local residents and European expatriates and inserted into photography's increasingly popular conduit for picture display: the photographic album.[23] The professional photographers, however, were also hired by institutions associated with colonial governmental authorities, commercial enterprises, and church and missionary bodies to record specific events visually. The taking of school photographs was one such event.

Two class photos taken in the 1890s in Freetown, capital of the British West African colony of Sierra Leone, exemplify this kind of venture and reveal a great deal about photography's modern imperial role.[24] The first image (fig. 1.6) presents male students at the Anglican Church Mission–sponsored, and Durham University–affiliated, Fourah Bay College, West Africa's first European-style university. The second (fig. 1.7) depicts female students and teachers, as well as children from the affiliated elementary school, photographed jointly at the Wesleyan Mission Society's New Town West Secondary School, the city's principal high school at the time.

In all likelihood, the students in the two photos (as well as the children in the front row of the New Town West school picture) are all Sierra Leone Creoles (Krio)—colony-born descendants of emancipated and liberated slaves brought as settlers to Freetown and the Sierra Leone peninsula over the course of a half century starting in the 1780s through British humanitarian and abolitionist efforts.[25] In Freetown, and in what in 1808 became the Crown Colony of Sierra Leone, the British ideologues that conceived the "Sierra Leone experiment" expected these students' parents and grandparents to stand at the forefront of a "civilizing mission." Each free black settler, exposed to European culture and religion by missionaries and white colonial agents, came to be considered a living illustration of what the directors of the royal chartered company that established Freetown had called "the Blessings of Industry and Civilization" for indigenous Africans "long detained in Barbarism."[26] Indeed, in a situation where tropical diseases significantly hindered large-scale European settlement, the black settlers and their Creole children were groomed as "Black English." Their British rulers came to view them as frontierspeople better able to adapt to West Africa's disease environment—the "climatic condition," in the language of the day—who would spread European "civilization" beyond the line non–Africa born whites could penetrate.[27]

Sober and formal in appearance, the students in these two Sierra Leone photographs are staged to project and ratify European notions about what constitutes careful grooming, dignity, and order. The Fourah Bay College photo is especially revealing in this regard. It shows a score of students,

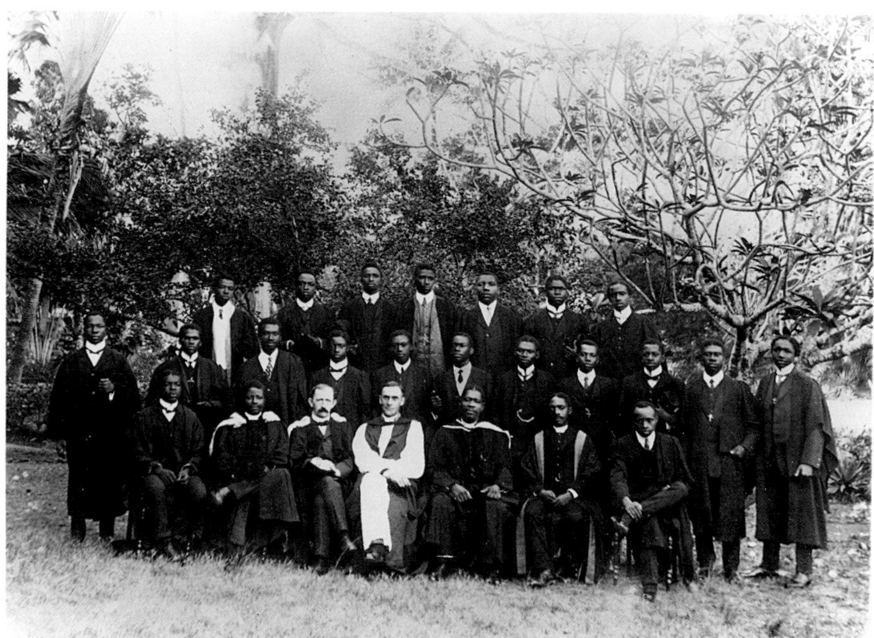

FIGURE 1.6. Fourah Bay College graduating class and their teachers in the 1890s in Freetown, Sierra Leone Colony. The students and the African teachers are colony-born (Creole/Krio) descendants of emancipated and liberated slaves brought to Freetown starting in the 1780s. (Spitzer collection)

the graduating class, standing and seated next to their British and African professors in an outdoor setting lush with palm trees and tropical vegetation. The students are wearing dark academic gowns and are carrying their mortarboard caps and tassels; their teachers—all excepting the white-and-black-gowned man (probably the principal) seated front and center—wear hooded robes, denoting their academic degrees, and hold their tasseled mortarboards in the lap. Faculty and students are elegantly dressed in fancy collared white shirts and ties and well-cut three-piece wool suits made from the heavy materials imported to Sierra Leone from European textile centers. In the steamy, hot tropical environment, their dressy outfits could hardly have been comfortable, but this detail remains invisible in the photograph.

The students are presented as newly successful arrivals within the black colonial bourgeoisie. Despite the status disparity between them and their professors based on age and degree of educational attainment, and the visible skin color difference with the centrally seated white teachers—emissaries

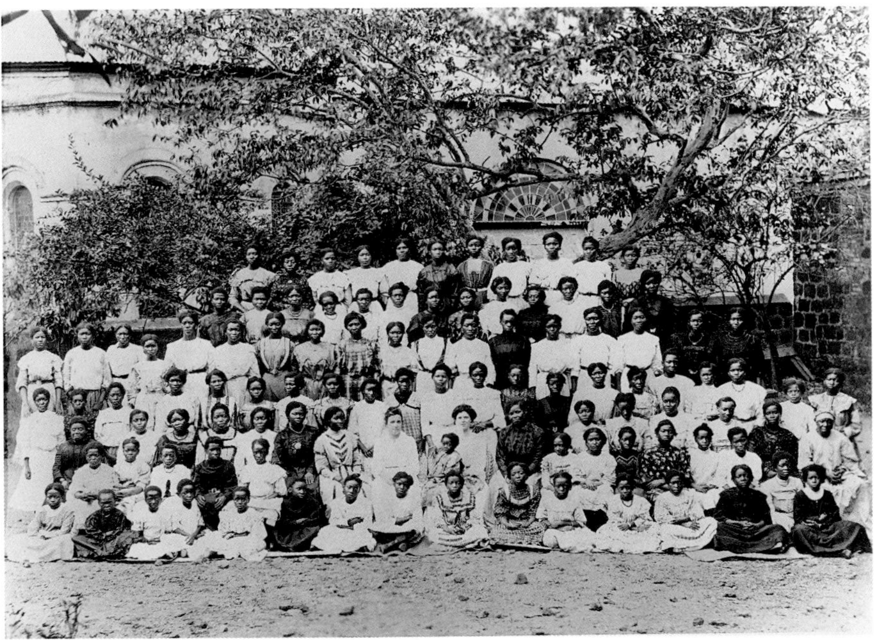

FIGURE 1.7. Students and teachers at the Wesleyan New Town West Secondary School, Freetown, Sierra Leone Colony, ca. 1890. The young girls in the front row are from the affiliated Wesleyan New Town West Elementary School. The occasion for the photograph is unknown. (Spitzer collection)

from the colonial metropolis—they do not look subordinate on this celebratory occasion. On the contrary, their faces and bodily stance seem to display pride and satisfaction in the status and recognition they have earned. They are young men receiving a graduate degree from an English-language African college affiliated with a leading British university who have conformed, in both scholarly achievement and outward appearance, to the dominant colonial order's expectations. The photo seems to proclaim that they have arrived: their transformation has been achieved; it is represented as immutable.

But the photo from the New Town West high school displays a more contradictory and thus shifting set of affects. In this image no one is in uniform or clothed in academic attire; instead, everyone is dressed up in Victorian-style light or dark long-sleeved, ankle-length dresses worn belted or highlighted with ruffled or embroidered collars and necklaces. The girls and women stand or sit up straight in front of a stone wall that separates them from a church building visible behind them, most probably the Ebenezer Methodist Church that housed the Wesleyan Mission's primary school in its basement. The students' arms and hands are by their sides or folded on their laps, and they face the camera and photographer. Their hair is carefully arranged, parted in the center or on the side of the head according to contemporary European fashion and pulled back or set closely to one side, de-emphasizing its natural texture, thickness, and curl.

The group largely consists of adolescents of high school age, but there are also some two dozen much younger girls—possibly siblings of enrolled students, or students in the Wesleyan primary school, who were brought together with the high school girls for "photo day." A number of women in the photograph are older, including two white women near the front center—likely teachers and staff members associated with the institution. Unlike in the Fourah Bay College graduation photo, no specific occasion is revealed for the taking of this school photograph. As a commercial picture, however, of a large group of young African Creole women in Victorian-era dress together with their missionary teachers, it served institutional goals. The image is housed in the Methodist missionary archives, suggesting that images such as this one were used to gain acceptance and financial support for missionary work in Africa. It shows success in transforming African subjects into European emissaries. At the same time, institutional images such as these were also addressed to families who might want to purchase them as a record of their children's educational progress. The expressions of the girls and young women in the New Town West photo are more ambiguous and opaque than the college graduates', however. They seem to accept their new status and the path of transformation in which they are engaged, but they do not uniformly project pride or accomplishment. The photograph establishes acquiescence as a trait appropriate both for a feminine and for a colonized subject. But it cannot convey what contradictory or resistant attitudes— what compromises or refusals—might underlie this quiet appearance.[28]

The role that photography played in furthering European imperial aims in Africa is perhaps even more ambiguous in a fascinating school photo taken at Zonnebloem College in the British Cape Colony in South Africa (fig. 1.8), almost certainly in the mid-1870s. Found in the Western Cape Provincial Archives of South Africa, where the photograph is described as "Group of students, sons of African Chiefs, Zonnebloem College, Woodstock," it probably shows sons, of a wide range of ages, of the chiefs and councilors of what was then known as Basutoland—an African state that became a British protectorate in 1868 and that was annexed into the Cape Colony three years later.[29]

Zonnebloem College was founded in 1858 as a combined venture of the Anglican Church and its bishop in South Africa, Robert Gray, and the British government, represented by Sir George Grey, governor and high commissioner of the Cape Colony. Principally but not exclusively intended as a place that would Christianize and educate male and female children of African chiefs along European lines, the institution was developed to satisfy both imperial political and Christian missionary objectives. Bishop Gray envisioned Zonnebloem as a focal hub from which British-educated African evangelists, converted by Anglican missionary teachers, would carry Christianity back to their homelands. The college, he observed,

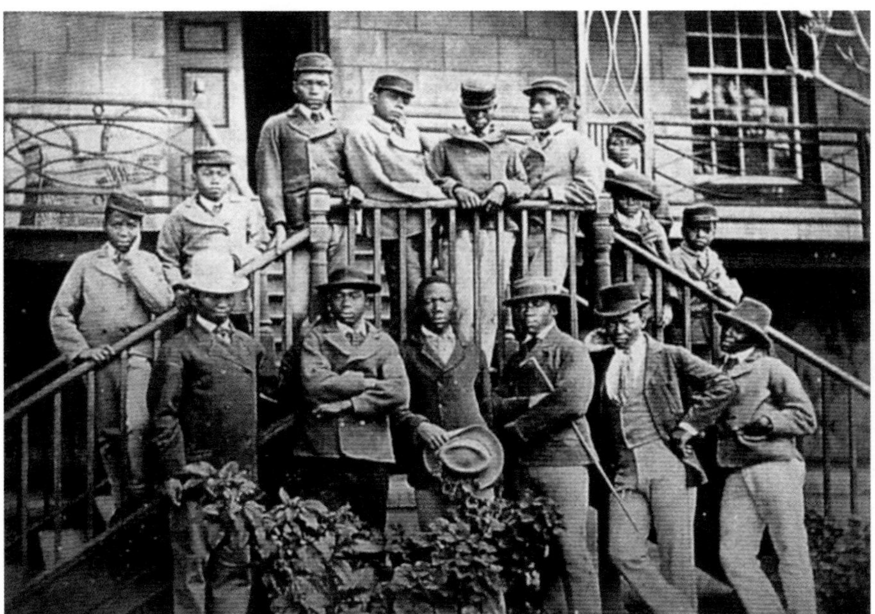

FIGURE 1.8. Sons of baSotho chiefs at Zonnebloem College, Cape Colony, South Africa, possibly 1876. (National Archive of South Africa, Cape Town/Western Cape Archive)

*will place Cape Town . . . in its proper position, as the point to
which the eyes of native chiefs and races from all parts of Africa
shall turn, as the centre of religious life and civilization; and I pray
God that it may become the school of prophets of South Africa,
and that within its walls may be trained many who shall hereafter
become burning and shining lights amidst the darkness which sur-
rounds their homes, witnesses for Christ, messengers of the gospel
of peace.*[30]

Governor Grey, for his part, viewed Zonnebloem College as a key to Great Britain's goals in areas of southern Africa beyond the boundaries of direct British colonial control. He also highlighted the institution's Christian conversionist potential but stressed its political dimension and possibilities—the place, in Janet Hodgson's words, where the sons of chiefs, "future leaders of the African people, would be transformed into black English gentlemen, imbued with the virtues of Victorian culture and loyalty to the Queen and British Empire."[31]

Given Zonnebloem's Anglican connection and the Church of England's evangelizing ambitions in Africa, school photos like this one and the Fourah Bay College graduation photograph in the British-ruled Sierra Leone colony were almost certainly used to propagandize the transformative successes of Anglican missionary and educational efforts in Africa. They could serve to raise additional funding to continue this work from potential supporters in Britain and locally. Copies of this photo may also have been brought or sent to the photographed students' parents and relatives—the chiefs and councilors back home—in order to demonstrate the students' well-being and their transformed Europeanized appearances. At the same time, however, this photo, showing sons of chiefs specifically, would also underscore the colonial project's totalizing transformative ambition: its success, as Bishop Gray expected, "not merely to make the sons of chiefs Christians, or expert workmen, or good English scholars, but to give them as deep and intelligent an insight, as the time will allow into the blessings of civilization; to awaken in them a sympathy with its institutions; and so to influence their whole tone and manner as to qualify them, if possible, to become leaders along the same path."[32]

This photograph, of fourteen students who are connected not by membership in a class and common grade but by their status as sons of African royalty and aristocracy, does not conform to other school photos from this era, however. Taken on steps to what probably was the entrance to the main college building, the chiefs' and councilors' sons are photographed in two rows. The younger ones, in identical uniforms and caps, stand behind a banister above their older siblings and schoolmates. The senior students, smartly dressed in European-style pants, jackets, and hats, stand on the ground below, leaning against the railing. One of them carries a fashionable walking cane tucked into the bend of his arm. But the expressions of the older students, especially, are ambiguous.

Seeing them perform the roles of imagined, if not stereotyped, "black Englishmen" in this exaggerated way, one wonders whether they are being mocked by the photographer who posed them in this manner, or whether they themselves are mimicking, ironizing, or parodying the "black Englishmen" role. Viewed by a white member of the British Anglican establishment, this image might serve to announce conversionist success that, through condescension, marks the subjects' inferiority. It would, in other words, communicate praise for the transformation and disdain for the transformed. But how would the students and their parents have seen the photograph? These students look directly at the photographer, each projecting an individual expression that exhibits considerable distance from the compliant role that subjects of school photos are generally positioned to perform. Wearing or carrying their hats, with arms crossed or on hips, in pockets, or holding the side of a face, they are cast as dandies or flaneurs. But some of them challenge that role with some irony visible in their bodies, arms, and telling glances. It is as though they wanted to emphasize the artificial nature of the setting they are inhabiting. They are aware of their performance. Their mimicry, and the control of the image it let them seize, might have enabled them to preserve the aristocratic status they felt to be innately theirs. Read in this way, the photo can be said to undo the finality of assimilative transformation. In highlighting its fluidity and ambiguity, we leave some agency to the image's subjects, weakening the photographer's and the institution's assimilative imperial frame.

Here and there you peek out
From behind history's veil

CARRIE MAE WEEMS

2

Framing Difference

CREATING NATIONAL SUBJECTS

What may be the first photograph of American Indian (Tulalip) schoolchildren (fig. 2.1), together with their Catholic missionary schoolmasters, was taken around 1865, early in the history of reproducible photography in North America. We do not know the occasion for the photo, but a simple label by an unidentified source tells us that it was taken in the American Northwest, in the territory that in 1889 would be incorporated into the United States as the state of Washington, and that one of the teachers in the photo is Eugene Casimir Chirouse, a layman belonging to the Catholic missionary order Oblates of Mary Immaculate.[1]

This photograph provides one of the earliest examples of what would become a pervasive ideological application of the institutional camera gaze: the use of school photos to display the conversion and cultural transformation of indigenous children to the hegemonic, white, Euro-American mainstream and its beliefs. Indeed, it is likely that the photo was intended for Catholic and other viewers as a visual advertisement to elicit financial and political support to further the missionaries' educational efforts.

The Tulalip boys in this photograph—younger ones in front, older ones behind them—may have constituted more than one school grade. Made to shed their indigenous clothing and to wear light uniforms and a variety of different, seemingly ill-fitting, military-style shaded caps, and to hold their hands at the sides or folded in front in solemn gestures of prayer or entreaty, they present an image of acquiescence, docility, and conformity. By 1860, according to visual anthropologist Carolyn J. Marr, the Reverend Chirouse had trained these pupils to work as a boy's musical band that entertained in neighboring mill towns and earned money to support the mission school. It is thus likely that the boys' uniforms in this photo are their band costumes, and that the taller young man on the right, wearing a dark uniform, is their bandleader.[2]

As in the daguerreotype school and group images taken some years earlier, the individuality of the children in this photo is submerged into a collective, group identity. Their missionary teachers, wearing black priestly

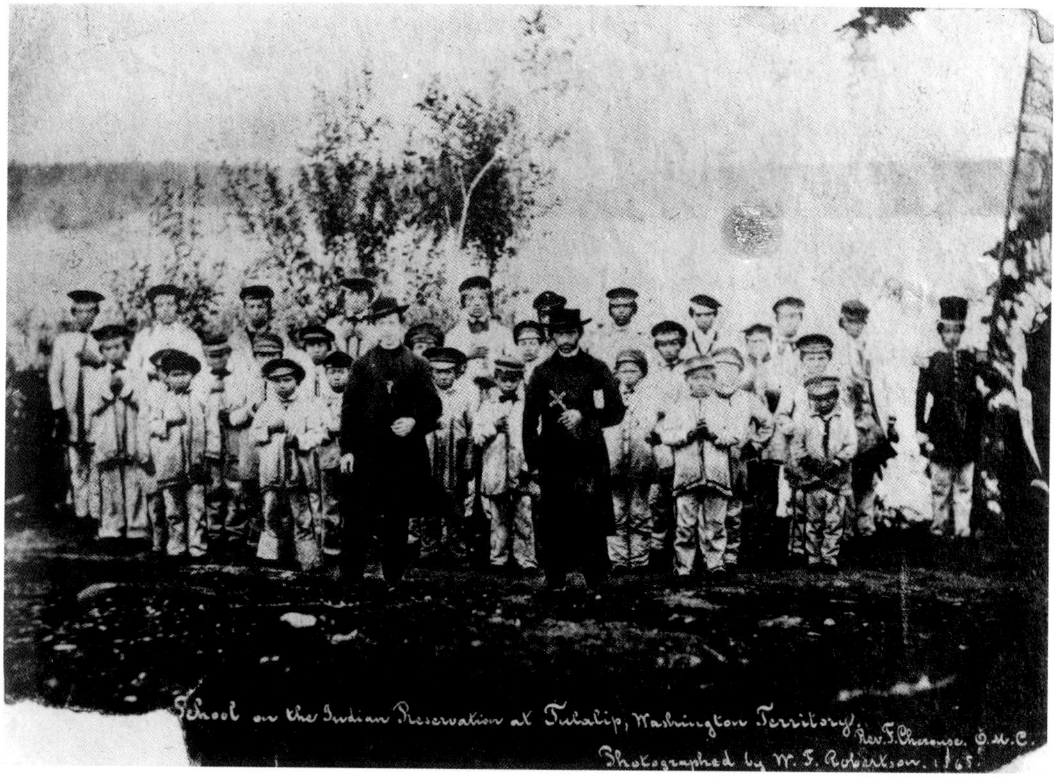

FIGURE 2.1. Group of young boys in uniform standing behind Catholic missionary Eugene Casimir Chirouse, OMI, and another priest, Tulalip Reservation, Washington Territory, 1865. Photo by William Francis Robertson (University of Washington Libraries, Special Collections, NA 1499)

apparel that contrasts with the boys' light uniforms, stand closest to the camera, some steps in front of the group. One of them grasps a crucifix and holds a book (the Roman Catholic bible?) in the bend of his arm; the other wears what, in the low-contrast print, appears to be a dark cross around his neck. Both draw the viewers' attention toward themselves and their roles as missionary agents for Christianity and Anglo-European cultural transformation. They seem unconcerned that their front-row positioning blocks several students from view. Indeed, their stance and bearing gesture hierarchy and separation—instantiating the institutional gaze that shapes the photo by visually proclaiming a status and cultural distance and hierarchy that their young Tulalip charges, even after their religious conversion, are not meant to overcome.

SCHOOLING, PHOTOGRAPHY, AND TRANSFORMATIVE ASSIMILATIONISM

In the United States, Canada, Australia, and New Zealand—Anglo-European-dominated colonial settlement societies that expanded their territorial frontiers by conquering indigenous and aboriginal populations—numerous indigenous children were removed, many of them forcibly, from their parents, families, and communities and sent to government boarding or missionary schools, often hundreds if not thousands of miles away. Once the children were there, school officials made an effort to strip them of their cultural customs, religion, and languages in exchange for those of the dominant whites.

Boarding and missionary schools used photography in calculated and sophisticated ways to record and promote their assimilationist ideologies and practices (fig. 2.2). But despite their promotion of national and institutional agendas, photos taken at the schools can also offer illuminating resources for a historical and theoretical analysis of how photography manages social differences. This is especially true when we join a study of photographic images with contemporary experiential accounts—letters, diaries, memoirs, and recorded oral histories—by participants in the boarding/missionary school experience. These accounts reveal a system of education and cultural transformation that was fundamentally coercive and harsh, frequently brutal and traumatic, and, much too often, lethal.[3] But they also reveal moments of community and accord among students, instances of friendship and solidarity that bridged linguistic and ethnic differences and stimulated powerful bonds forming a Pan-Indian political and cultural identity. They record individual and collective determination and resistance and the growth of a new group consciousness—and they thus enjoin us to reexamine institutionally made school photos for responses that they might otherwise not readily disclose.

Initiation procedures upon arrival at the residential schools were similar everywhere. Students were "cleaned up": washed, bathed, and started on their instruction in personal hygiene. If it was deemed necessary, school officials washed children's hair with pesticides or kerosene to kill lice before cutting it. Euro-American whites associated Indians' long hair with what they saw as the "primitive," if not "savage," state of their lifeworld, and therefore shearing off their hair became a fundamental starting step in their transformation.[4]

In their accounts, former students often recall the humiliation of haircutting. "They shut the door and about that time I get excited and they got a chair," Guy Quoetone, a young Kiowa noted about his haircutting experience at the Methodist Mission's Methvin Institute in Oklahoma:

> *This man set me there and they commence to hold me. . . . This
> barber . . . he come from behind and cut one side of my braid
> off. . . . About that time I jumped up and they grabbed me and hold
> me down. And I turned tiger! I commenced to fight and scratch
> and bite and jump up in the air! They had a time, all of them, holding me down. Cut the other side. . . . It was almost an hour before
> he finished cutting my hair. And you ought to see how I looked. I
> sure hate a haircut![5]*

"I remember being dragged out [from a hiding place under a bed], though I resisted by kicking and scratching wildly," Zitkala-Ša, a Lakota woman, wrote in her memoir; ". . . I was carried downstairs and tied fast in a chair. I cried aloud, shaking my head all the while until I felt the cold blades of the scissors against my neck, and heard them gnaw off one of my thick braids.

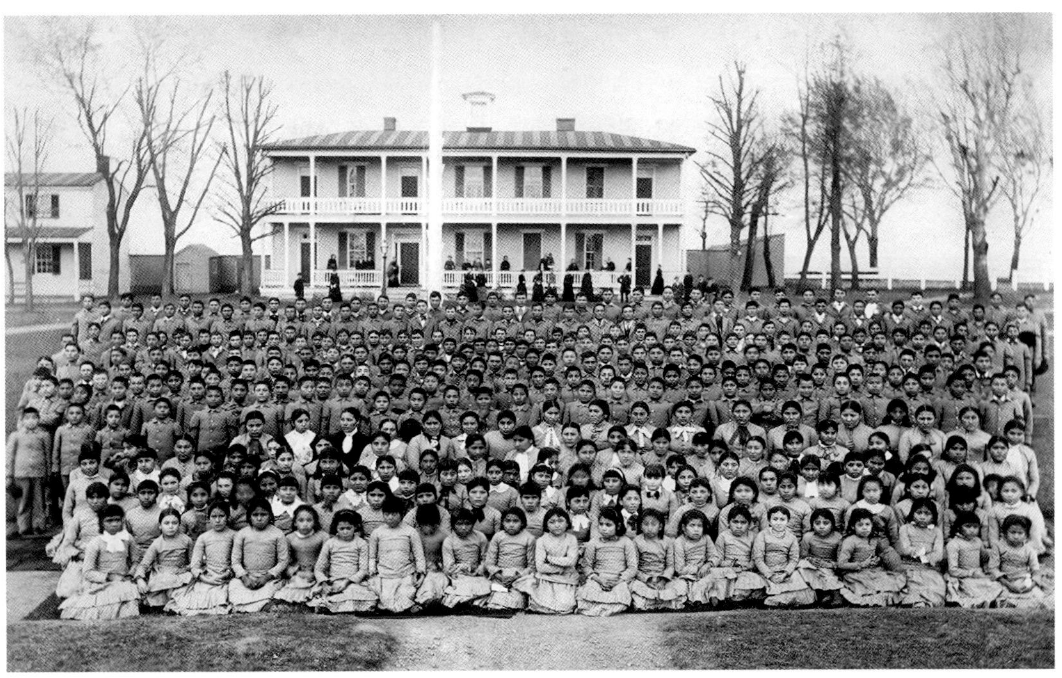

Then I lost my spirit. . . . Among our people, short hair was worn by mourners, and shingled hair by cowards!"[6]

Carrying out the process that Carlisle Indian Industrial School's founder and first superintendent, Richard H. Pratt, had so bluntly described as "Kill the Indian, Save the Man," teachers and school officials forced newly arrived children to remove the indigenous clothing and bodily decoration they had brought with them, exchanging these for school uniforms.[7] Girls were given prim dresses, usually in a similar design and color, and boys were made to wear military-style trousers and jackets, much like the uniforms worn by cavalry soldiers that had subjugated Indian peoples in the frontier wars of dispossession. This exchange, school officials asserted, was intended as a way to strip Indian children of their indigenous identities and create an appearance of conformity and similarity, if not interchangeability, that school photos reinforced. But the military-style uniforms also permitted the exhibition of military-inspired ranking differences between older ("more advanced") students, rewarded by school officials and granted some limited oversight and disciplining powers, and younger or more rebellious ones.[8]

School officials also compelled children to drop their Indian names in exchange for new ones soon after their arrival, echoing the name changes that were common to all imperial assimilationist practices, from Central Europe to Africa, India, and the Americas.[9] In the residential schools, teachers and other authorities chose names like Ruth, David, Esther, Mary, Joseph, and Sarah for the students—biblical names from the Judeo-Christian tradition—as well as the names of US presidents, like George or Ulysses, or conventional forenames like Connie, Daisy, Don, Guy, Jean, and Lewis. At Carlisle, Superintendent Pratt argued that Indians needed "civilized" names, pronounceable by teachers and others, in order to function in the world of white Anglo-Americans. "Symbolically," Brenda Child observes in *Boarding School Seasons*, "the casting off of the Indian name and the assumption of a 'Christian' name was the first sign that 'civility' had indeed touched the savage. . . . Nothing less than a complete assumption of a new identity was expected of the boarding school student."[10] "They marched us into a room," recalled Daklugie, a Chiricahua Apache brought to Carlisle, "and our interpreter ordered us to line up with our backs to a wall. . . . Then a man went down it. Starting with me he began: 'Asa, Benjamin, Charles, Daniel, Eli, Frank.' . . . I became Asa Daklugie. We didn't know till later that they'd even imposed meaningless new names on us. . . . I've always hated that name. It was forced on me as though I had been an animal."[11]

But perhaps the most insidious means school authorities employed to obliterate Indian cultural identity were their concentrated efforts to restrict students' use of their native languages. Already by the 1880s, English, "the language of the greatest, most powerful, and enterprising nationalities beneath the sun," as commissioner of Indian Affairs J. D. C. Atkins had boasted ethnocentrically, was proclaimed the *only acceptable language* in US government–funded schools.[12] Teachers and school officials meted out severe punishments for infractions of the "English only" rule. "When we entered the Mission School," recalled Francis La Flesche, who in the mid-1860s attended a Presbyterian-run boarding school for Omaha Indians, ". . . we encountered a rule that prohibited the use of our own language, . . . [a] rule which was rigidly enforced with a hickory rod, so that the new-comer, however socially inclined, was obliged to go about like a little dummy until he had learned to express himself in English."[13]

"Beatings, swats from rulers, having one's mouth washed with soap or lye, or being locked in the school jail were not uncommon punishments," writes Brenda Child.[14] "In my childhood," recalls Simon Ortiz from Acoma Pueblo, "the language we all spoke was Acoma, and it was a struggle to maintain it against the outright threats of corporal punishment, ostracism, and the invocation that it would impede our progress toward Americanization. Children in school were punished and looked upon with disdain if they did not speak and learn English quickly and smoothly, and so I learned it."[15]

From the day they came to the boarding schools, after being removed from their homes and familial lives and enduring long journeys, students faced physical and emotional dangers—perils and vulnerabilities that school photos rarely, if ever, recorded. Recent arrivals and new residents, moving into Euro-American disease environments that they had never encountered, were especially at risk from contagious illnesses like trachoma, influenza, diphtheria, measles, and tuberculosis, "the foremost infectious disease among American Indian children during the first half of the twentieth century."[16] Large-scale outbreaks of these and other infectious diseases were common, and numerous students succumbed to them, died, and were buried near the institutions. Many hundreds of children's graves are today visible in the cemeteries associated with Indian boarding schools.

And yet illnesses from diseases were certainly exacerbated by the devastating effects of homesickness, a malady that deeply affected the children's spirits and minds—and a malady totally absent from photographic representation. "I was so homesick, and sick, I just thought I would die," wrote a student at the Chilocco Indian School in Oklahoma, recalling his own feelings shortly after getting there, but no doubt also expressing emotional reactions that were widespread among boarding school students.[17] Many new and recent arrivals at institutions far removed from their homes felt lonely and deeply sad in what they perceived as alien and unfamiliar environments. They longed for parents, families, friends, and playmates; they yearned for their native lands and for familiar environments; they missed their home languages, which white school officials and teachers forbade them to speak. As Louise Erdrich writes in her poem "Indian Boarding School: The Runaways,"

> *Home's the place we head for in our sleep.*
> *Boxcars stumbling north in dreams*
> *don't wait for us. We catch them on the run.*[18]

Many students responded to their regimented and unhappy life at boarding school by attempting to flee in order to return home. Running away was a drastic and potentially dangerous move that usually involved clandestine foot and rail travel over vast distances, as well as punitive confinement in school "brigs" or jails if caught. School officials were seriously concerned about runaways, or "deserters," as they sometimes referred to them, using military terminology. They offered rewards for assistance in identifying and capturing runaways and used truant officers, law enforcers, and Indian Bureau agents to seize and return fugitives to their institutions for disciplining and possible lockup. As Erdrich's poem concludes, "We know the sheriff's waiting at midrun / to take us back."[19]

FRAMING CHILDREN

The remarkable images these boarding schools used to promote their assimilationist mission have been exhaustively discussed in historical accounts of these schools in the United States, Canada, and Australia, as well as in analyses of photography and race.[20] Significantly, however, they have not been discussed as *school pictures* in particular, nor have they been chronologically or historically connected to school photos taken elsewhere in the world.

Two particular sets of photos from the two pioneering boarding schools in the United States—the Hampton Normal and Agricultural Institute in Hampton, Virginia, and what some have labeled "its daughter institution," the Carlisle Indian Industrial School in Carlisle, Pennsylvania—offer rich examples, and we will spend some time with these images and their role in shaping the mission not only of these schools but also of racially segregated American schools more generally. Officials in these schools engaged professional photographers to document how black and Indian students were being changed through their daily curricular activities in academic classes and vocational workshops, as well as through their extracurricular participation in sports and music.[21]

Contemporary reformers specifically created both boarding schools to be transformative institutions—federal Congress– and state-chartered establishments for what they termed the "civilizing betterment" of black American youth after the Civil War and emancipation and of Native American young people after the American Indian Wars and the launching of the reservation system.[22]

The Hampton Institute, established in 1868 in the waning years of the short-lived Reconstruction era following the Civil War, preceded Carlisle by eleven years. From the very start, Hampton's founder and first principal, General Samuel Chapman Armstrong, designated it as a "normal" school—a two-year training institution for prospective teachers. By the mid-1870s and the successful undermining in the South of ex-slaves' efforts to become full-fledged citizens, the school's primary mission became the education of its sizeable black student population—most of which had originated in the American South—to become schoolteachers for the South's segregated, black educational system.[23] But in 1877, in part stimulated by funding available through the US Congress's first general monetary appropriation for Indian education, Hampton also began a much smaller program to educate Native Americans.[24] They too were to be instructed like the black students, in the same classes, possibly to become teachers as well (fig. 2.3). The prime aim of Indian education, however, was *not* to enable them to return to their reservation origins in order to instruct and work with communities from which they had come. Instead, it was to activate what white reformers termed their "progress to civilization"—their complete cultural transformation: "the replacement of tribal identification with race and American citizenship, of communal landholdings by individual homesteads and private property, of native languages by English, and of the Great Mystery by Christianity."[25] The larger aim was to destroy the social and cultural fabric of these indigenous communities altogether.

In keeping with chauvinistic ideological beliefs about enforced cultural re-education, educators and governmental "experts" concerned with the acculturation of both indigenous and formerly enslaved populations developed curricula that combined academic and practical/vocational learning. At Hampton, Carlisle, and the many schools for which these served as models, the fundamentals taught were reading, writing, spoken English, arithmetic, and science—subjects intended to provide essential language and analytical skills and comprehension enabling students to gain basic access to what George Wilson, in an 1882 *Atlantic Monthly* article, called the "civilized world of books" and "civilized branches of knowledge."[26] The curricula also included US history—exposure to a national narrative from the dominant Anglo-American perspective that included justifications for the westward sweep of US empire and the dispossession of Indian lands, as well as for a belief in the just victories of what those who deemed themselves reformers considered "civilization" over "savagery."

But in a more or less equal division of daily instructional time, the boarding schools also emphasized gender-differentiated vocational training. Manual trades like carpentry, metalworking, forestry, and farming were largely reserved for male students, and sewing, cooking, laundering, ironing, and various domestic work skills for females.[27] For Hampton's black future teachers intending to return to work in southern black communities, as James D. Anderson has argued, such personal manual labor training and experience offered a way to embody and transmit the ethic of hard work and the dignity of labor. While Hampton's educational ideology appeared to promise its postemancipation students and future teachers a path to democratic citizenship, it was actually designed to make them into vehicles who would help persuade black southerners, during the post-Reconstruction decades that came to be called the Jim Crow era, to accept and perpetuate economic and racial hierarchies.[28]

The founding superintendent of the Carlisle Indian School, Captain Richard Pratt, and Hollis Burke Frissell, who became head of Hampton Institute in 1893 after the death of founder Samuel Armstrong, were both keenly aware of the powerful publicizing role that photography could play to win political and financial support for their institutions' culturally transformative goals.[29] As Pratt explained in an 1880 letter to US congressional representative Thaddeus Pound, an important supporter of his school: "I send you today a few stereo views of the Indian youth here. You will note that they came mostly

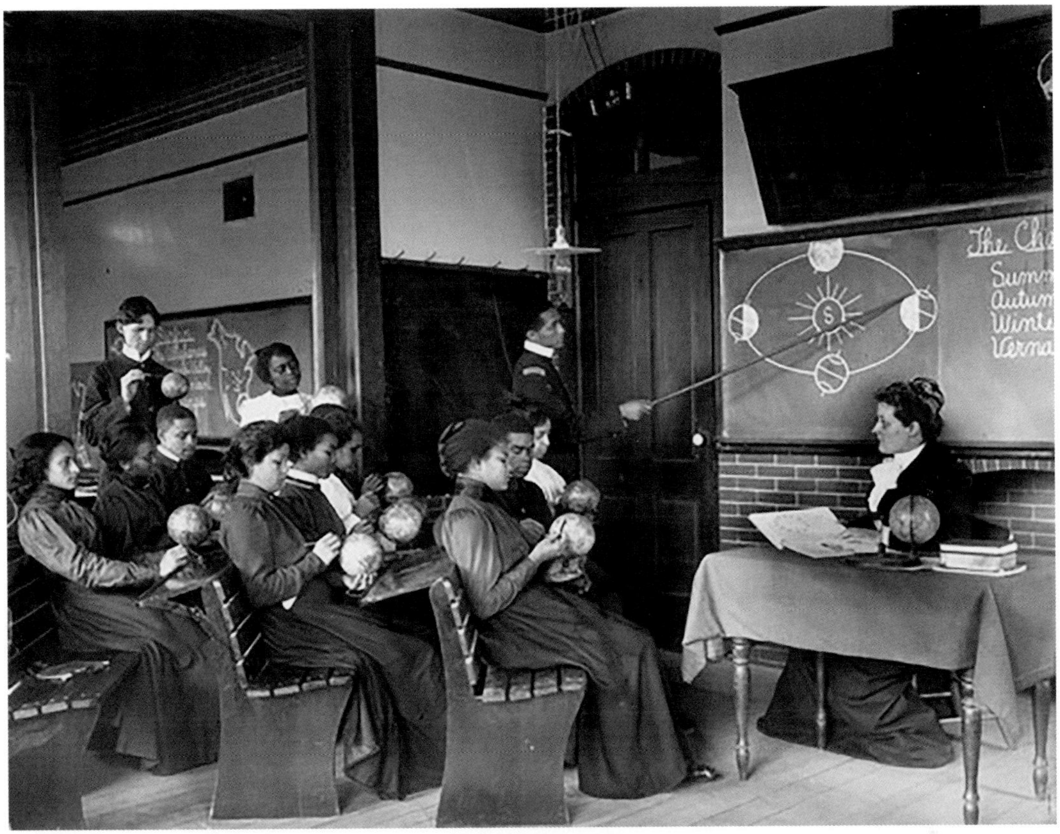

FIGURE 2.3. *Geography. Studying the Seasons*, Hampton Institute, 1899. Platinum print photograph by Frances B. Johnston from *The Hampton Album*, 1899–1900. (Digital image © The Museum of Modern Art. Licensed by SCALA/Art Resource, NY)

as blanket Indians.[30] A very large proportion of them had never been inside a schoolroom. I am gratified to report that they have yielded gracefully to discipline. . . . Isolated as these Indian youth are from the savage surroundings of their homes, they lose their tenacity to savage life . . . and give themselves up to learning."[31]

Professional photographers took hundreds of photos of students in large and small groups, in class activities, and individually and mass-reproduced them as albumen prints on sometimes colorized cardboard-backed postcards and in stereoscopic images viewable in three dimensions (fig. 2.4).

The intended audiences for these images were members of Congress and the presidential administration who were central in funding the institutions, as well as philanthropic agencies and the public at large. Photos were also delivered to Indian notables back in the reservations—persons needed to support the ongoing transportation of Indian youth eastward, hundreds or even thousands of miles from their homelands.

BEFORE AND AFTER

A prevalent way for school officials to display the success of the boarding school experience was through photographs that became popularly known as "before-and-after" images: images that deliberately staged what white officials wanted to present as the students' cultural "degeneracy" upon arrival at the schools and their dramatically visible physical transformation

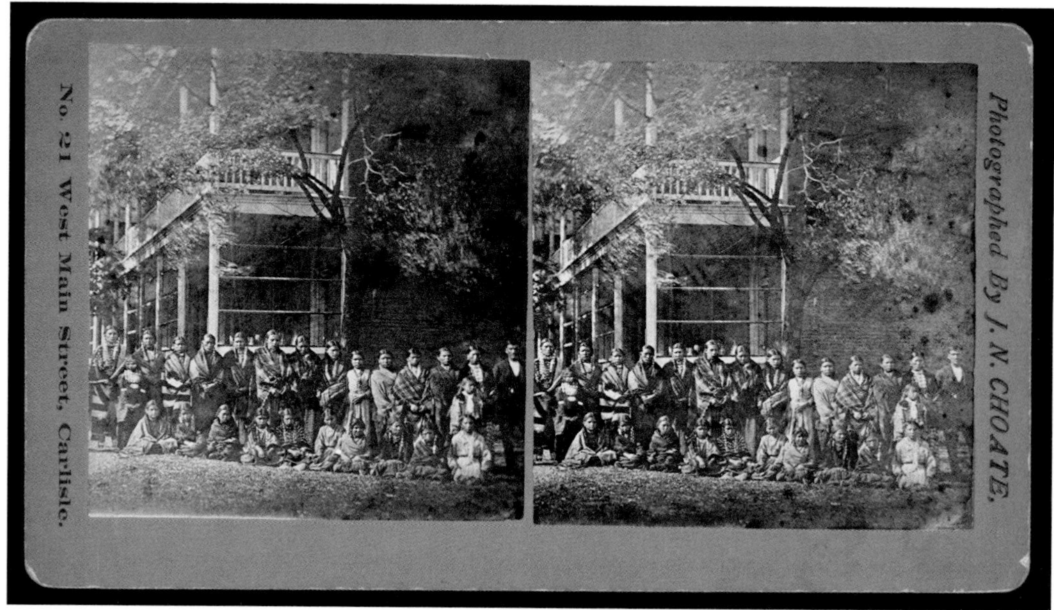

FIGURE 2.4. Stereoscopic albumen prints intended for popular viewing of the arrival of the first Sioux (Lakota) girls at Carlisle in 1879. Photos by John N. Choate. (Courtesy of the Carlisle Indian School Digital Resource Center, from collections at Dickinson College)

some months afterward, after the schools' conversionist practices had had a chance to take effect (fig. 2.5).

As Jacqueline Fear-Segal and Eric Margolis have argued, such a use of photography to visually stage transformation over time was not invented at these boarding schools. Social reformers in the United States and in Europe from the mid-nineteenth century onward employed before-and-after photography and developed it into a genre. More than fifty thousand such photos, for example, were taken between 1874 and 1905 by photographers hired by the Home for Working and Destitute Lads in England—"systematic records of the children as they entered the institution and then, 'scrubbed and clean', as they were released."[32] In the United States after the Civil War, as part of a campaign to raise funds and to convince northerners that ex-slaves and their offspring could become respectable citizens, the Religious Society of Friends (Quakers) commissioned and distributed before-and-after photos of southern black children who had been brought north and educated at the Quaker Philadelphia Orphans Center.[33] In the early 1880s, before-and-after photographs were also being used in the medical field as visual evidence of physical improvement over time.[34]

Although we have no confirming evidence, it is likely that Captain Pratt and other boarding school officials, as well as some of the professional photographers they employed, were inspired by these pioneering applications of the before-and-after practice. "We wish a variety of photographs of the Indians," Samuel Armstrong wrote to Richard Pratt, who had brought a group of young Native Americans, captured during the Indian wars, to be enrolled at Hampton in 1878. "Be sure and have them bring their wild barbarous things. This will show whence we started."[35] We do know that starting at Carlisle with photographer John Nicholas Choate and then imitated at other boarding schools in the United States and elsewhere, the "before" photos of the Indian youngsters were usually taken on the very day of their arrival. Such arrival group photos were staged to address the imaginary of their largely white, Euro-American viewers. Most of the incoming group had come to their respective schools after long journeys—often transcontinental, in the case of Carlisle and Hampton. They were photographed outdoors with long, mostly disheveled, hair, wearing indigenous dress, buckskin or rawhide moccasins, beads, feathers, and blanket coverings. Reproduced in multiple

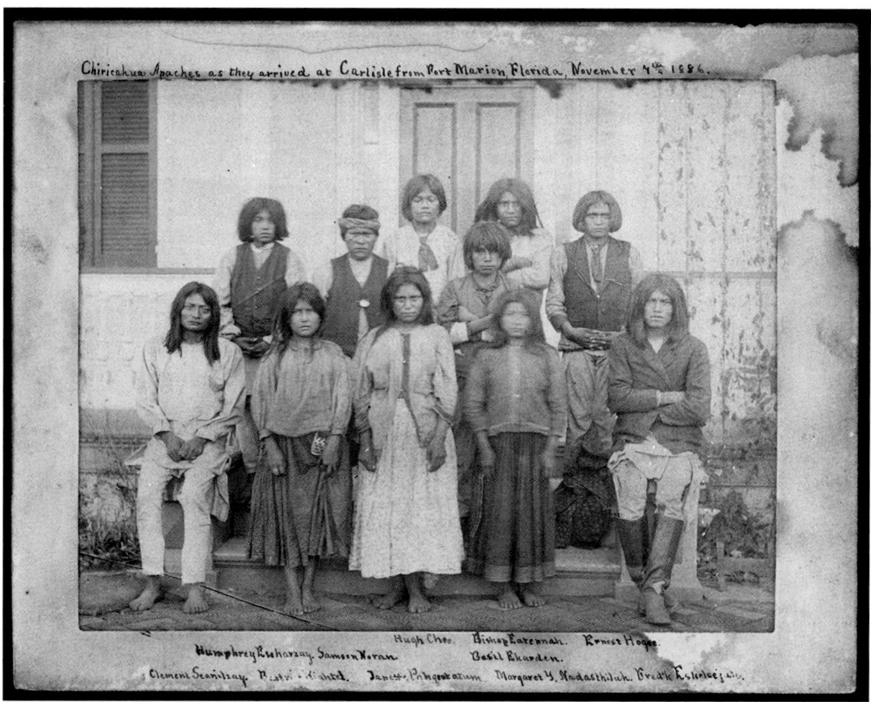

FIGURE 2.5. Chiricahua Apaches as they arrived at Carlisle from Fort Marion, Florida, November 4, 1886 (*above*), and four months later, March 1887 (*opposite*). Photos by John Nicholas Choate. (2.5 [above] courtesy of the Carlisle Indian School Digital Resource Center [http://carlisleindian.dickinson.edu], from collections at Dickinson College; 2.5 [opposite] courtesy of Beinecke Rare Book and Manuscript Library, Yale University)

copies for distribution, sale, and display as "Cabinet Cards"—widely popular cardboard-mounted albumen prints typically measuring 4¼ × 6½ inches— they were staged to reinforce dominant white stereotypes about Indian "savagery."

At some subsequent point, sometimes within a period of a few months or perhaps a year or so later, a second photograph was taken of the same group posed identically to show a dramatically transformed appearance and demeanor that would signal to white viewers that a "civilized" norm, contrasting sharply with the earlier "wild barbarous" state, had been achieved.

Photographers also took before-and-after photos of individual young Indians as well as sibling groups, most often of children or kin of chiefs still

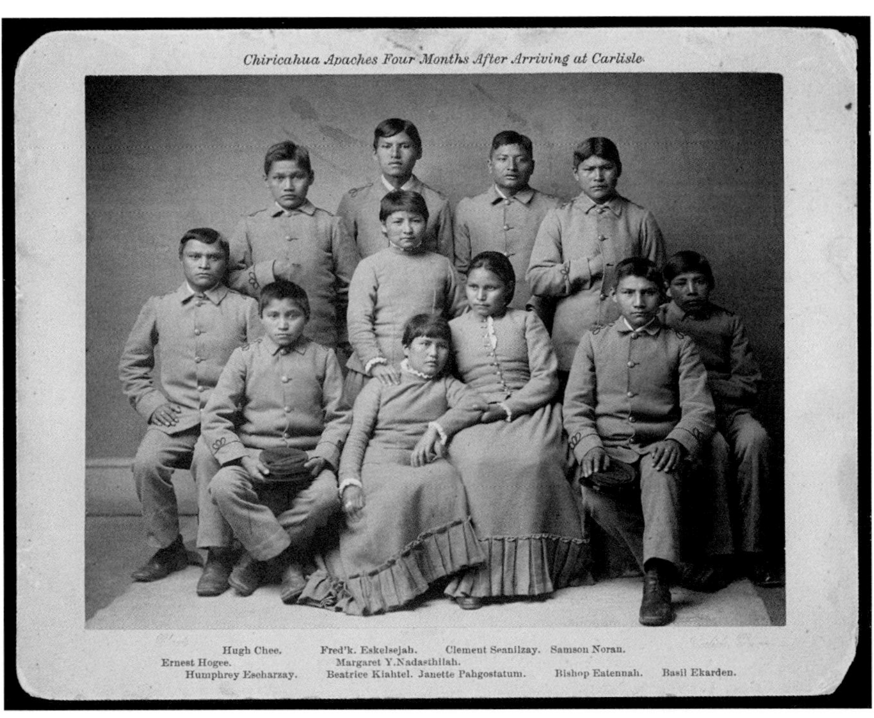

living on reservations. Unlike the large-group images, however, these were carefully staged and lit studio portraits that addressed a different version of the white American imaginary (fig. 2.6). Here the "before" photos also show young Indians in tribal garb, but they are not unkempt and tousled like the newly arrived ensemble in the large-group photos. Instead, they are posed to perform a dignified bearing and a proud, inscrutable demeanor—physical and affective qualities that white viewers idealized and filtered through the lens of a romanticized primitivism and what anthropologist Renato Rosaldo has termed "imperialist nostalgia," the nostalgia of victors for the past that they participated in destroying. Conforming to the Noble Savage stereotype, they are presented as "vanishing Indians"—elegiac figures who, in the aftermath of white military subjugation of Native peoples and the large-scale absorption of their lands, could now, paradoxically, be mourned by the victors for their "passage into oblivion."[36] In lieu of "degeneracy" and "depravity," these "before" images highlight "uprightness" and "dignity"—positive qualities that many Europeans viewed as innate in the character of Indians, and that they expected to be enhanced and developed by a "civilizing" exposure to state- or mission-run boarding school education. And it is this enhancing development that the "after" photographs are meant to display: young Indians, still inscrutably dignified and noble in bearing and appearance, but now, with hair neatly cut, dressed in military-style uniforms like those of the armies that had defeated them, seemingly prepared to be further inserted into the white-dominated Euro-American working world. As

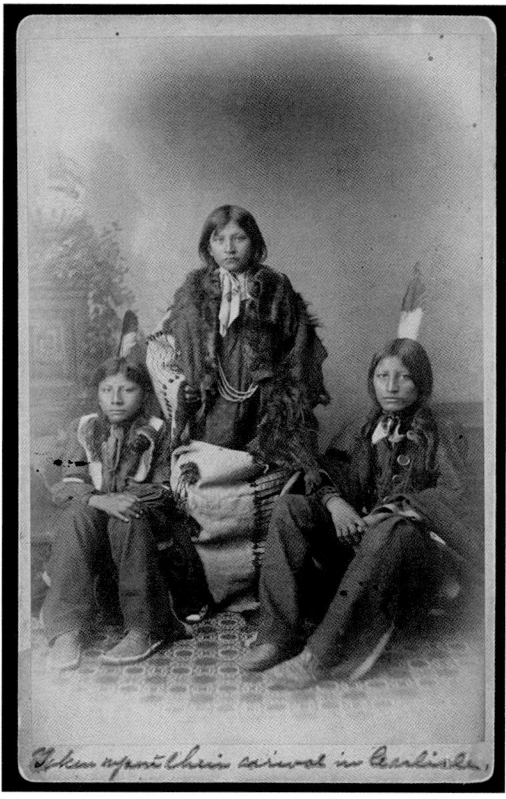
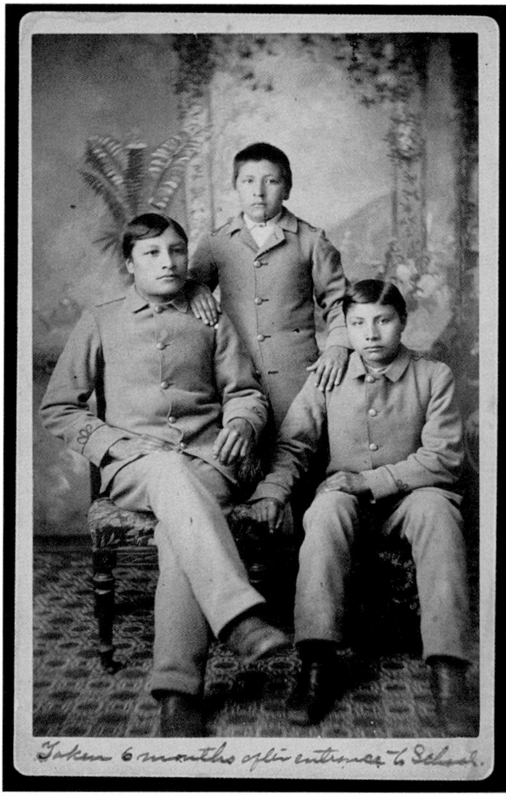

FIGURE 2.6. View of Wounded Yellow Robe, Timber Yellow Robe, and Henry Standing Bear on November 15, 1883: "Taken upon arrival at Carlisle" (*left*); and six months after they entered the school (*right*). (Courtesy of the Carlisle Indian School Digital Resource Center [http://carlisleindian.dickinson.edu], from collections at Dickinson College)

Jacqueline Fear-Segal argues, what the public sought, and thus produced, in the before-and-after images of either type was not the "after" but the primitivized and romanticized "before": "it was the image of 'savagery' that most Americans wanted to see."[37] These photos of Indian chiefs' children are staged to make the journey of assimilation appear linear, final, and irreversible.

The extensive use of before-and-after images in school photos in the United States and throughout the world highlights widely shared assumptions about photography's indexicality and the medium's evidentiary ability to visually display change—or lack of change—from one moment in time to another. They are, as Kate Palmer Albers and Jordan Bear have written, "visible temporal bookends"[38] unable to reveal anything visually specific about the practices occurring in the time gap between the photographed moments, and later, throughout the children's boarding school education.[39]

SCENES OF INSTRUCTION

Frances Benjamin Johnston, who had previously taken and produced hundreds of school photos in Washington, DC, to illustrate a series of booklets on progressive educational principles, was commissioned in 1899 by the Reverend Hollis Burke Frissell to take more than 150 photographs at the Hampton Institute. Johnston was recognized quickly at Hampton for her photographic artistry and representational talent, and her commissioned photos were subsequently featured in "The Exhibit of American Negroes" at the 1900 *Exposition Universelle* in Paris.[40] Arranged by subject matter and displayed on the movable leaves of a large upright cabinet, their role there, as back at Hampton, was to propagandize successes—institutional as well as national—in assimilating black people into the dominant Euro-American culture and economy. They were intended, in other words, to provide visual evidence and convince an international, predominantly white viewing audience what Thomas Calloway, the African American lawyer, educator, and primary organizer of the exhibit, had wanted: evidence of "the Negro's development in his churches, his schools, his homes . . . [and] his professions."[41] The exhibit also contained an album of images of types of African American subjects, mainly from Georgia, assembled by W. E. B. Du Bois, plus numerous other images and artifacts. Significantly, however, it was displayed in the Palace of Social Economy and not in the United States national building that contained the principal US exhibition.

How did Johnston's images serve the needs of institutions like Hampton and the assimilationist project they furthered? In a rich discussion in her *American Archives: Gender, Race, and Class in Visual Culture*, Shawn Michelle Smith comments on the complexity of Johnston's representations. On the one hand, they counter explicitly racist visions of American national identity and the racialized biological determinism of iconic photographers like Francis Galton. Rather than essentializing racial difference, Smith argues, Johnston shows her subjects performing American identity through a set of rituals and behaviors that align them with Euro-American norms. Yet, Smith finds, Johnston's camera scrutinizes the students from a distance: eyes averted, they never meet the white photographer's gaze. Johnston thus subtly affirms social distance and racial hierarchies.[42] In Laura Wexler's eloquent reading, moreover, Johnston's images avert their gaze to the social realities of white supremacy and racial- and gender-based oppression. They record, she writes, "a myth on the eve of its explosion."[43] These images do not actually show a *process* of transformation any more than the "before-and-after" images do: in fact, as we will show, they conflate the before-and-after sequence into several single timeless moments. Static, or dry, in Jeff Wall's terms, they communicate a sense of inevitability about the events being staged. In Wexler's reading, "they privilege achievement over transition, accomplishment over struggle, and the gentler work of transition over the brutal labor of beginning."[44] "Time, in Johnston's representation of Hampton," Wexler continues, "is quiet too. It seems almost to stand still and wait, with an exquisite tenderness, for the forsaken races to catch up."[45]

And yet the images themselves, and the heterogeneous knowledge they carry, can reveal more than the quiet mythic stasis that their camera setup would seem to allow. Building on Smith's and Wexler's insights, we aim to read them in a way that can dismantle their inevitability, allowing us to glimpse beyond the images' frames and into what Walter Benjamin would term their "optical unconscious." It is there that we can perhaps sense the insidious and contradictory work of assimilationism from the perspectives both of the institution and of the children themselves.

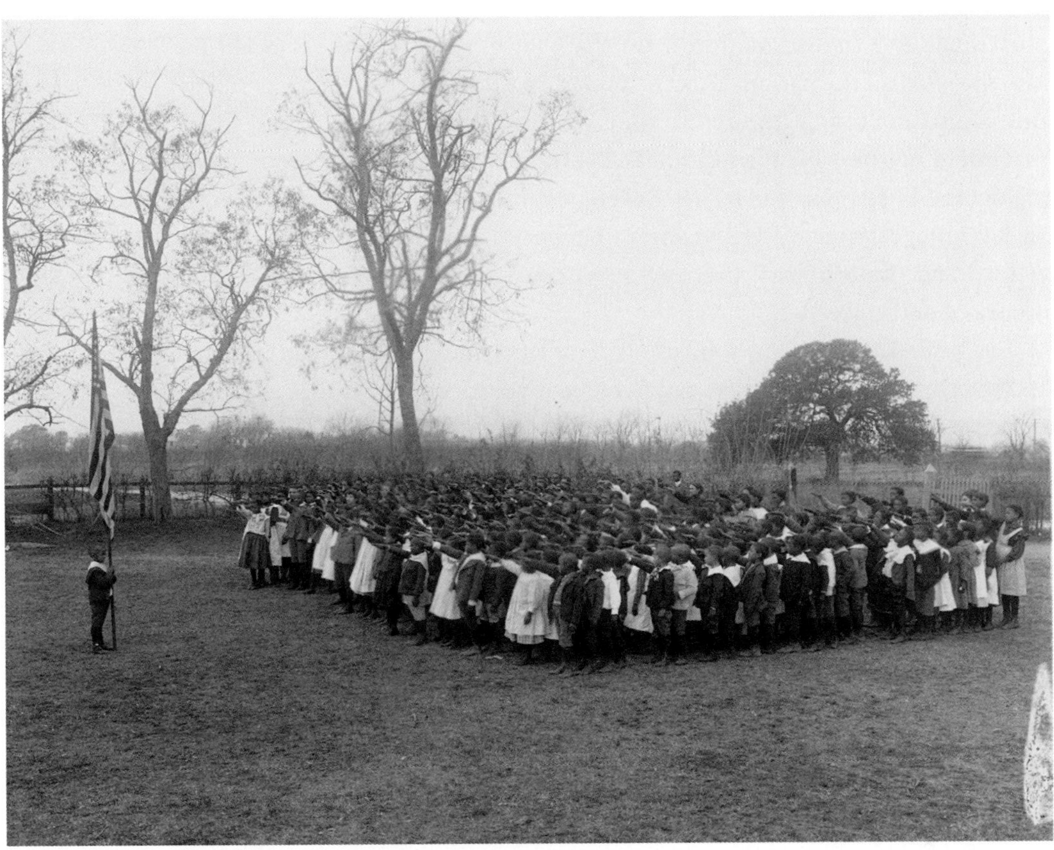

Saluting the Flag at the Whittier Primary School (fig. 2.7) is an excellent example of a distant wide-angle side view that reveals the overt staging of assimilationism at work. Placed in a choreographed triangular formation, the students and teachers of Hampton's elementary school subsidiary, dressed in dark or white uniforms, all raise their right hands in a flag salute, while their left arms hang down by their sides. A little boy facing the multitude holds up a giant US flag that dominates the domesticated outdoor landscape. In saluting the flag and raising their hands, these black children carry out a symbolic act of patriotic citizenship—a performance of their generational movement and transformation from the chattel slavery of their forebears into the space of the national American body politic. Ironically, they perform this in a school totally devoted to their racially segregated education, a fact that could not have escaped them. The setting of the triangular group, on a manicured lawn separated by a visible fence from an overgrown field in the background, reinforces the separation between their transformative "cultivation" and the originary, presumed "wildness" that their schooling both produced and corrected.

Two years later, in 1901, Johnston's now recognized skill in constructing and photographing impressive academic and vocational classroom tableaux earned her another commission, this one from Carlisle's Superintendent Pratt, to take a series of photographs at the Indian boarding school. Her work at Carlisle concentrated primarily on in-class pictures: among others, of English, history, and mathematics classes; of art and singing lessons; of bread-baking instruction; and of training in pharmacy and library work.

Like the Hampton images, Johnston's photos here were also meticulously staged and carefully executed performances of curricular learning activities. But as historian Jacqueline Fear-Segal observed, one class picture from this set especially references before-and-after photography most ingeniously, "elevating it to a new level of sophistication"[46] that skillfully combines the time elements of before-and-after photography into a single photo.

Simply titled *Ninth Grade Class, 1901* (fig. 2.8), the photograph shows a group of students, with a teacher, engaged in reading a text—presumably (as the questions on the blackboard indicate), Henry Wadsworth Longfellow's 1855 epic poem, *The Song of Hiawatha.*

Indeed, Frances Johnston posed and photographed these Carlisle students to represent the process of their assimilation as a linear journey. The distance traveled in that journey is highlighted in the photo by wall hangings in the rear of the classroom—blankets, buckskin clothing, beads, ceremonial sticks, a bow with arrows, and woven and pattern-ornamented shoulder bags—and by a chalk drawing on the blackboard of a tepee and hammock. Patterned and hand-crafted storage baskets also sit on the desks of the three students closest to camera. Many of these indigenous items had probably been worn or used by young Indians when they first arrived at Carlisle. Largely relegated to a background display, however, and exhibited like decorative ethnographic

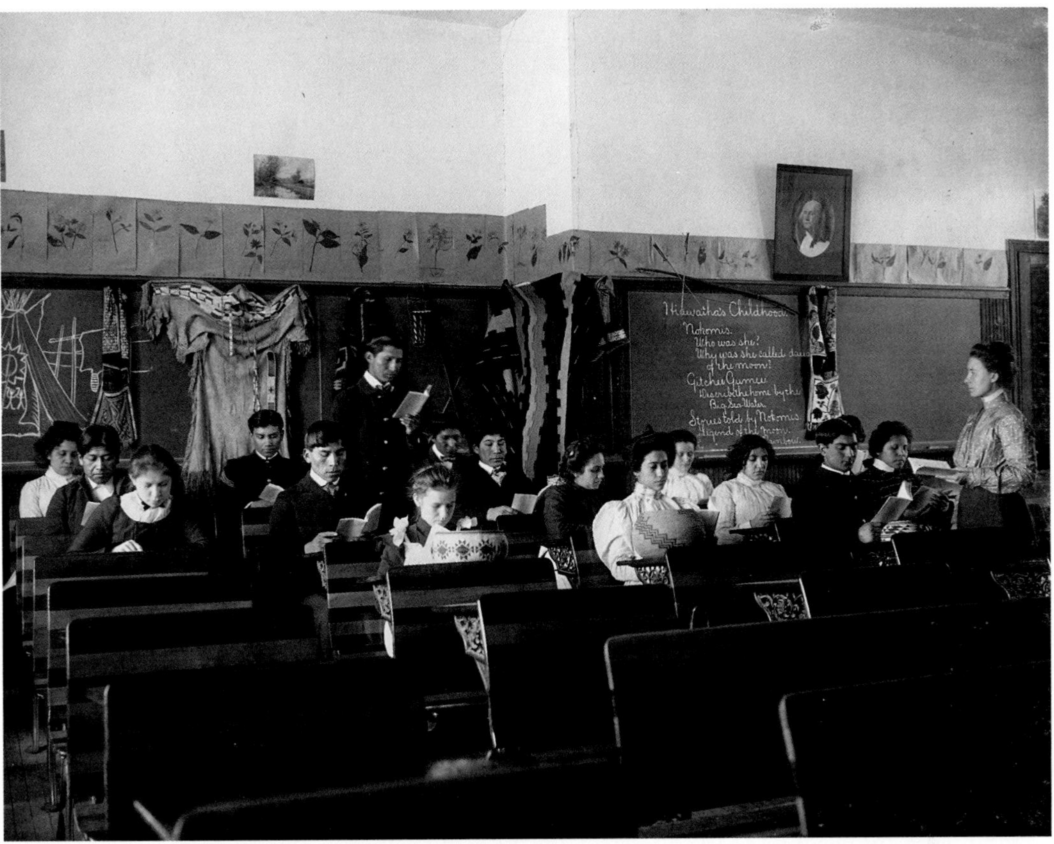

FIGURE 2.8. *Ninth-Grade Class, 1901.* Carlisle Indian School. Cyanotype photograph by Frances B. Johnston. (Library of Congress Prints and Photographs Division)

museum pieces, they are undoubtedly also intended to indicate a past that these well-dressed Europeanized students have left behind and made timeless and mythic—for all practical purposes, discarded. As the objects move into an ethnographic timelessness, the students pass into modern capitalist time.[47]

That message is further underscored if we scrutinize the instructional event taking place and being depicted in the photograph. Looking at *Ninth Grade Class, 1901*, we see an apparently disciplined group of students, closely attentive to their teacher and to the text being read. We can almost hear the section of *The Song of Hiawatha* the standing student is reading to his classmates. The well-known narrative of Longfellow's American epic—one that, at the turn of the twentieth century, many educated readers in the United States would have known and, perhaps, been able to recite by heart—certainly supports the transformative ideology of cultural conversionism at the heart of the Carlisle Indian School's mission. At the same time, it offers yet another instance of imperialist nostalgia made visible and palpable in the photograph.

The epic's narrative, as Roy Harvey Pearce has observed, is set "in a past far enough away in time to be safe and near enough in space to be appealing."[48] Hiawatha, the Ojibwe hero of the poem, is a romanticized Noble Savage—not the hostile, menacing warrior of the Indian wars but a larger-than-life figure with legendary supernatural powers for good. Performing many great deeds, some magically, he instructs his people in corn planting, picture writing, and healing arts. But he is also a peacekeeper who, by action and example, indicates the path to what the epic represents as progress, civilization, and Christian salvation. This becomes explicit in the closing section, written on the blackboard, which tells of a birch canoe arriving at Hiawatha's village. The canoe, containing "the Priest of Prayer, the Pale-face," the "Black-Robe" missionary who brings word of Jesus Christ and the Christian message of redemption, is elatedly welcomed by Hiawatha. Set to exit the scene and depart forever, he bids his people: "But my guests I leave behind me / Listen to their words of wisdom, / Listen to the truth they tell you."[49]

For the Indian students in the Carlisle class, the poem would have reinforced the rightness of the conversionist and assimilationist changes they had been made to undertake and would have blessed their entrance into the Anglo-Christian American white world. And yet despite the framed portrait of George Washington that overlooks the class, we cannot know from Johnston's brilliantly staged photograph if these students will ever be granted or receive—or even want to be granted—equal citizenship and integrated rights within the white-ruled America that Washington's image indexes. At the very time this Carlisle class photo was taken, Estelle Reel, who believed that Indians (and, in her words, other "colored races") were inherently limited by heredity to be less than whites, was superintendent of Indian Schools, appointed in 1898 by President William McKinley. Under Reel's racist oversight, curricular emphasis in Indian schools shifted. Reel's educational ideas, based on a

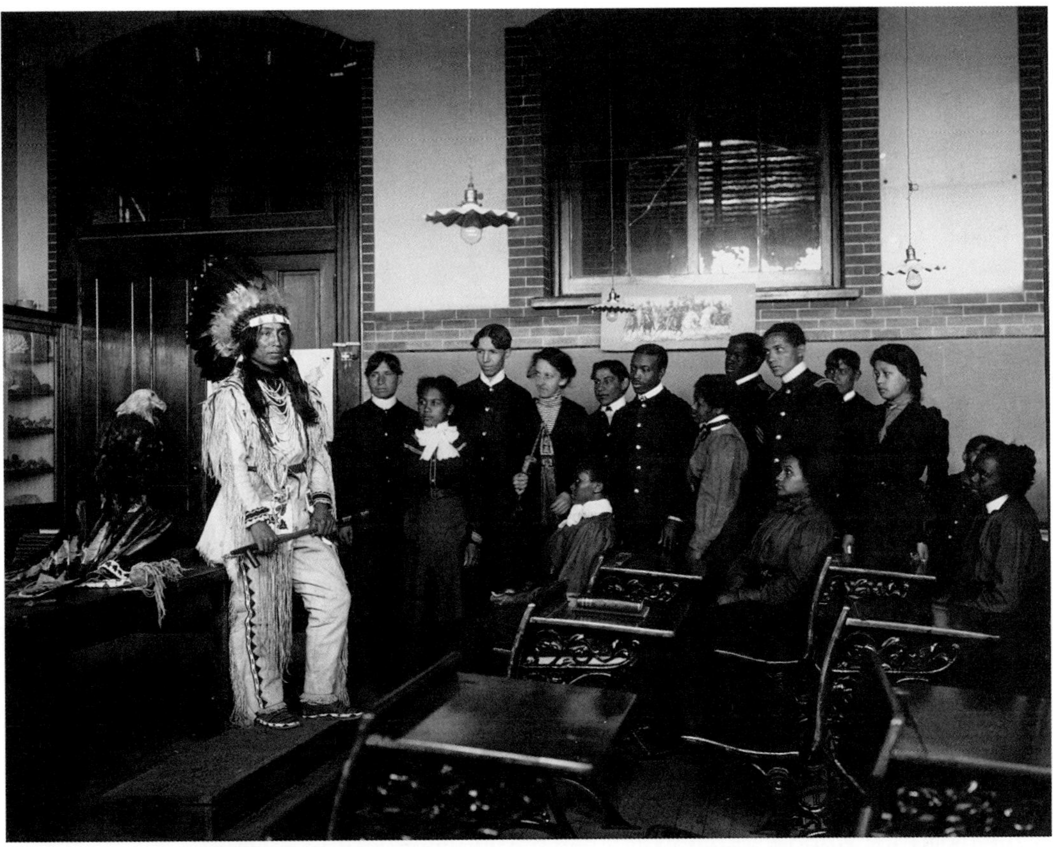

FIGURE 2.9. *Class in American History* from the *Hampton Album*. Platinum print by Frances B. Johnston [1864–1952]. (Gift of Lincoln Kirstein. © The Museum of Modern Art. Licensed by SCALA/Art Resource, NY.)

belief that native peoples "were destined to labor in the fields, farms, shops, and homes of white America," stressed manual and domestic over academic training. Challenging the relatively more "progressive" assimilationist and culturally transformative philosophies of Captain Pratt and the founders of boarding schools modeled on Carlisle, Reel's racist curricular designs were increasingly implemented over the course of the first two decades of the twentieth century in government-funded and -certified Indian schools.[50]

Johnston also ingeniously conflated before and after in her *Class in American History* photo (fig. 2.9), taken two years earlier at the Hampton Institute.

Here, black and Indian students in uniforms study history by looking at several displays prepared for their instruction: a stuffed American eagle, a Remington print on the wall depicting a US cavalry raid on Indian territory, and a live Indian dressed up in tribal regalia. Laura Wexler calls this photograph "a virtual maelstrom of conflicting currents" and argues that Johnston is a witness who does not critique what she sees.[51]

And yet the contradictions in this image cannot escape even the most casual of viewers employing a civil, rather than an institutional, gaze. Visually it relegates the violent reality of Euro-American expansionism and its "civilizing mission" (illustrated, without apparent irony, by the Remington print) to the background while foregrounding the achievement of the children's assimilative transformation. When Native American children in a school class can look at an "Indian" presented in tribal garb as an illustrative *object* in a history lesson, then their process of cultural alienation would seem to be complete. And, we might add, that objectified Indian reflects back on them, highlighting the ways in which they too are staged as motionless, outside of time in Johnston's diorama-like photographic display.

If we try to insert Johnston's images into liquid time, we would have to reconceive assimilation as a trajectory shaped by the instrumentalization and objectification we see in this static tableau and, of course, by imperial persecution, murder, and genocide. Presenting Johnston's *Hampton Album* at the 1900 Paris World Exhibition as a demonstration of African American modernity can in no way belie the human costs and the occlusions of the mythology of "progress" that photography was mobilized to foster.

LISTENING TO IMAGES

The failure of the many hundreds of photos from Hampton, Carlisle, and other boarding schools to account visually for the children's own experiences enjoins us not just to *look at* or to *watch* them but, indeed, to *listen* to them and to the aural and affective resonances that they carry. The firsthand personal narratives and observations, mainly from students but also from teachers and parents, manage to describe and convey a sense of the assimilative process's emotional impact. These accounts enable us to examine the photos we do have more closely, attentive certainly to the visual information that they carry but also sensitive to what Tina Campt calls their "quiet soundings." We can, in other words, "listen to [these] images" not only for what they can "tell" us but also for what they can't, thus for the resistances and refusals they might nevertheless be able to disclose and animate.[52] "Listening to images," Campt writes, "is constituted as a practice of looking beyond what we see and attuning our sense to the other affective frequencies through which photographs register. It is a haptic encounter that foregrounds the frequencies of images and how they move, touch, and connect us to the *event* of the photo."[53]

"We Wear the Mask," a famous poem by African American Hampton graduate Paul Laurence Dunbar, begins to testify to affects that structured the looks on the children's faces:

> *We wear the mask that grins and lies*
> *It hides our cheeks and shades our eyes—*
> *This debt we pay to human guile;*
> *With torn and bleeding hearts we smile,*
> *And mouth with myriad subtleties.*[54]

Sounds and rhythms permeated and shaped daily life at the schools. Primary among them was the ringing of bells marking timed intervals in every student's schedule. Wakeup time, toilette and cleanup time, mealtime, classroom and work time, bedtime: these and other events were announced by bell clangs that established a repetitive rhythm in everyday life, a program of regularly expected, clocked periods.[55] "At school we just went by the bell," Frank Mitchell, a Navajo student, recalls. "Every time that bell rang, it meant that we had to get in line, or go to bed, or get up and get ready for breakfast, or dinner, or supper."[56]

Time markers and clocked reminders are also present in photos taken to show extracurricular activities—in images of students engaged in rhythmic, precisely timed marching drills or parades, as well as playing instruments in school bands (fig. 2.10). And they can be perceived in photographs of boarding or missionary school sporting teams involved in timed athletic events, including in those that would in due course be considered "national pastimes": football and baseball.

These images were largely taken by institutional photographers to tout the sporting successes of their school's teams or of outstanding athletes (like Carlisle's future 1912 Olympic double gold medal winner, Jim Thorpe).[57] But the rhythmic resonances in photos of these clocked and choreographed extracurricular events and activities also reveal how closely connected they all were to the boarding schools' overall assimilationist goals. As Indian children were infused into frameworks molded and defined by Euro-American conceptions of time, they were being disciplined and taught to abandon native temporal notions and to internalize a schedule of regulated intervals appropriate to the capitalist work world they were being schooled to enter.[58]

Individual accounts of coercive, even punitive, discipline that constituted the pedagogy of these schools help us watch and listen to these photos, enabling us to appreciate the surveillance and control to which the children were subject in body and mind. But it would be a mistake not to listen also to accounts of individual and communal resourcefulness, agency, and

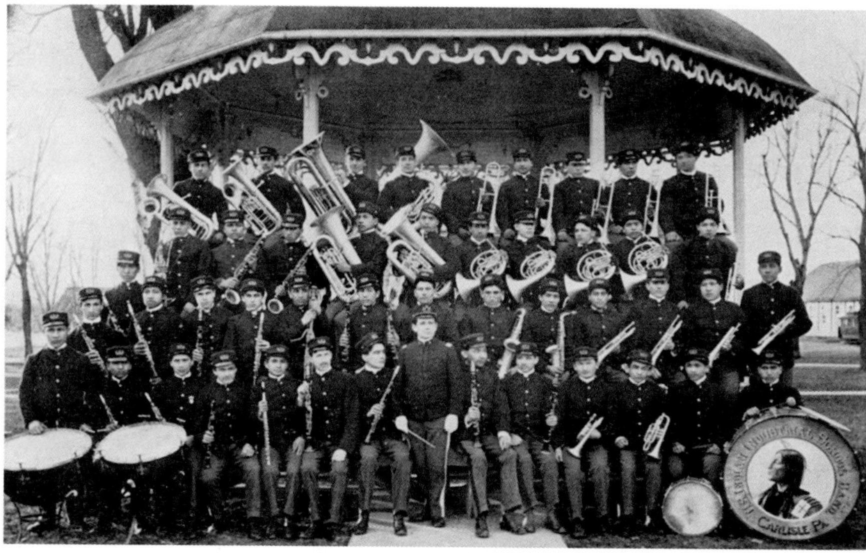

FIGURE 2.10. *The Famous Indian Band of 1901.* Photo by John N. Choate. Could the members of band not have noted that the cover of one of the large drums on which they were beating depicted an Indian dressed with a traditional headdress? (Courtesy of the Carlisle Indian School Digital Resource Center [http://carlisleindian.dickinson.edu], from collections at Dickinson College)

resistance—of the sustaining communities students were able to build and the bonds they were able to form. While these aspects of boarding school life might be less visible in the photos, they are immensely important to highlight in any critical examination of these schools. As K. Tsianina Lomowaima writes about the Chilocco Indian School in Oklahoma, "students successfully exercised their own power in resistance."[59] A former student from the Riverside Indian school, also in Oklahoma, recalls: "I didn't learn my Indian ways at home; I learned them right here [Riverside]."[60] Inevitably, Indian children affiliated emotionally not only with each other but also with the schools that provided them with a complex and contradictory personal and collective transformative experience. These schools could not fully erase their indigenous identities and affiliations. As a Kiowa graduate of Rainy Mountain School, also in Oklahoma, emphatically states "when asked if schools took his cultural identity away: 'They couldn't, I didn't let that happen. People are all the time asking me who I am. Who am I? I am a *Kiowa.*'"[61] In sharing resistance stories, Lomowaima argues, former students communicated and built a communal spirit that survived and bourgeoned despite concerted efforts to impede and destroy such affiliations. It is in these schools that multitribal Pan-Indianness began to take shape and to fuel larger resistance movements in the future.

ACTS OF WITNESS

In 1937 E. Beverley Brown, a young Kwak'wala girl, was taken from her family and sent to St. Michael's Indian Residential School in Alert Bay, British Columbia, Canada. Beverley was a second-generation student in the school; her father had been there before her, and it is he who brought her a camera and, with it, the possibility of not just being *an object* of a camera gaze but of becoming an image maker in her own right. The scores of photographs she and her friends took with that camera over the next years—pictures she donated to the University of British Columbia Museum of Anthropology— provide a very rare record of the residential school system seen through the eyes of a student who participated in it.[62]

St. Michael's, which was in operation for nearly a century (1879–1974), was a residential school for aboriginal children in Canada—one of 140 such schools that Canadian law mandated aboriginal children to attend to satisfy a government policy unabashedly called "aggressive assimilation."[63] The last such Canadian residential school closed in 1996, followed by a massive Truth and Reconciliation campaign that led to formal apologies by numerous religious orders and the Canadian state itself for wrongs and suffering committed and inflicted on aboriginal children.

Beverley Brown's black-and-white photographs of small and large groups of children of different ages who attended St. Michael's during her stay have formed the basis of several exhibitions and e-books designed to fulfill a pedagogical mission: to teach today's schoolchildren about the residential school system's catastrophic effects. In one recent exhibit in British Columbia, *Honouring: Project of Heart / Speaking to Memory*, her photos, accompanied by thirty testimonies by former St. Michael's students, present both pictorial and written accounts of life at the institution.[64] Like testimonials from US boarding schools for Indian children, these also display a range of responses; some former students express satisfaction with the education received, while others stress humiliation, mistreatment, hunger, depression, and unbearable suffering.

Though many were taken clandestinely, Beverley Brown's photos illustrate only the more positive accounts. Informally set up and intimately photographed from a short distance and at their subjects' eye level, her photographs show smiling children who seem happy to be together, exuding pleasure and a sense of community (fig. 2.11). The pictures are taken outdoors, in front of or near the brick school building. Children squint into the sun, laugh jokingly, hold each other's hands or bodies. They are comfortable with the photographer and visibly seem to enjoy the photographic event. And Brown made sure they would be recalled by name. In the photos she included in subsequent exhibits, she inscribed every child's name on the image's skin with a blue pen.

Certainly, the conventions of group photography do not easily lend themselves to expressing the abjection found in the retrospective testimonies that

FIGURE 2.11. School photos taken by Beverley Brown (or by fellow students using her camera) at the St. Michael's Indian Residential School, Alert Bay, British Columbia. (Courtesy of University of British Columbia Museum of Anthropology, Vancouver, Canada)

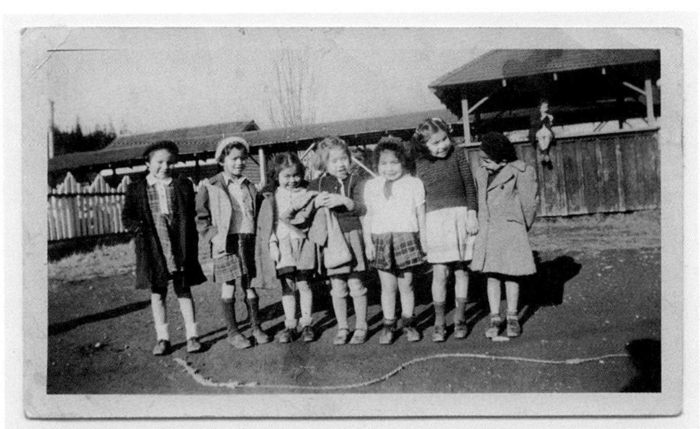

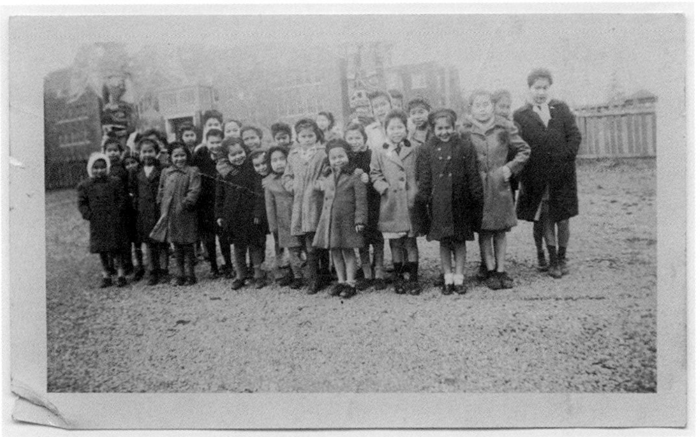

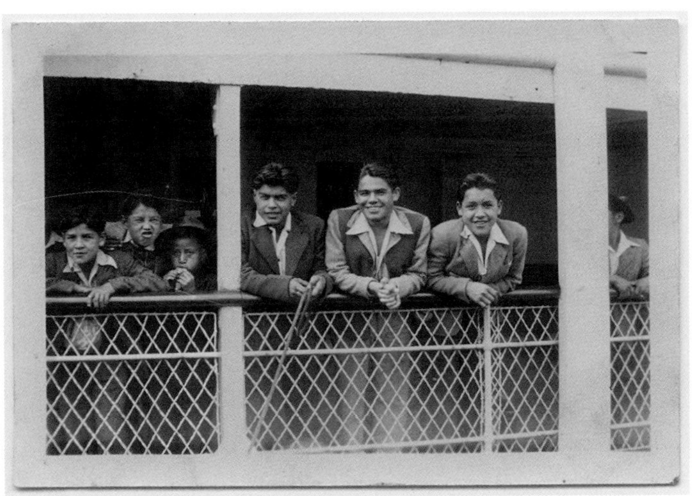

exhibit organizers felt compelled to include along with Brown's images. But some of that abjection and objectification can be seen in the institutional images of indigenous children in boarding schools. Brown's images are different: the relationship between the camera lens and the images' subjects is visibly closer, more intimate than any in photos by Frances Johnston, Nicholas Choate, or any of the other institutional photographers—images in which the children are observed and put on display rather than directly engaged by the photographer.

Beverley Brown's daughters, Bessie Brown and Pam Brown, eloquently describe the collection of images their mother took at St. Michael's:

> *St. Mike's was "home" to Beverley for eight years.*
>
> *Beverley and her brother, Peter Mason Jr., were the second generation of the Mason family to attend St. Mike's. Their father, Peter Mason Sr., also attended the residential school.*
>
> *Peter Sr. clearly understood the hardships of being away from family and friends at such a young age. In between fishing and trapping, Peter would make time to visit his children in Alert Bay. It was during one of these visits he gave Beverley a Kodak camera.*
>
> *Despite the challenges of being away from her family, Beverley created lifelong friendships with many students from villages up and down the coast.*
>
> *The camera became a passion for Beverley and her friends. Wherever they went, they took the camera along. Beverley's father generously ensured they had enough film to take as many photos as they wanted. Peter would then send the film to Vancouver to be developed.*
>
> *The photos in Beverley's collection provide a unique lens into the lives of students at St. Mike's. The young photographers snapped most of the images out of the sight of St. Mike's staff and away from the confines of the school. Their photos give voice to students who were often silenced or invisible. They are a testament to the strength and courage of the girls and boys who attended Indian residential school, and whose friendships became lifelines for one another.*
>
> *The photo collection is not meant to extol the virtues of St. Mike's or justify the wrongdoings that have been publically documented. Rather, it pays tribute to the resilience, spirit and strength of these students.*[65]

As Bessie and Pam Brown make clear, it is not that the children at St. Michael's did not suffer; it is that the photographic events themselves might have provided a hiatus in the school's routine—a respite from institutional surveillance. Offering the children a chance to become agents of their own representation, Brown's camera provided an alternative—in bell hooks's terms, "oppositional"—view.[66]

EMANCIPATION DAY

"Before racial integration, there was a constant struggle on the part of black folks to create a counterhegemonic world of images that would stand as visual resistance, challenging racist images. . . . The camera was the central instrument by which blacks could disprove representations of us created by white folks."[67] Bell hooks's late twentieth-century celebration of the affirming powers of the camera, and especially the snapshot, as a space in which she can "love" her own image echoes Frederick Douglass's nineteenth-century view of photography, discussed earlier. Unlike W. E. B. du Bois, who coined the term "double consciousness" to characterize the internalization of the racist view of the other, Douglass believed in the emancipatory qualities of the external view the camera provided—both for the photographed subject seeing herself positively reflected in the image and for white viewers who would be able to perceive, in photographs, the humanity of black subjects.

This emancipatory vision of the camera explains the smiles on the children's faces in Beverley Brown's snapshots of St. Michael's, as well as the difference between her look and the white institutional gaze wielded by professional school photographers documenting boarding school and segregated education for Indians and blacks. But in the United States, after the brief opening offered by Reconstruction, school segregation persisted, especially for black children. The "separate but equal" public education system legally ratified and mandated in the 1896 *Plessy v. Ferguson* Supreme Court case would not be overturned until the court's ruling on *Brown v. Board of Education* in 1954. In this difficult period, African American image makers could use photography in ways suggested by Frederick Douglass—as a liberatory technology of self-representation. In their case, this is true even of institutional images like school photos. In their book *Envisioning Emancipation:*

Black Americans and the End of Slavery, Deborah Willis and Barbara Krauthamer discuss the visual legacies of emancipation by way of a photographic archive of "Emancipation Day" celebrations in the American South. Variously observed on January 1 in commemoration of the signing of the Emancipation Proclamation or on one of several other significant days, the day, whenever celebrated, occasioned numerous photographs over several decades.[68]

In a photo from a black neighborhood in St. Augustine, Florida, taken between 1922 and 1927 (fig. 2.12), the young schoolgirls from St. Benedict Parochial School are photographed on their float along with their black teachers. The float is decorated with flowers and the American flag. The girls, dressed in white outfits, some with white bows in their hair, look proud as they proclaim their freedom, their social standing, and, by way of the flag, their citizenship.

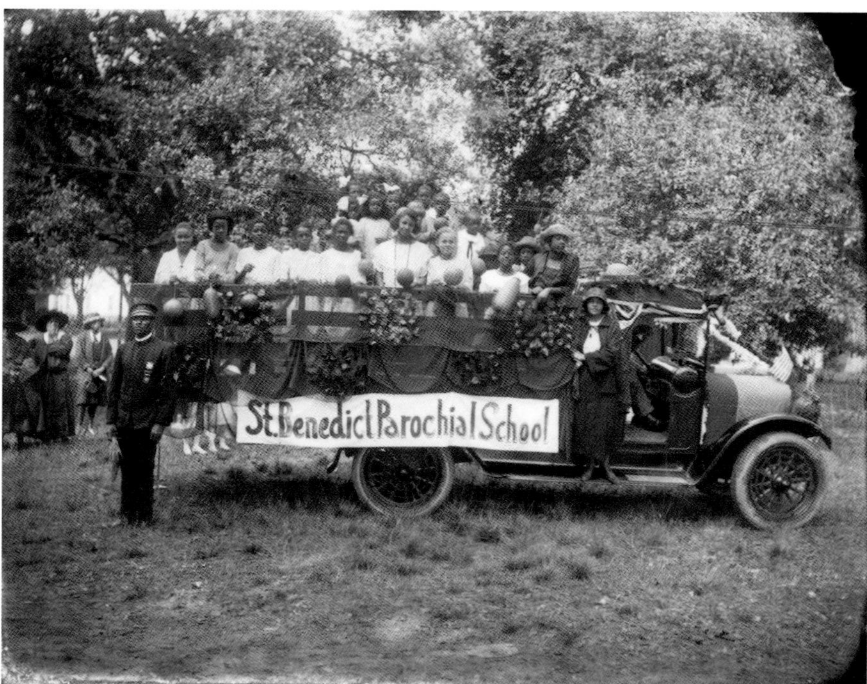

FIGURE 2.12. St. Benedict Catholic School "Emancipation Day" parade float, Lincolnville, Florida, between 1922 and 1927. Photo by Richard Aloysius Twine, 1896–1974. Black & white photoprint, 8 × 10 in. (State Archives of Florida, Florida Memory)

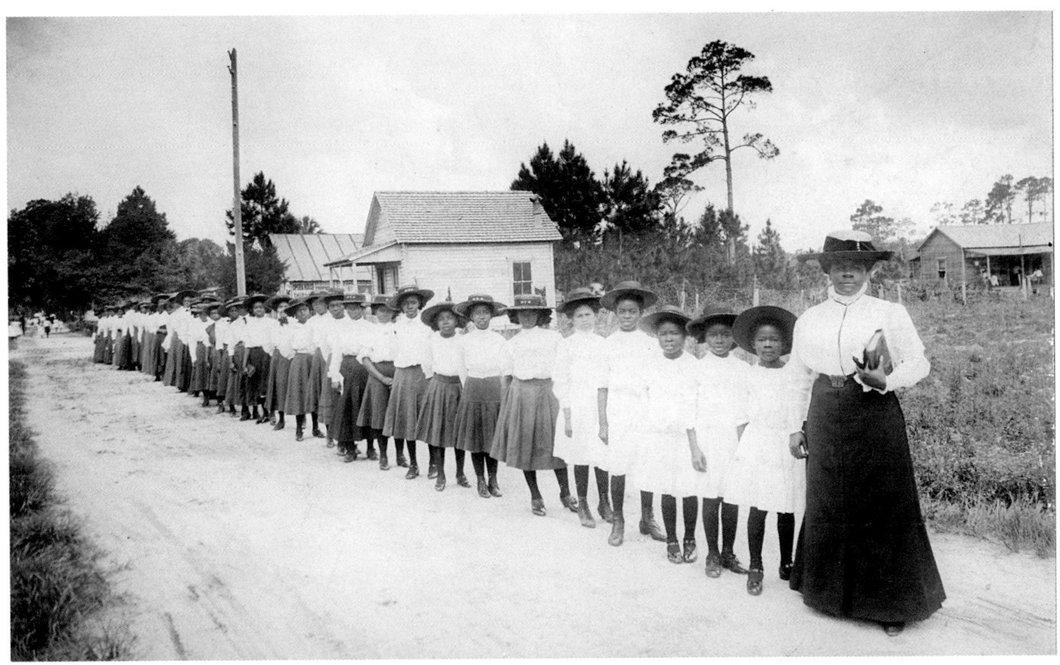

FIGURE 2.13. Educator Mary McLeod Bethune with a line of girls from the Daytona Literary and Industrial School for Training Negro Girls, Daytona, Florida, ca. 1905. This school was established in 1904 in a rented cabin by Mary Bethune with five girls and $1.50 cash. By 1918 there was a four-story building called Faith Hall, a two-story kitchen building, and a new $40,000 auditorium on 20 acres. In addition to the education of teachers and nurses, the school offered classes in sewing, dressmaking, domestic science, gardening, poultry raising, raffia work, rug weaving, chair caning, and broom making. Black and white photonegative. (State Archives of Florida, Florida Memory)

Another school photo, taken by an unknown photographer around 1905 (fig. 2.13), shows the young Mary McLeod Bethune, who would become a well-known educator and civil rights activist, accompanied by "a line of girls" from the school for African American girls she founded in Daytona, Florida, to compensate for the desolate state of public schools open to African American children there.[69] (Eventually the school would become Bethune-Cookman College, with Bethune as its president.) The photograph was taken early in the school's history, after its student population had grown substantially from the original six students in 1904. We might surmise that it served

Bethune and her dedicated helpers and supporters in her legendary efforts to raise funds from white donors and to secure the black community's backing. The diagonal line that the students and their teacher form on an unpaved country road with a few modest houses, one of which might be the two-room frame house that served as the school building, shows the school's dynamism and forward-looking spirit. Bethune and the girls all wear matching white blouses, dark or white skirts, dark stockings and shoes, and, most strikingly, dark straw hats. The careful setup of girls in ascending age and size, with the white-skirted in front of the dark-skirted ones, exhibits conscious self-representation and belief in the photograph's influence. One can imagine the determination and investment that this setup must have taken in an impoverished community and school where the girls had to produce their own pencils out of charred wood and ink from elderberry flowers. The contrast between this image, taken by an unknown but most probably black photographer, and the statically posed boarding school photos could not be more radical. This photograph projects energy, pride, and hope; though standing still for the photographic take and smiling timidly but directly at the camera, the girls are in motion behind their teacher. Unstoppable, they look ahead to the future. It is a photograph in which, as bell hooks would write many decades later, the girls could "love (them)sel(ves)," even as officials in their town deemed them unworthy of an adequate education.

Photographs of segregated school classes taken by African American photographers and studios abound throughout the era of segregation, even as black educators and communities, however ambivalently, fought for integration and equal opportunities for black and other minority children. The Scurlock portrait studio in Washington, DC, for example, documented schools devoted to educating black middle-class children in the city between the 1930s and the 1960s (fig. 2.14).

FIGURE 2.14. Scurlock Studio: Freedmen's Hospital nurses, 1930, above, and a graduation (school not identified, no date), below. Despite the fact that Washington, DC, was a historically and legally segregated city (and would remain so into the 1960s), a substantial African American middle class continued to grow and prosper in the city. The Scurlock photographic studio (1911–94) specialized in recording individual and group portraits of this middle class and its successes. (Archives Center, National Museum of American History, Smithsonian Institution. Scurlock Studio Records)

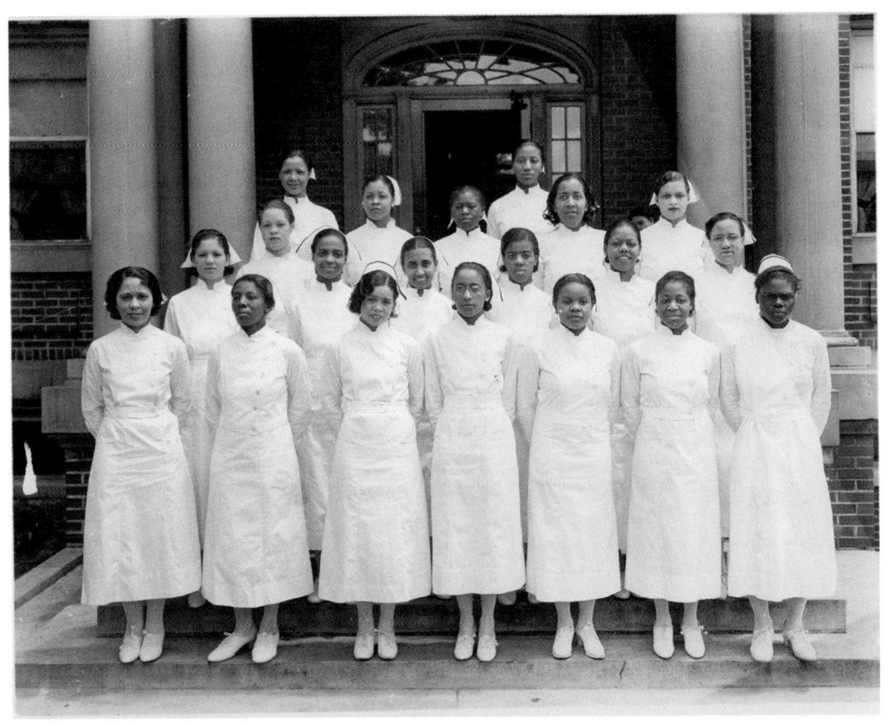

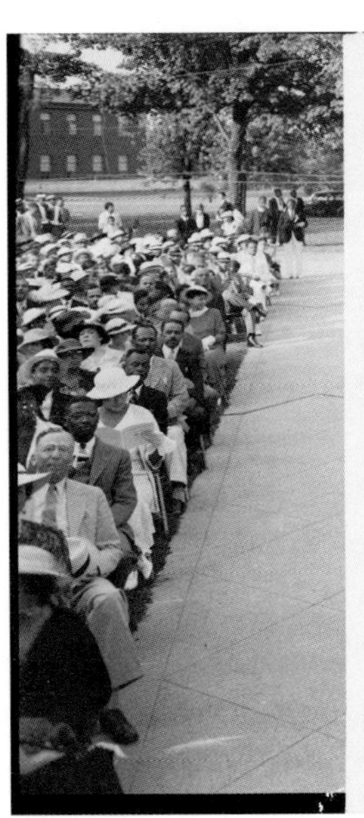
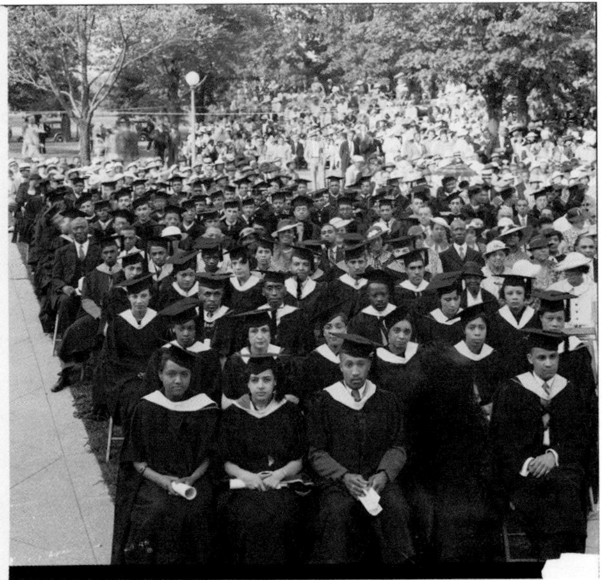

The carefully posed pictures show ballet, drama, and music classes, as well as more conventional class and graduation photos of well-dressed smiling students, comfortable in their communities, who, in the words of Sara Catalina "embody [. . .] black uplift" in their "refinement and restlessness."[70] They also show the devotion of black teachers. Nowhere in these images do we see the radical inequalities that this supposedly "separate but equal" educational system perpetuated, or the fight for integration that the NAACP was carrying out in preparation for legal challenges to the *Plessy v. Ferguson* ruling. Segregation by neighborhood, and by law, shaped the school system in the United States—a system that in its instructional curriculum also promised integration and citizenship.

"I WAS PHOTOGRAPHED"

In the spring of 1942, Dorothea Lange took a photo (fig. 2.15) that echoes numerous images of minority subjects pledging allegiance to the US flag and proclaiming their citizenship. But this picture of Japanese American children's earnest performance of patriotic feelings was taken on the eve of a new wave of racial separation, exclusion, and incarceration, one that would occasion a number of telling school photographs.

Indeed, the sense of order and ordinariness conveyed by figures 2.16 and 2.17 is astoundingly deceptive. We appear to be looking at smiling teenagers of Japanese background, together with their teachers, posing in seemingly conventional indoor/outdoor school photo settings. But these class images are anything but conventional or ordinary. Instead, they are photographs of incarcerated Japanese American students, one taken at Rohwer Relocation Center in McGhee, Arkansas, and the other at Manzanar War Relocation Center in Newell, California—two of the ten concentration camps built in remote west-central inland areas of the United States to house approximately 120,000 Japanese Americans (about 80,000 of whom were US citizens) who were forcibly removed from their homes during World War II, following President Franklin D. Roosevelt's Executive Order 9066, issued in February 1942.[71] They were stripped of their rights without accusation of crime and without benefit of a hearing or trial; their deportation and incarceration was fueled by racism and anti-Japanese hysteria in the aftermath of the 1942 attack on Pearl Harbor that occasioned the US entry into World War II. A contemporary editorial in the *Los Angeles Times* proclaimed this racism succinctly: "A viper is nonetheless a viper wherever the egg is hatched," it declared, "so a Japanese-American, born of Japanese parents [. . .] grows up to be a Japanese, not an American."[72]

These photos of Japanese American students were taken at about the same time that Jewish children and teenagers were being photographed surreptitiously in clandestine school classes in Nazi-established ghettos and concentration camps in Central and Eastern Europe. And, like in Nazi-occupied Europe, in the United States, photography played an important role in Japanese Americans' forced removal and incarceration. In fact, as Jasmine Alinder shows in her illuminating book *Moving Images*, the "struggle over photography figured in nearly every aspect of the incarceration."[73]

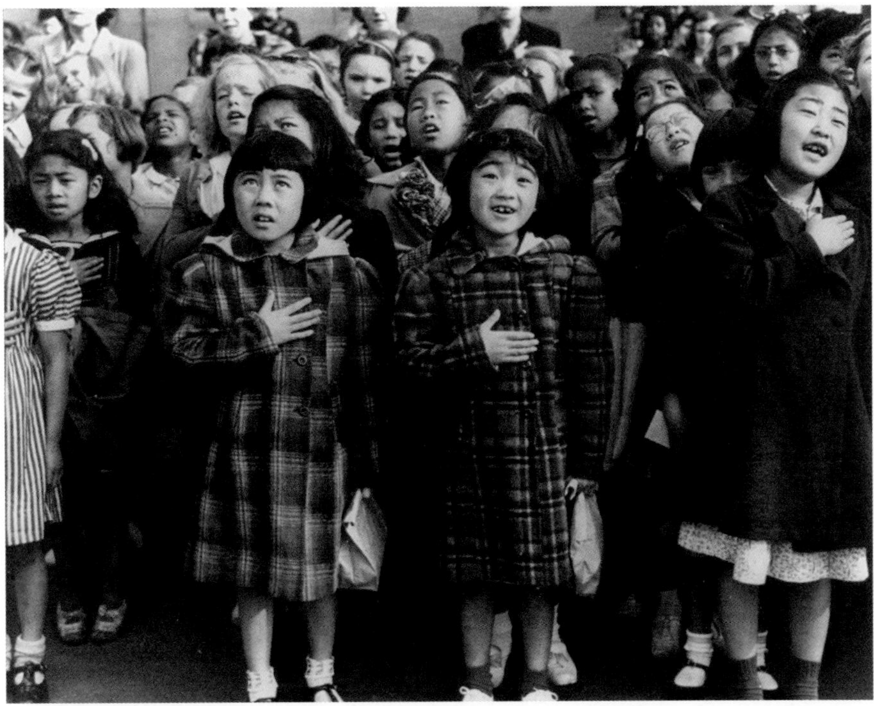

FIGURE 2.15. Flag of allegiance pledge at Raphael Weill Public School. San Francisco, California, April 1942. Photo by Dorothea Lange. (From Central Photographic File of the US War Relocation Authority. National Archives.)

But Alinder also emphasizes that "while Holocaust photographs stress the extraordinary nature of the concentration camp, Japanese American photographs seem to portray the concentration camp as somehow normal. . . . In the thousands of photographs made of the incarceration process by government photographers, independent documentarians, and prisoners themselves, it is much more difficult to find photographs that portray suffering than it is to find smiling faces."[74] The images that have survived the US camps have thus been at cross-purposes with postwar critical historical accounts and indictments of the cruel injustices perpetrated by the US government.

The bulk of photos of these US camps taken between 1942 and 1945 were produced for the federal government by "official" photographers working

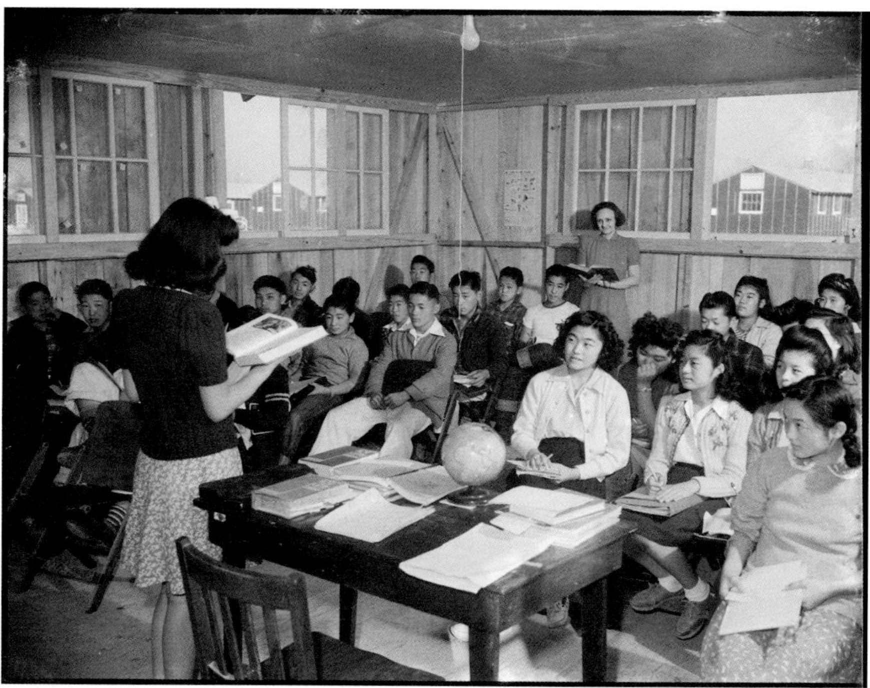

FIGURE 2.16. Archival caption reads: "Mrs. Ziegler oversees her 9th grade class at the internment camp in Jerome, Arkansas." 1942. Classes were typically set up in military-style barracks. Photograph by Tom Parker. (From Central Photographic File of the US War Relocation Authority. National Archives.)

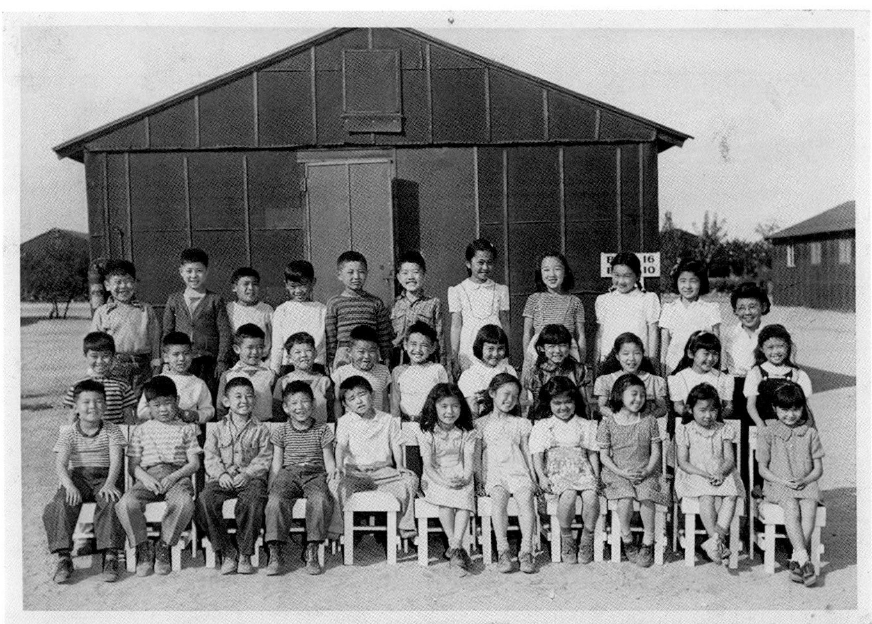

FIGURE 2.17. Untitled (Seiko Ishida's class picture). Manzanar Relocation Center, Manzanar, California, November 1944. Photo probably by Jack Iwata. (Hood Museum of Art at Dartmouth College Collection)

for WRAPS, the War Relocation Authority's (WRA) Photographic Section. Initially in 1942–1943, following the implementation of Roosevelt's executive order, the WRA hired professional photographers to work for the agency under short-term contracts—including Dorothea Lange and Russell Lee, who had photographed for the Farm Security Administration during the Great Depression years of the 1930s, and Clement Albers and Francis Stewart, who had worked for West Coast newspapers and print media. Their charge was to photograph the assembly, transport, and "internment"[75] of Japanese Americans so as to create a visual archive of these wartime actions. At the same time, the WRA outlawed the use of cameras among incarcerated Japanese Americans, although at least one Japanese American photographer, Toyo Miyatake, smuggled his cameras in and courageously documented the incarceration clandestinely.[76]

The WRA's official employment of photographers who were known to be politically progressive during this initial stage of the Japanese American forced removals implies that officials hoped that this archive would be exonerating in content: that despite the implementation of extraordinary wartime measures, it would counter allegations of mistreatment and show that the displaced and incarcerated were being treated in an orderly and humane manner in keeping with standards of international law.

Dorothea Lange would have seemed ideally suited to carry out this job. When she worked for the Farm Security Administration and took her powerful portraits and images of migrant farmworkers and Dust Bowl refugees she was, as her biographer Linda Gordon indicated, "comfortable with her job description: to bring rural Depression conditions to public attention and to do it in a manner that showed its victims as citizens, worthy of help and able to make use of it."[77] She had been recommended for hire to the War Relocation Authority precisely "because her previous work had so perfectly advanced the [Farm Security Administration's] agenda," and she was expected to do the same with her WRA photos.[78]

But Lange quickly defied these expectations. She considered the removal and incarceration a grave injustice, and her photos underscore this sentiment. During April and May 1942, Lange photographed incessantly throughout California. She covered Japanese American life in the days immediately before the start of the forced removals and then took photos of roundups, evacuations, and temporary "assembly centers" in San Bruno, Stockton, Sacramento, and Salinas. In June and July she photographed at the Manzanar War Relocation Center, the first established of the ten Japanese American concentration camps.

Linda Gordon has insightfully argued that Lange's overall aspiration in undertaking her WRAPS photographic work was to "tell . . . the story from the point of view of its victims," even as she refused to treat or to show them as victims.[79] Strategically, at the very start of her task, she wanted to document the "normal life" of Japanese Americans and visually establish "the respectability, Americanism, work ethic, good citizenship, and achievements of . . . people now being treated as criminals."[80]

Lange took school photos after arriving at Manzanar—images that reveal continuity under adverse conditions rather than the patriotic fervor of the earlier photos. The children in her images are not enjoined to sport radiant "smiles," as so many of the other incarcerated Japanese American subjects

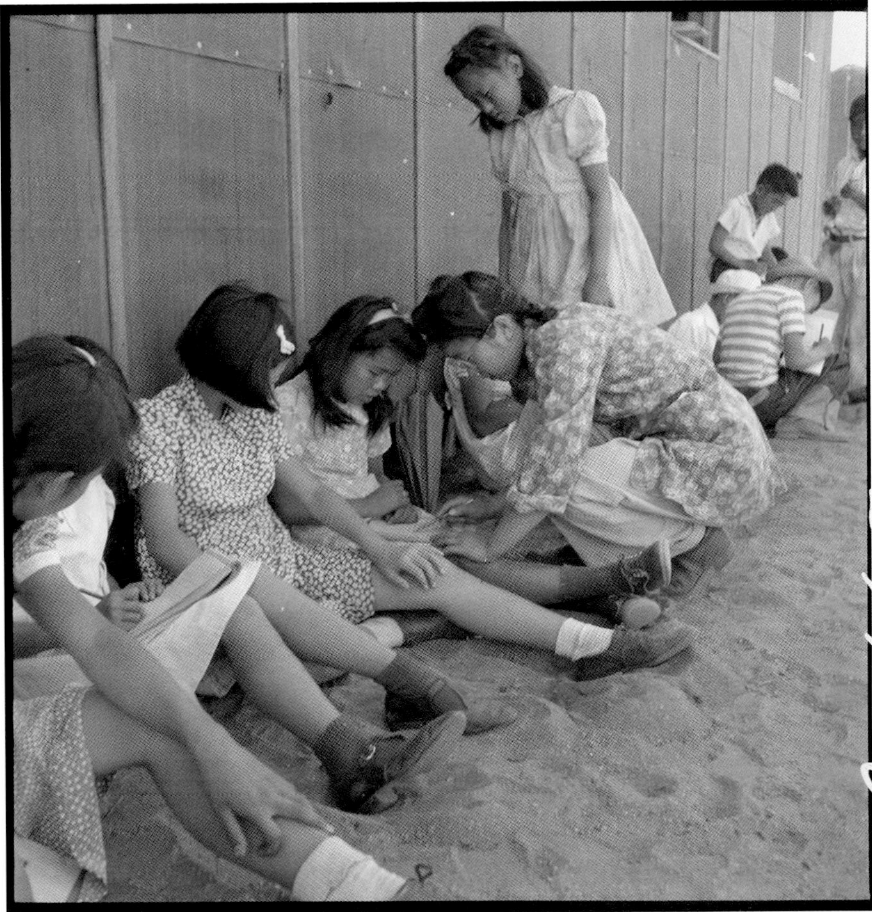

FIGURE 2.18. According to the archival caption, "An elementary school with voluntary attendance has been established with volunteer evacuee teachers, most of whom are college graduates. No school equipment is as yet obtainable and available tables and benches are used. However, classes are often held in the shade of the barrack building at this War Relocation Authority center." Manzanar Relocation Center, Manzanar California, 1942. Photo by Dorothea Lange. (From Central Photographic File of the US War Relocation Authority. National Archives.)

do in photos, complying with the intent of well-meaning photographers to counter stereotyped images that cast them as the enemy (fig. 2.18). Lange shows both children and teachers passionately eager for the structural regularity of schooling and for the curricular engagement that would create a sense of everyday life in their disrupted existence. In doing this, these photos echo the resilience and defiance, and the hope for a better future, that are also apparent in some of the sanctioned and clandestine school photos made almost at the very same time in the Jewish ghettos in Nazi-occupied Europe. The intimacy of Lange's images from Manzanar, an intimacy that is tender without being intrusive, conveys dimensions of schooling that offer hope through a passion for learning in contexts of community and conviviality. They show school classes arranged in informal settings by determined evacuee teachers, lacking facilities and materials. Lange's images come as close as possible to aligning themselves with the perspective of their incarcerated subjects. It is precisely through this alignment that Lange practiced her "disobedient gaze" and offered her trenchant critique. She shows these students to be just like any other American children, thus pointing to the injustice they suffered.

Throughout her employment by WRAPS, Lange faced subtle censorship, obstacles, and harassment both from the WRA and from military authorities of the Western Defense Command that policed the roundup and the camps. The WRA changed Lange's extensive captions, thus using the images to serve their own purposes. Repeatedly scrutinizing all of her negatives, which she was required to turn in to officials as a condition of her employment contract, military censors eventually determined that many of Lange's images were unacceptable for public consumption in wartime and quarantined the majority of her Japanese American removal and incarceration photos. After the war ended, these photos—many of them stamped "impounded"—were deposited in the National Archives, where they remained largely unexamined and unstudied for decades. Lange, herself, did not see the photographs for over twenty years—until 1964, the year before she died.[81]

Paradoxically, restrictions on photographers and, in some places, control of their work began to soften in late 1942 when the Wartime Civil Control Administration—which was part of the US Army and in charge of all Phase One preparations leading up to the exclusion and incarceration of Japanese Americans on the West Coast—relinquished its jurisdiction fully to the War Relocation Authority. Within months, in what came to be called Phase Two of the incarceration, that agency's directors decided that a central component of their mission was to "facilitate the release of 'loyal' Japanese Americans back into the larger society while the war was still in progress, *if they* could pass security evaluations, *if* they could find a job, and *if* they would sign an oath to comport themselves as good Americans and avoid contact with ethnic compatriots."[82]

Photography—and especially photography of school classes and extracurricular activities—became important as a vehicle to show a viewing public the plan's progress and to convince them of its successes. At this point, Lange's contributions, which would have supported this mission, had been sequestered. Photographers like Thomas W. Parker, Frances Stewart, and Charles Mace were hired by WRAPS to present Japanese Americans and the camp experience in a light that would favorably support eventually closing the camps and potentially releasing the incarcerated inhabitants. Ansel Adams, a personal friend of Manzanar's director, Ralph Merritt, was also invited in 1943 to take photos at this camp (fig. 2.19), presumably in the hope that he would apply his immense photographic talents and reputation

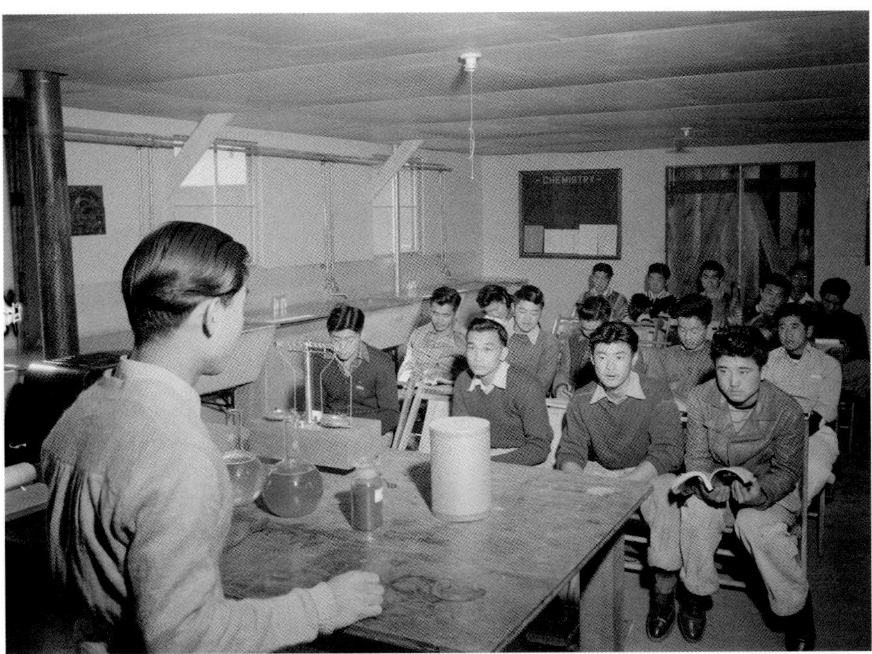

FIGURE 2.19. Science lecture, Manzanar Relocation Center, 1943. Photo by Ansel Adams. (Library of Congress Prints and Photographs Division)

toward a positive and sympathetic rendering of the place and its residents. Most interestingly, around the same time the interdiction against Japanese Americans possessing cameras and taking photos was lifted—a change that resulted in numerous photographs, including school photos, taken by Japanese American photographers, including Toyo Miyatake and Jack Iwata (fig. 2.20) at Manzanar and Hikaru Carl Iwasaki and Bill Manbo at Heart Mountain. But even at that time, their work was monitored by the WRA and camp authorities.[83] Adams agreed not to show barracks or barbed wire in his images.

Given that the school photos—like the more general camp photos of individuals and groups made by WRAPS photographers in this Phase Two photography—were intended to present their subjects in the positive light of loyalty to the United States, engaged in the assimilative process and practices of Americanization, it is not surprising that they have been subject to considerable criticism for their "normalization" and propagandistic and staged presentation of camp life and existence. Too many people smiling, too performative, too neat, too compliant and nice.[84] The conventional genre of the class photo and its surface opacity actually facilitate this positive representation, and the images taken in this second phase are more conventional than the more disorderly photographs Lange took when the camps were first opened. Yet clearly both Japanese American photographers and their subjects, enjoined to demonstrate loyalty to the United States as a condition of freedom, found themselves in a bind. As Jasmine Alinder explains, in this particular situation, "smiling for the camera became charged with new meanings."[85] Distance, critique, and subversion had to take on subtle, if not covert, forms. We find it the inclusion of barracks and barbed wire in the remarkable two high school yearbooks produced in Manzanar in 1943/44 and 1944/45, with photos by Miyatake, for example. The choice of the yearbook's final image, "Our World," which depicts a looming guard tower photographed from a very low angle, is less subtle in its subversion: it registers it, but only at the very end of an otherwise conventional yearbook.[86]

Miné Okubo, a Japanese American artist who worked as an art teacher in the Tanforan Assembly Center in California and subsequently in the Topaz War Relocation Center in Utah, implicitly underscores this critique and opens up the complexity of the photographic events, enabling a deeper

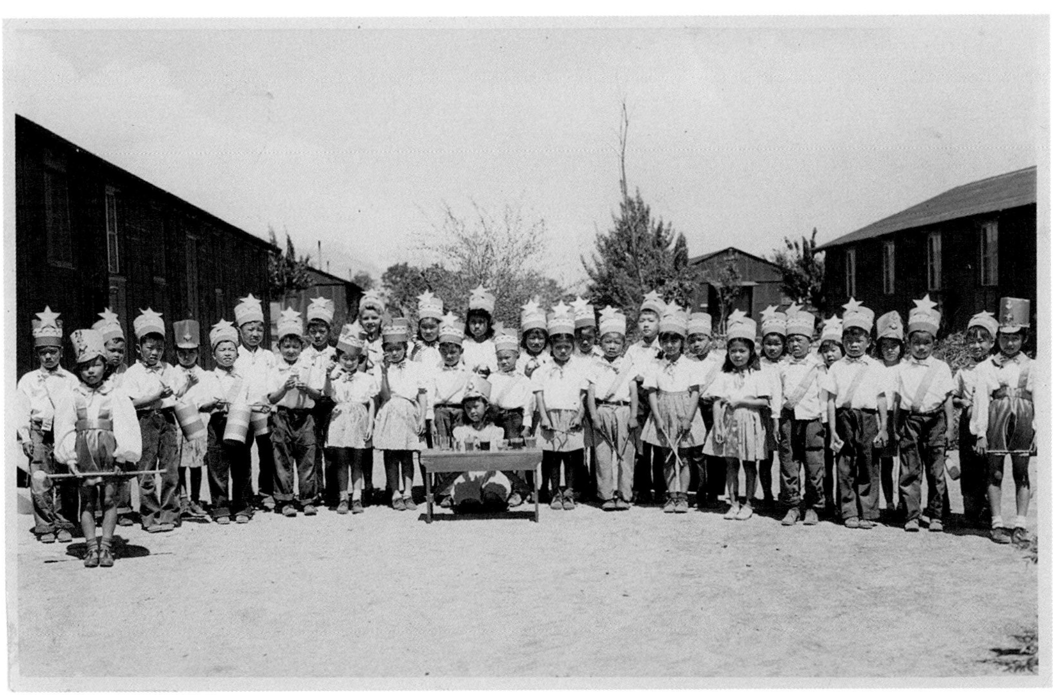

FIGURE 2.20. Untitled (schoolchildren in band uniforms at Manzanar), ca. 1944. Photo probably by Jack Iwata. (Hood Museum of Art at Dartmouth College Collection)

appreciation of the images. Okubo was not a photographer. But she recorded the camp experience, as she witnessed and experienced it, in sketches, drawings, and written commentary (figs. 2.21–2.22). In 1946, after her release from Topaz, Okubo published a graphic memoir about her incarceration, *Citizen 13660*.[87] Interestingly, this "first personal documentation of the evacuation story," as she described it, was fully supported by the WRA for publication as a documentary work that might serve to normalize the camp experience for postwar readers, enabling them to identify with the incarcerated narrator.[88] As Christine Hong notes in her introduction to the latest edition of *Citizen 13660*, it was hoped that Okubo's visual and verbal work would help undo previous visual caricatures of Japanese subjects as "other" and reinscribe Japanese Americans squarely into "American" identities and lifeways.[89] Her graphic memoir, as such, could serve as a medium of exoneration in the aftermath.

Okubo's comix portrayal of the camp school experience, however, diverges profoundly from most school and class pictures taken by Anglo- or Japanese-American photographers. Indeed, far from buttressing the message of Japanese American compliant conformity that the WRA wanted to convey at this time, her critical work seriously undermines it.

A classroom scene in Tanforan, for example (fig. 2.21, left), shows an unruly group of students, inattentive, spilling paint and drawing on each other, talking and fighting while the teacher looks back helplessly as though wanting to control the scene. Okubo writes that "schools were late in opening and difficult to organize because of the lack of buildings and necessary supplies."[90] In Topaz, where, Okubo reports, "school organization was an improvement over Tanforan" and the "curriculum followed the requirements of the state of Utah," the class depiction shows only marginal improvement (fig. 2.21, right). Her Topaz image shows a class in which the children, though now seated in rows in more orderly fashion, play cards, knit, talk, read, or simply look bored. A cat is in the foreground. The teacher's facial expression is sour if not desperate, as she stands in front of the room holding a pointer to use on the globe on her desk. A girl standing behind her looks on, ready for her geography lesson, but the class remains disjointed and distracted, contributing to the critical picture of camp life that animates the memoir.

Okubo's last image of schooling (fig. 2.22), a high school graduation scene depicting the 150 students in the Topaz War Relocation Center's first gradu-

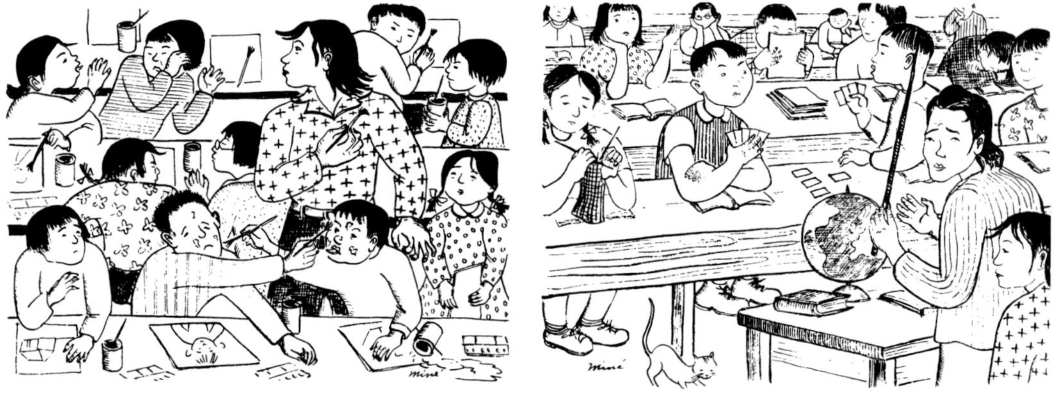

FIGURE 2.21. Miné Okubo, two "school images" from her illustrated memoir, *Citizen 13660*. (Courtesy of Miné Okubo Estate)

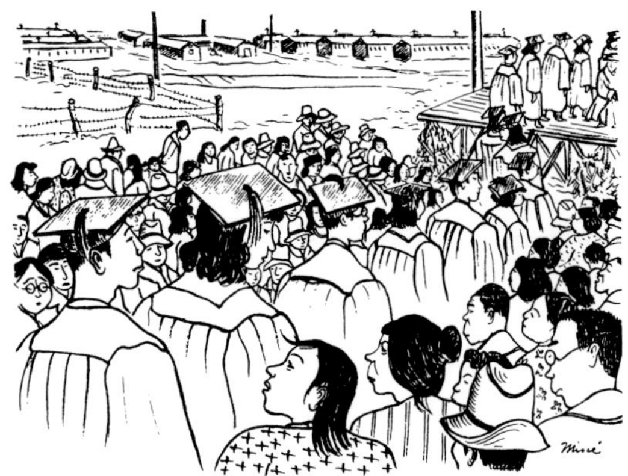

FIGURE 2.22. Miné Okubo, *Graduation*, from her illustrated memoir, *Citizen 13660*. (Courtesy of Miné Okubo Estate)

ating class, wearing rented caps and gowns, is similarly subtly disturbing. "The graduates were very serious," Okubo writes, and indeed, she draws that seriousness on their faces and those of their onlooking families. But this serious graduation scene, marking success and apparent admission into a future of possibility, is marred by the image's composition. In the right foreground, we see large groups milling outdoors around the row of marching graduates who are approaching a tall podium. All are crowded into the lower right side of the frame. In the background are barracks, surrounded by barbed wire, in a sprawling, utterly barren landscape. This is a scene marking incarceration and confinement that remain less blatantly visible in the photographs of the camps.

The graduation scene comes late in Okubo's memoir, preceding her own liberation. Her descriptions of the bureaucracy of evacuation and relocation, and of the injunctions to sign attestations of patriotic loyalty as a condition for being released, culminate in a drawing in which we see her sitting at a desk with a frame and camera on a tripod facing her. Her face is barely visible. Here Okubo comments directly on the event of photography and what she presents as its bureaucratic impersonality. A Japanese American photographer is about to snap her picture. "I was photographed," she writes.[91] Her first-person graphic memoir gives us insight into her subjective experience while also showing how, as a Japanese American, she is seen, categorized, judged, and labeled, and how, through this process, she is turned into an object of surveillance.

AFTERLIVES

Japanese Americans returning to former home communities, or relocating east at the war's end, re-entered a society shaped by racism and xenophobia. School segregation—allowed by law for African American children during the first half of the twentieth century and maintained for many other persecuted groups by housing separation and glaring social and economic inequalities—became the ground for intense activist efforts to gain equality and integration, particularly for African Americans. The 1954 Supreme Court ruling on *Brown v. Board of Education*, mandating integrated schooling, was an important step in this effort, but the fight for equality in education continues to this day.

Photography has served these efforts powerfully. Introducing her book *Imprisoned in a Luminous Glare: Photography in the African American Freedom Struggle*, Leigh Raiford argues that "we cannot comprehend the African American freedom struggle in the twentieth century without making sense of its photographic representations."[92] The iconic photos through which we most vividly remember the *Brown* case, however, are not so much photos of civil rights uprisings and demonstrations, such as the ones Raiford discusses, though many of those exist. They are images of schoolchildren: a photo of the six black children on whose behalf the case was brought, among them little Linda Brown; photos of newly integrated classrooms with a few black children sitting alone at the back of the room; photos of newly integrated classrooms where white and black children stare at each other across the aisle; photos of children attempting to enter previously all-white schools and being heckled or blocked by white students and adults or being escorted by police. The white students' and parents' hateful faces survive in memory alongside the black children's determination to go to school.

Elizabeth Eckford was one of the Little Rock Nine, nine African American high school students registered by the NAACP to integrate Little Rock Central High School in 1957. The photograph of the first day of school that made her famous is unusual but telling. It shows Elizabeth holding books in her left arm, wearing sunglasses, keeping her head down. She is walking away from the school from which she was barred by National Guard troops the governor deployed in violation of the court order that mandated integration. Behind her are adults and other high school students, some also carrying books, jeering or laughing. One girl's face in particular is twisted with hate. Reportedly, she was shouting insults at the black girl. Police are standing by.

Adrian Piper includes this picture as the middle panel in one version of her series of 1992 photomontage triptychs, titled *Decide Who You Are*. *Decide Who You Are, #15: You Don't Want Me Here* (fig. 2.23) frames the 1957

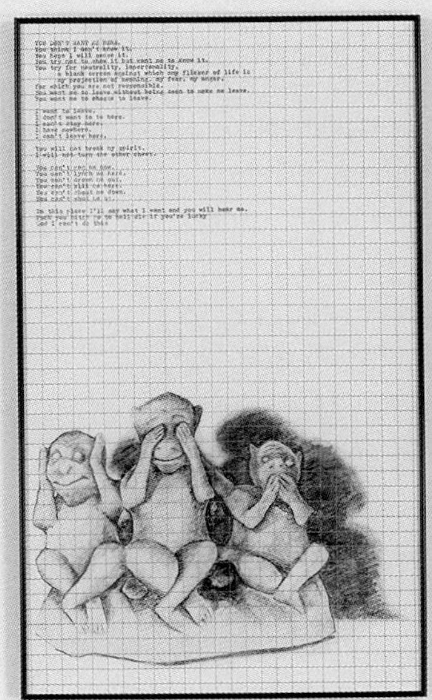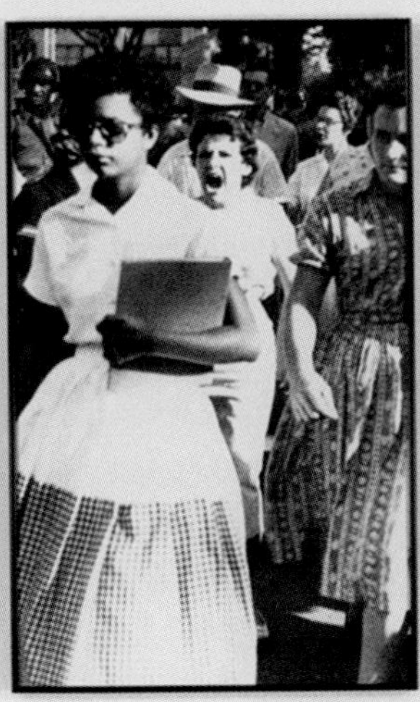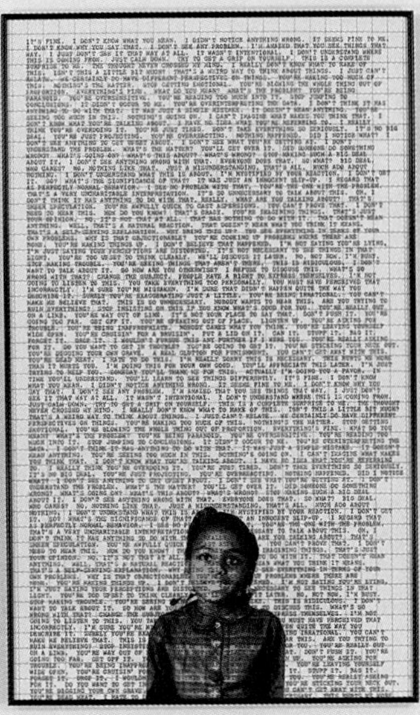

FIGURE 2.23. Adrian Piper, *Decide Who You Are #15: You Don't Want Me Here,* 1992. Three silkscreened image-text collages printed on paper and mounted on foam. See also plate 5. (Private Collection. © Adrian Piper Research Archive Foundation Berlin.)

photo of Elizabeth Eckford with two other panels. At the artist's request, our discussion separates a description of the work from our interpretation.

Describing the work, on the right, we see one of Adrian Piper's iconic images of a smiling little black girl, with hair pulled back, standing at the very bottom of the large rectangular frame. Printed above and over her is a long text in red composed of short phrases in a direct address by an "I" to a "you:" "It's fine. I don't know why you say that. I'm amazed that you see things that way. It wasn't intentional. Just calm down. Isn't this a little bit much? You're making too much of this." On the left, there is a drawing on grid paper of three monkeys holding their hands over their eyes, ears and mouth, respectively. The text, in red on the blue grid above them, is, again, a direct address, containing phrases like: "you don't want me here; you think I don't know it."

In our interpretation, this picture of the socially isolated and unwanted child at the center of this work, rather than one of the more conventional images of groups of younger children in mixed classrooms from this moment of integration, creates a scathingly critical school photo, questioning even the possibility of integrated schooling in the face of entrenched racial hatred. The three panels together powerfully stage the hostile exchange we witness in the 1957 photo of Elizabeth Eckford. As we read them aloud and actually hear them, the phrases on the right panel are phrases that white people whisper or shout at black children, silencing and intimidating them—phrases Elizabeth Eckford no doubt heard all her life. Negating the child's feelings and responses, the voice overwhelms her with a logic of denial and erasure. The three monkeys on the left, holding their hands over their eyes, ears, and mouth, perform a version of "see no evil, hear no evil, speak no evil." In a reversal of violent stereotypes, whites are represented as apes while a black voice tries to break through their hostility, demanding to be heard. We can imagine that this is the voice of the silent Elizabeth Eckford, whose presence at the white high school is so unwanted.

As we see them, the three separate, unconnected rectangular panels perform the isolation of the black child under segregation. The two voices speak or shout across the figure of the student who is being denied entrance to school. They do not hear each other. But they enable us to listen to the 1957 photograph itself, to hear the ugly commotion in front of that school. The two black children—the little girl on the right and the older high school student in the center—are edged out of the pictures' frames. Piper's triptych enlarges the frame of the archival image and places it into liquid time—the *longue durée* of racist exclusion that produced this scene, a scene that reverberates across time and space.

Two artists, Carrie Mae Weems and Steven Deo, offer equally scathing commentaries and responses to images set in an earlier period—the Hampton and Carlisle photographs—and their works also enable us to view and "hear" these iconic school images more expansively and critically. Breaking through the surfaces of the Hampton/Carlisle photos, Weems and Deo reinsert them into time and history, restoring the different gazes that shaped the photographic encounter in their creation. They thus succeed in rupturing the logic of the assimilationist project and of the archive that both contains and hazards replicating it. Their images and installations allow both the photos' subjects and us as viewers to envision a past and a future that is occluded in the static tableaux on which the works are based. That past is one that precedes colonization and its practices of schooling, and the future is our own present, when these images reemerge in liquid time, provoking the attention of a civil gaze that cannot "bear another's control over the visible."[93]

Carrie Mae Weems's large installation piece *The Hampton Project* (fig. 2.24), which was commissioned and first exhibited in 2000 at Williams College, alma mater of Hampton Institute's founder, Colonel Samuel Armstrong, scathingly deconstructs Frances B. Johnston's *Hampton Album*. It also indicts the legacy of oppression, deleted traditions, and dashed hopes that are unacknowledged or suppressed within Johnston's project. Selecting from Johnston's Hampton photos—but also, among others, pictures of Ku Klux Klan parades celebrating "white supremacy," white missionaries baptizing Native Americans, and African Americans sprayed with fire hoses by police to break up 1960s civil rights demonstrations—Weems created large sepia-toned wall prints and prints on free-hanging diaphanous muslin banners that are suspended across the gallery space. Walking through these banners, we as viewers encounter Johnston's images in new ways that encourage us, in Weems's terms, to "invade history."[94]

Using captions and texts as overlays for these, as well as poetic audio commentaries in her own voice, she provides ironic observations on Johnston's "before" and "after" photographic depictions of the assimilationist success. The bloody "before" histories of initial contacts between Europeans and indigenous American and African peoples, the history of slavery, of westward expansion and Indian land dispossession, as well as the continuing bloody "after" of the Jim Crow era and the civil rights conflicts of the twentieth century—none escape her beautiful but eminently unsettling work. Nor does the fact that despite transformative promises implicit in assimilation, the children depicted in the Hampton school photos would remain, at best, only *second-class citizens* of the nation by which they were being schooled. They were made literate in English and educated into a Euro-American worldview, to be sure, but for the most part, they would also remain subordinated and regimented workers serving to assure whites of the continuing hegemony of an economic, cultural, and political value system from which they were largely excluded. By reframing the images and the ideologies that shape them, Weems highlights these contradictions and aftermaths. Suspending and superimposing images from different time periods, and combining these multiple images with a voice that narrates an alternate history, Weems reclaims the larger temporality shrouded by the photos and the official account of American history.

Steven Deo's acrylic and canvas mixed-media collages *Indoctrination #3* (2001) and *When We Become Our Role Models No. 2* (2004)—much smaller-scale works than Weems's but no less powerful—engage American Indian schooling through the artist's personal life history. A Muskogee Creek born in Oklahoma in 1956, Deo was sent to public schools by parents who, according to him, "made the deliberate choice to acculturate their sons into the public school system and mainstream American culture."[95] His work as an artist explores the "indoctrinated identity," as he calls it, that he and his Indian companions received through the public educational process.[96] But he does this by embedding his own and his companions' personal experiences within the larger story of native children's dislocations to "transformative" educational institutions, like the Carlisle Indian School, that his work references directly.

In his mixed-media *Indoctrination #3*, Deo uses a section of one of the Carlisle "after" school photos of neatly coiffed children in uniform and, in a visual metaphor for the silencing and submersion of native languages and cultures, he covers their mouths with red paint strokes. Over this image he superimposes the words "equal, to equal, to be equal, equally" and the corresponding terms in Euchee, the indigenous language of the Muskogee Creek group into which he was born. "Today," Deo explains in an exhibit catalog, "[Euchee] . . . is spoken fluently by only a handful of elders. As with most Native languages, [it] . . . was beaten, threatened, and coerced out of the children in federal and religious 'education' and 'civilization' programs during the past two centuries." "In my wake," he continues, "I continually think about the people I came from. The language they spoke became clouded by

FIGURE 2.24. Carrie Mae Weems: *"Before Columbus . . ."* from *The Hampton Project.* Installation views. Williams College Museum of Art, Williamstown, MA, March 4–October 22, 2000. Photo credit: Arthur Evans. See also plates 6–7. (2.24, top, courtesy of the Williams College Museum of Art; 2.24, bottom, courtesy of Carrie Mae Weems Studio)

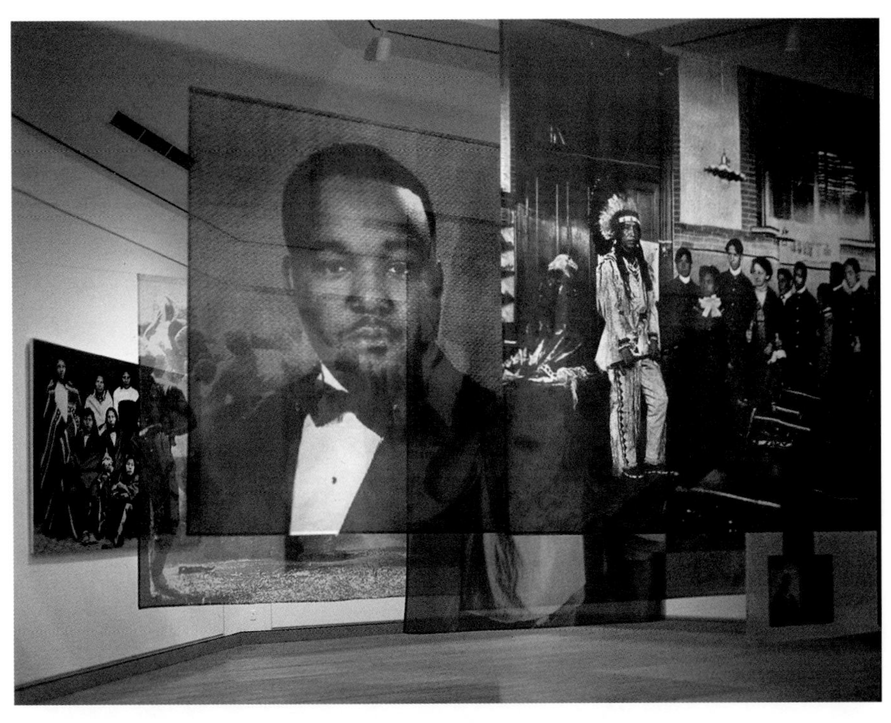

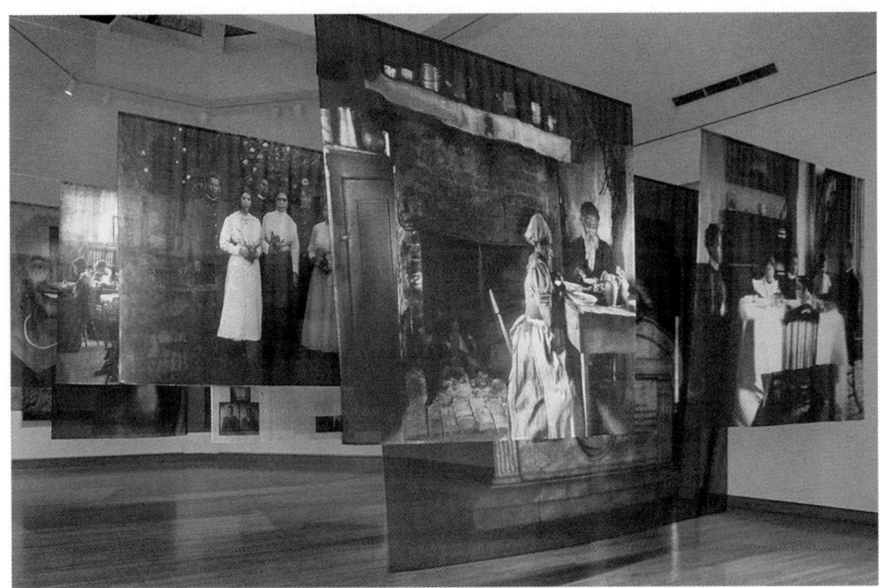

time and daily life. The songs from the beginning of creation resonate in my daydreams, and solace is found in that sacred place called art."[97]

Like *Indoctrination #3*, Deo's collage *When We Become Our Role Models No. 2* (fig. 2.25) uses an archival school photo as a central image. The "we" in the work's title focuses our gaze on the image's subjects, the boy and girl who pose on the lower right—modern American Indian children, shaped by a century-long process of acculturation with which, on the surface at least, they seem to be in smiling agreement. Their background consists of a black-and-white photograph of an unsmiling multitude of early twentieth-century indigenous and black schoolchildren—ghosts that utterly overwhelm the space and practically occlude the boy and girl themselves. This large image is surrounded by car keys and kitschy cutout drawings from

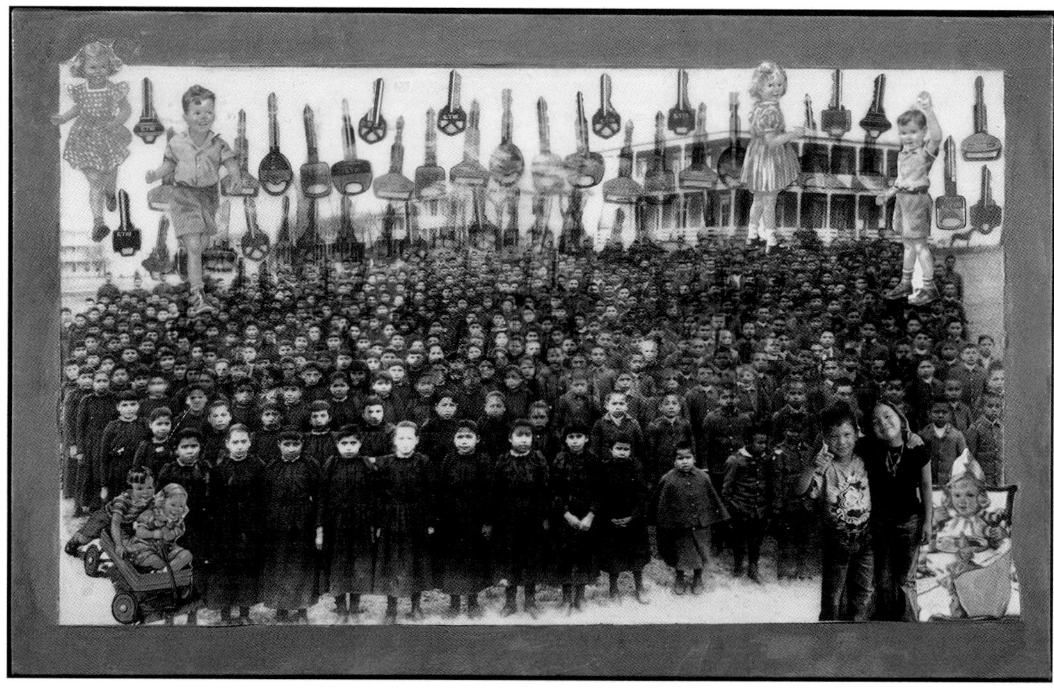

FIGURE 2.25. Steven Deo (Muscogee/Euchee, 1956–2010), *When We Become Our Role Models No. 2*, 2004. Mixed media; acrylic and collage on canvas. See also plate 8. (Hood Museum of Art, Dartmouth College. Purchased through the Hood Museum of Art Acquisitions Fund; MIS.2004.65.)

a Dick and Jane elementary school primer from the same period. In contrast to the quiet pose of the modern native boy and girl and the static children in the school photograph, the blond Dick and Jane figures are on the move, walking, running, riding their red handcart, waving. Moving forward at a fast pace, they seem to be offering a tempting choice, beckoning, "Come with us, leave behind your ancestral ways, move upward, gain success, grasp the tempting keys that open houses, start cars, and access the material 'goodies' of Euro-American modernity!"

But are their beckoning and the car keys they offer as a horizon of expectations genuinely tempting? Deo's work suggests an alternative pathway. If we read the smiles of the native girl and boy not as a gesture of agreement but rather as one of ironic dismissal, it would indicate resistant defiance. It would signal their rejection of both a compromised past and the lures of a materialistic and deracinated future. Indeed, it would confirm what Deo's title of the collage suggests: that they had turned away from the ghosts of the past and had truly "become their [own] role models."

Since we weren't allowed to study,
studying became a forbidden, desirable fruit.

RUTH KLÜGER

3

Exclusionary Frames

FRAGILE ACCEPTANCE

On May 6, 2008, I received a surprise email from a woman named Irene Slabyj, who, searching the internet for clues to her family history, discovered an intimate connection between us: "I was pleasantly surprised to find posting of your mother's school photographs, Hoffmann Gymnasium," she wrote, referring to the photographs (fig. 3.1) that my mother, Lotte Hirsch, had donated to the United States Holocaust Memorial Museum in Washington in an effort to supplement its small collections on her native city of Czernowitz:

> *What caught my breath was seeing my mother in these three photos. . . . My mother, who died in 2001, was a member of the class of 1936 and was then named Olha Ostaficiuc. In reading the descriptions included with these photographs, I realized that we share another connection since my grandfather, Ivan Ostaficiuc, also worked for the railroad [like your father]. Since I have no information or photographs from my mother regarding this school, I wonder whether your mother may recall the address of the school. Possibly she may have a photograph of the school itself that you may be able to share with me.*
>
> *For my own interest and to share such with my children, I have been eager to gather as much pertinent information as possible.*

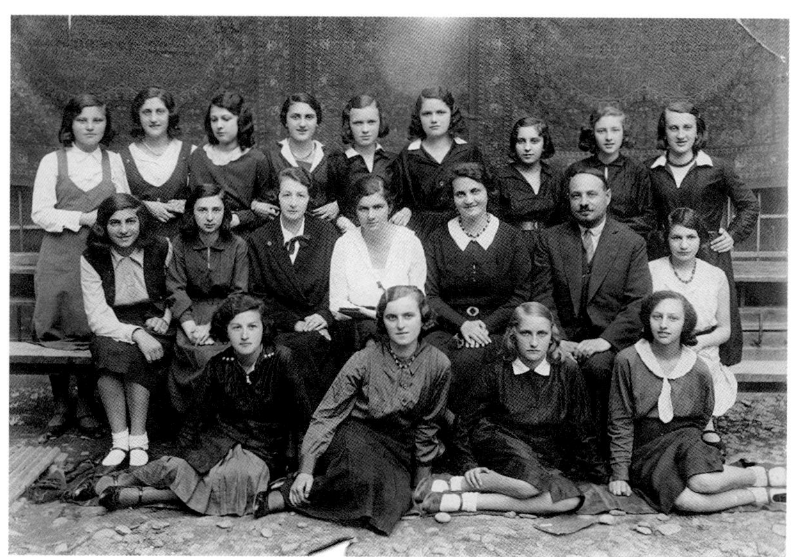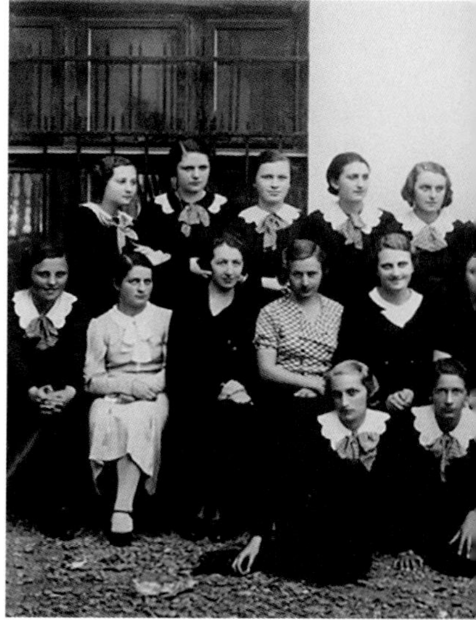

Although by 2008 my mother's memory had become quite spotty, she
clearly remembered Olha Ostaficiuc as a Ukrainian school friend and was
able to identify her in the pictures. And I was able to send Irene a photograph of the school building my mother had pointed out to us on our 1998
visit to what had become the Ukrainian city of Chernivtsi.

My email exchange with Irene Slabyj may appear quite ordinary, a
by-product of new research technologies in the digital age that indeed
make the world seem smaller. But in view of the history of growing ethnic
intolerance and discrimination in interwar Greater Romania and the catastrophic events that ensued after our mothers graduated from what both
would have referred to as the Hoffmann Gymnasium, my twenty-first century meeting with Irene Slabyj would have seemed unlikely, if not improbable.[2] By 1936 that private girls' secondary school in Romanian Cernăuți,
which was founded and directed in the early 1920s by Leo Hoffmann, a

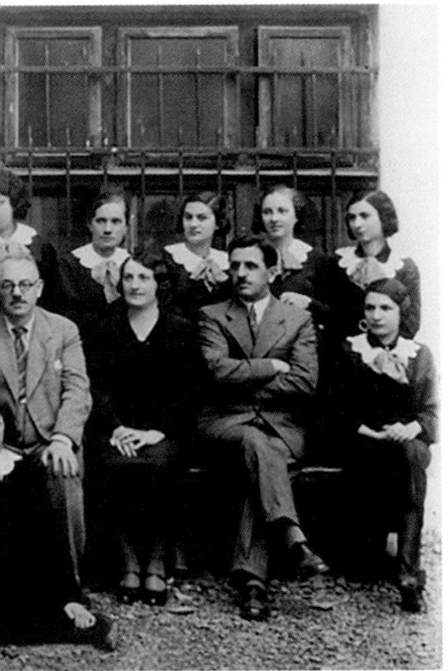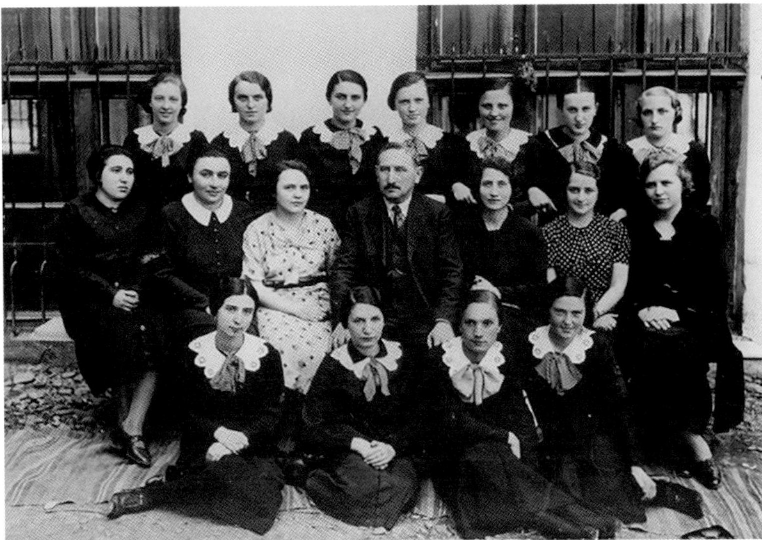

FIGURE 3.1A–C. School classes, Hoffmann Lyceum, Cernăuți, Romania, 1930s. (Hirsch Family collection)

Jew, had been compelled to appoint a Romanian director and to change its name to a more acceptable Romanian one, Liceul Julia Hașdeu.[3]

Clearly, however, a Jewish girl and a non-Jewish Ukrainian girl, both students at the same private school in the mid-1930s, could be friends; they could visit each other's houses; they could study together for their baccalaureate exams. Ukrainians and Jews could also both work for the railroad administration, as Irene's grandfather and my father did. And yet a mere five years later, in 1941, Jews would be deported en masse from Cernăuți and the surrounding region by Romanian authorities collaborating with their Nazi German allies; the city would try to rid itself of their presence. Cernăuți's sizable Ukrainian population was also subordinated under the fascist Romanian regime, but many anti-Semitic Ukrainians, especially in rural areas, initiated or participated in atrocities against Jews during the ensuing years. My mother managed to evade deportation and survive the Romanian Holocaust and, after the defeat of Nazi Germany and the triumph of the Red Army, succeeded in fleeing what had become Soviet Chernovtsy for Romanian Transylvania in 1945. I was born there, in Timișoara, a few years later. Olha Ostaficiuc remained in Soviet Chernovtsy, and Irene was born there. Later, we all emigrated to the United States, but Olha and Lotte would never meet again. Certainly, when Olha and Lotte faced the school photographer in mid-1930s Cernăuți, they could not yet know how fragile their world had already become and how vulnerable their friendship would prove to be.

For me, the email from Irene—the knowledge it brought as well as the recollections it engendered from my mother—was a complete surprise. I had known from my mother's stories that the Hoffmann school was a Jewish-attended private school for girls that prepared students for the national baccalaureate exam that my mother was proud of passing on a first try, in spite of Romanian examiners' blatant anti-Semitic discrimination.[4] *Until I asked her about Olha Ostaficiuc, however, she had not told me that non-Jewish girls studied in the school as well, nor that she had had Ukrainian girlfriends. These details were simply not part of her narrative about her childhood and teens, a narrative that over the years had acquired a certain fixity, as all our life stories tend to do. But her school photographs, their collection in the United States Holocaust Memorial Museum photo archives, and the correspondence they engendered provided a trigger for connection and investigation and, indeed, an expanded understanding of Christian-Jewish cohabitation in interwar Cernăuți.*

The numerous photos of integrated school classes collected in archives like the United States Holocaust Memorial Museum and Israel's Yad Vashem, or online and in published collections such as *And I Still See Their Faces* and *Museum of Family History*, proclaim the success of Jewish emancipation and social integration well into the late 1930s.[5] Finding the range and multiplicity of schools children attended and social connections they forged, seeing the kinds of special occasions that warranted being photographed—class groupings, school excursions, end-of-year performances—all these allow later generations glimpses into past lifeworlds. In memorial archives, school photos of integrated classrooms reanimate the shattered dream of acceptance and integration. Minimizing differences and exhibiting uniformity by virtue of their generic features, school photos are particularly effective at obscuring the virulent anti-Semitic persecution to which the children depicted were, by then, subject, and which some of them were themselves perpetrating. As archival historical and memorial objects, they show both the extent and the fragility of Jewish acceptance and integration, the contradictions that shape this moment of transition to totalitarianism that still allowed, for a brief time, a hope for a Jewish future in Europe to persist.

In his memoir *My German Question: Growing Up in Nazi Berlin*, historian Peter Gay describes the extent to which his parents had been eager to integrate into the Berlin bourgeoisie by subordinating their ties to Jewishness. "They were Germans," he asserts, though he also tells us that he was circumcised and that his father lit candles on the anniversaries of his parents' deaths: "people are not consistent."[6] Gay includes school photos in the memoir, in addition to other images with childhood comrades and fellow members of his Jewish Boy Scout group. The school pictures of his early grade school classes—dating from around 1930, before Hitler came to power—illustrate the seeming integration of Jewish and non-Jewish students: they recall a class excursion and spotlight a special collective activity with friends. In one of them, Gay identifies himself as "the good boy, attentive, serious, with my hands folded." But a later photo from 1935 (fig. 3.2), "a collective portrait" of his gymnasium class with his Latin teacher, elicits a very different caption. "I am the second from the right in the [top] row," Gay

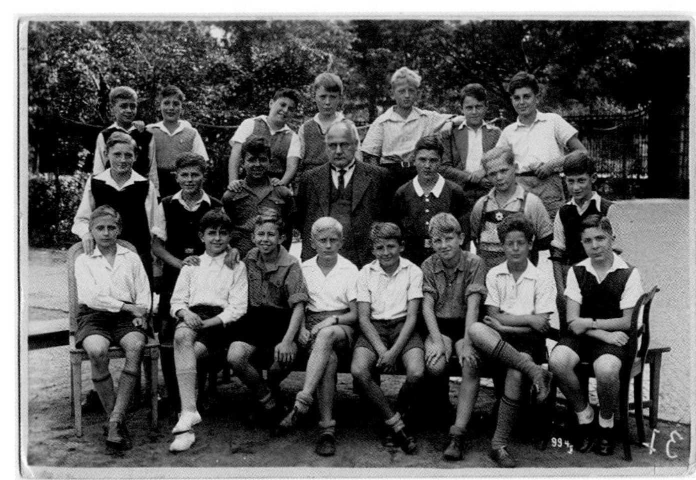

FIGURE 3.2. "To my mind an extraordinary photo from 1935." Photo printed in Peter Gay's memoir, *My German Question* (1998), with this comment. (Peter Gay Collection, Yale University)

writes, "with Hans Schmidt, already an intolerable Hitler Youth, leaning on my shoulder casually, amiably. Pictures do lie!"

Gay's caustic observation would, of course, have been widely applicable, during fascist anti-Semitism's virulent rise in 1930s Europe, to photos of multiethnic classes into which Jews had been integrated. It is startlingly supported, for example, by another German school photo taken in Frankfurt in the mid-1930s (fig. 3.3). This picture is of a group of girls dressed in white and posed outdoors with their teacher. The girls, wearing wreaths of flowers in their hair, are holding each other's hands, palms forward and upward, and they are smiling broadly. Behind them, centrally placed, looms a giant Nazi flag bearing a swastika. Quite likely, given the increasing spread of Nazi ideology in Germany during these years, the girls' harmonized white dress uniform and their neatly braided and arranged hair, in front of such a flag, would be meant as optical signals of an Aryan racial purity. The lie in this pic-

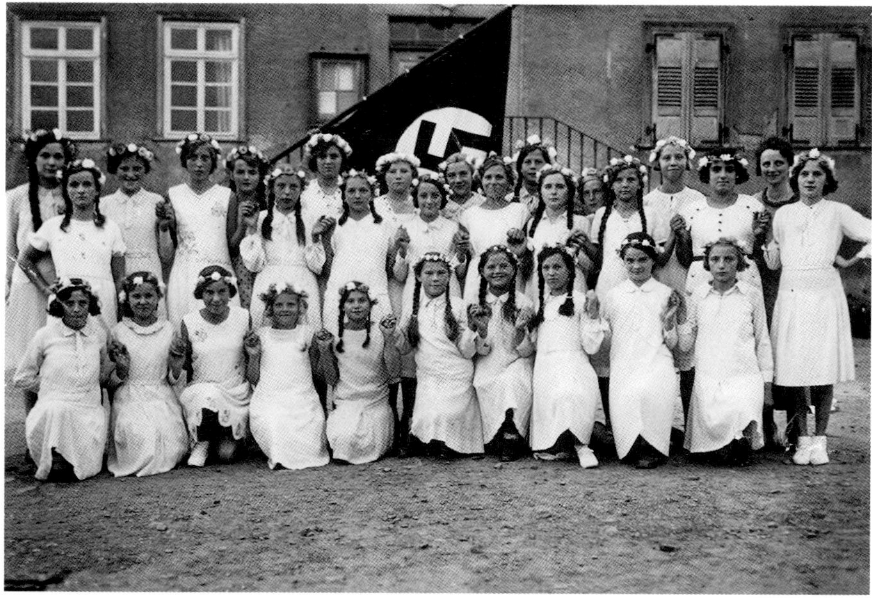

FIGURE 3.3. Group portrait of German girls posing outside their school in front of a Nazi flag in 1935. Among them is Lilli Eckstein (m. Stern) (*top row, seventh from left*). She was expelled six months later for being Jewish. (Courtesy of the South African Holocaust and Genocide Foundation)

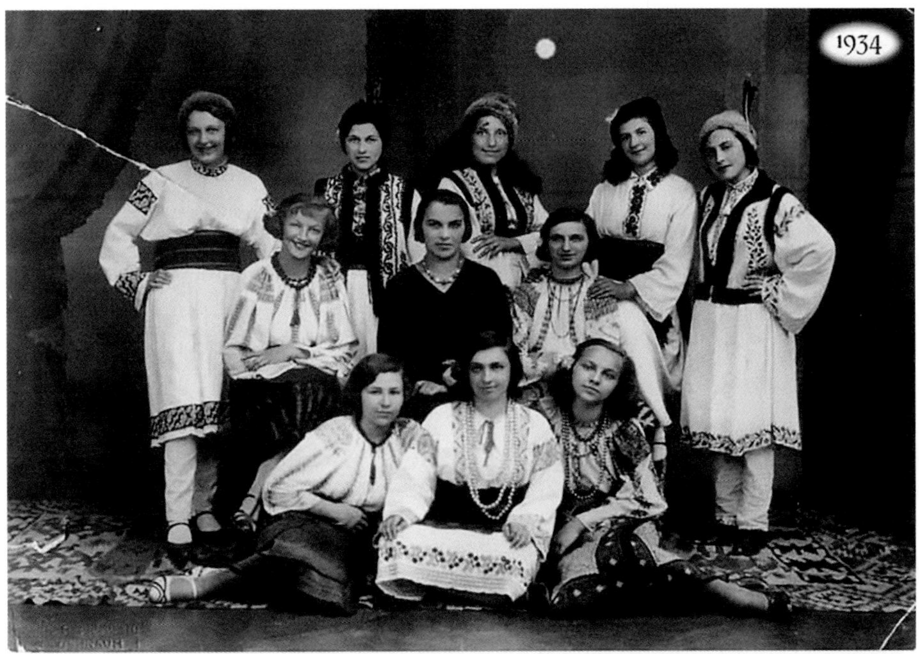

FIGURE 3.4. Celebrating the end of the school year, Public Girls' School LF2 in Cernăuți, Romania, 1934. There are Christians and Jews in the class, and the girls stem from German-language Jewish as well as Romanian and Ukrainian ethnic backgrounds. Romanian nationalism, expressed through the implementation of "Romanianization," and anti-Semitism are on a steep rise throughout greater Romania. (United States Holocaust Memorial Museum)

ture, however, consists of the fact that the class contains at least one Jewish girl—Lilli Eckstein (later Stern), whose father would be arrested on Kristallnacht in November 1938 and whose family, after a desperate flight, would find refuge in Cape Town, South Africa, after the war.[7] As with Peter Gay's photograph, or numerous other photos taken in Germany in the mid-1930s before Jews were no longer permitted to attend schools together with non-Jewish Germans, Lilli's increasingly consequential difference is unmarked: she smiles and poses just like her classmates.

The 1934 end-of-year photo of students from the LF2 public high school for girls in Cernăuți, Greater Romania (fig. 3.4), magnifies these contradictions. The girls smile and touch; the group seems friendly. Just at the very time when Romanian anti-Semitism became more virulent, occasioning violent outbreaks in integrated schools and elsewhere, both the Jewish and the Christian students wear traditionally embroidered Romanian peasant dresses, and they appear to wear them without detecting the irony of this visible symbol of an ever-increasing nationalism. What we see here, instead, is conviviality and community.

National costumes and flags (as we saw in images from the Whittier Primary School or from Japanese American schools) underscore the ironies of coercing children to demonstrate their allegiance to a state that mobilizes symbols of inclusive nationhood only to exclude, if not annihilate, groups that have been led to believe that they were successfully integrated and accepted. Encased by the civil frames of European assimilationism, school photos from interwar Europe, specifically, show us how Jewish children learned to blend in, to erase their differences, to aspire to full integration, even to believe they had achieved it. But though ostensibly integrated in the space of the school, Jewish children in late nineteenth and early to mid-twentieth century Europe were no less objects of social separation and discrimination than the black and Indian girls and boys from North American segregated schools. Over the 1920s and 1930s, invisible but always present countercurrents and blockages to their integration would become increasingly dangerous and vehement until they culminated in outright exclusion. Ruth Klüger describes this moment in her memoir *Still Alive*. The day after the Anschluss, when Austria was incorporated into the German Reich, she writes, "The school principal came to our class, told us we now had to use the Hitler greeting, and raised his right arm to show us how it was done—only the Jewish children weren't to use it. The class dutifully imitated him, while we five to six Jewish kids got to sit in back. Because the principal was friendly, and the teacher visibly embarrassed, I was unsure at first—such is the optimism of the young—whether our special status was a privilege or an insult."[8]

Those who embraced and those who contested the assimilationist project in Central Europe, those who integrated and those who developed alternative affiliations and ideologies ranging from diaspora nationalism to Zionism, equally became targets of the genocidal campaign that would erupt in the near future—a future toward which the children in these interwar images were looking as they faced the camera.

In many ways, this image of children lined up on a staircase (fig. 3.5) resembles school photos taken both in integrated and in ethnically separate schools throughout Europe during the 1920s and 1930s. It was probably taken sometime in 1941 in an unidentified ghetto school in German-occupied Eastern Europe, only a very few years after Lotte Hirsch and Olha Ostaficiuc had their photos taken in a multiethnic class in fascist Romania and Peter Gay was photographed, seemingly comfortably integrated with Christian students, in a Berlin school. But in this photo, the children are visibly marked by the yellow "Jew" star that each one of them is wearing. Each is framed as *different* by an emblem of identification and separation in much the way that Jews were marked as "other" in the era before the Edicts of Tolerance of the late eighteenth century, and in much the same way that black, Asian, or Indian subjects were cast as different by being racialized through what Frantz Fanon referred to as the "racial epidermal schema."[9] These ghetto children, moreover, look gaunt, if not hungry; their clothing is threadbare and ill-matched;

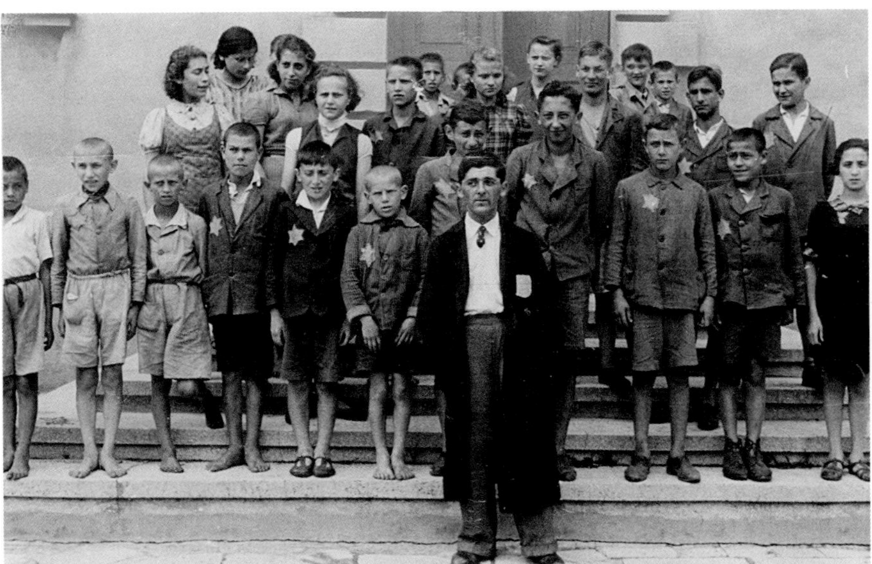

FIGURE 3.5. This unidentified Ghetto photograph, published in the Nazi propaganda rag *Der Stürmer*, was captioned "Satan's Brood." (Nuremberg City Archives)

some are barefoot. The looks on their faces and on the face of the teacher who stands in front of, not with, them suggest that the photographer was not a sympathetic or benign presence. The teacher's eyes glance slightly to the side, avoiding the camera, and the children look about in many different directions. A few look down, others smile hesitatingly, most look quizzical about what was undoubtedly a coerced photographic event. Their hands hang down by their sides.

Serving Nazi propaganda purposes, this photo of Jewish children published in the Nazi weekly tabloid *Der Stürmer* in 1942 is captioned *Satansbrut*—Satan's Brood. It was produced by an unknown photographer to display the degradation of Jews and their exclusion from societal norms of the human. And yet the diversity of the children and the very ambiguity of their self-presentation—the half-smiles on some of their faces and the dignified upright stance of others—complicate the intended Nazi message and the photographer's exclusionary gaze. These children enjoin viewers to see each of them separately, not as an undifferentiated "brood." They ask for a resistant civil encounter from those who might look at them at some different time.

A very different photographic gaze, and a different photographic event, shapes a graduation photo from the Lódź ghetto (fig. 3.6), as well as others taken in initially sanctioned and subsequently clandestine ghetto schools. Their incongruous existence and improbable survival enlarges our understanding of school photographs as historical and testimonial objects.

Although some of the boys in this Lódź image also wear the yellow star, they appear to be comfortable with one another, gathered around the centrally placed Nazi-appointed ghetto elder and head of the Jewish Council, Chaim Rumkowski. They hold school certificates in their hands, and one graduate casually hugs a classmate. All engage cordially with the photographer. Before the Nazis closed nonvocational Jewish schools in the Lódź ghetto in late 1941, Rumkowski posed for photos with schoolchildren on numerous occasions. He employed his core of German-authorized Jewish Council photographers by having them visually illustrate how well run (by him) and how "civilized" the ghetto was, thus satisfying Nazi propaganda demands. At the same time, however, he also seems to have wanted the images to help convince Nazi authorities that "his" well-educated Jews con-

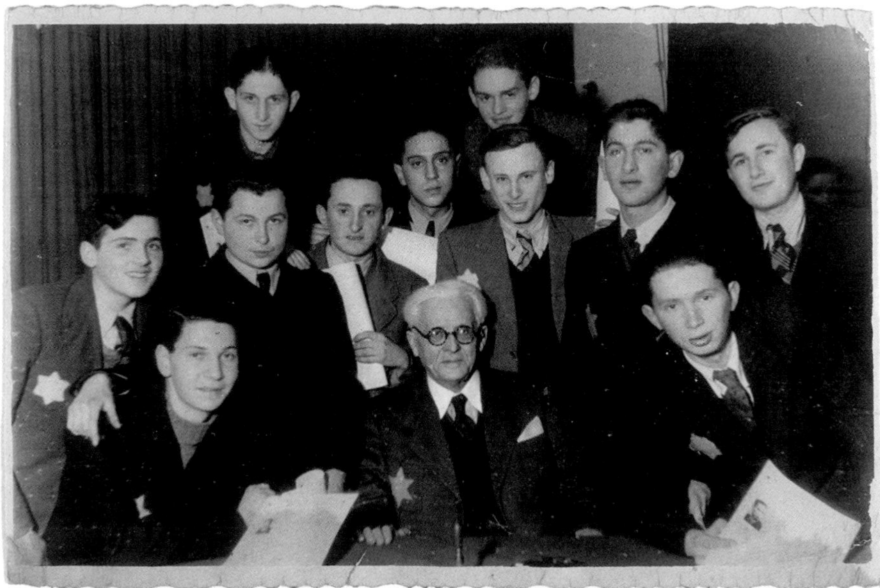

FIGURE 3.6. Graduating students holding their diplomas in the Lódz ghetto with the Nazi-appointed ghetto elder and head of the Jewish Council, Chaim Rumkowski, 1941. (United States Holocaust Memorial Museum, courtesy of Izak and Rosa Rosenwasser)

tinued to be necessary and worthy. And yet, facing the camera, the young men in the photo proclaim pride in their graduation and do not address Nazi viewers who disparage them. Were it not for the yellow stars they are compelled to wear, nothing would distinguish their picture from school photos taken elsewhere in more ordinary times. In its utter conformity to the genre of class photos, and its deployment of the civil gaze of prewar Jewish assimilation, this image, like many others taken in the Nazi ghettos, is a testament to ghetto inhabitants' will to continuity in times of extremity. It reflects a refusal of the Nazi camera's exclusionary gaze and documents an act of resistance against Nazi efforts to break incarcerated ghetto inhabitants' spirits and to destroy communal life.

Pictures such as this one, emerging from the Nazi ghettos during the war, function similarly to the school photos from the Japanese American and Japanese Canadian concentration camps in the United States and Canada. They offer yet another poignant case study of photography's instrumental work in framing children as different and expendable while also revealing photography's potential to reframe, and refuse, forms of difference that took on not only exclusionary but also lethal dimensions.

JEWISH CHILDREN AND SCHOOLING DURING THE HOLOCAUST

A staggering reality frames any discussion of children, schooling, and photography during the years of the Holocaust. Only approximately 11 percent of the 1.6 million Jewish children under sixteen who were alive in 1939–40 in what was to become Nazi-occupied Europe survived the war. For adult Jews, the survival rate was about 33 percent.[10] As noted by Nechama Tec, a Holocaust scholar who herself survived the war as a hidden child in Poland: "In line with the Third Reich's racial policies, all Jewish children were slated for murder."[11]

The timing and rate of genocide varied in occupied areas, influenced by wartime military and economic factors and needs, the demand for Jewish forced labor, and the establishment and use of large-scale concentrationary killing centers. Mass murder of Jewish women, men, and children by specially deployed killing squads, *Einsatzgruppen*, began soon after Germany invaded Poland in September 1939 and increased substantially after Germany invaded the Soviet Union in June 1941. The scale of killing, however, rose to the level of genocidal extermination after the January 1942 conference of senior Nazi officials on the Wannsee near Berlin, a conference that planned for the implementation of "the final solution of the Jewish question" in German-controlled territories.[12]

Given the immensity of the genocidal destruction of Jews and the special targeting of young children—whom the Nazis saw as seedlings of a Jewish future and potential revenge—it may perhaps seem odd that some officially Nazi-sanctioned schooling for Jewish children *did* continue to exist during the war years, on an on-again, off-again basis, in a few of the larger ghettos and transit camps. It may seem even odder that the schools that functioned were documented in school photos that, in large part, conform to the genre—and that many of these photos have survived, however damaged (fig. 3.7).

In Łódź, for instance, after the Jewish ghetto was formed and sealed in March–April 1940, Third Reich authorities allowed both elementary and secondary education to continue for most of the first year and a half of the ghetto's existence.[13] Under Chaim Rumkowski's supervision, the Council ran forty-five schools, including forty elementary schools, two preschools, two secondary schools, and one vocational school. Until October 1941, when school buildings were transformed into shelters for thousands of Western European Jews transported to the Łódź ghetto and all except officially authorized vocational schooling was effectively terminated, these served over 17,500 pupils (approximately 63 percent of the ghetto's school-age children) and were staffed by 648 teachers and over 110 caretakers/custodians.[14]

Unlike Łódź in the Wartheland, territory that was *annexed* by Nazi Germany into the Reich after the defeat of Poland in September 1939 and the start of World War II, Warsaw was located in the German-occupied region of Poland designated as a *protectorate* and known as the *Generalgouvernement*. Nazi authorities here permitted both elementary and secondary Jewish schools to open in October 1939. Briefly, for a month, some did hold classes, but officials then closed all Jewish schools on the pretext of the threat

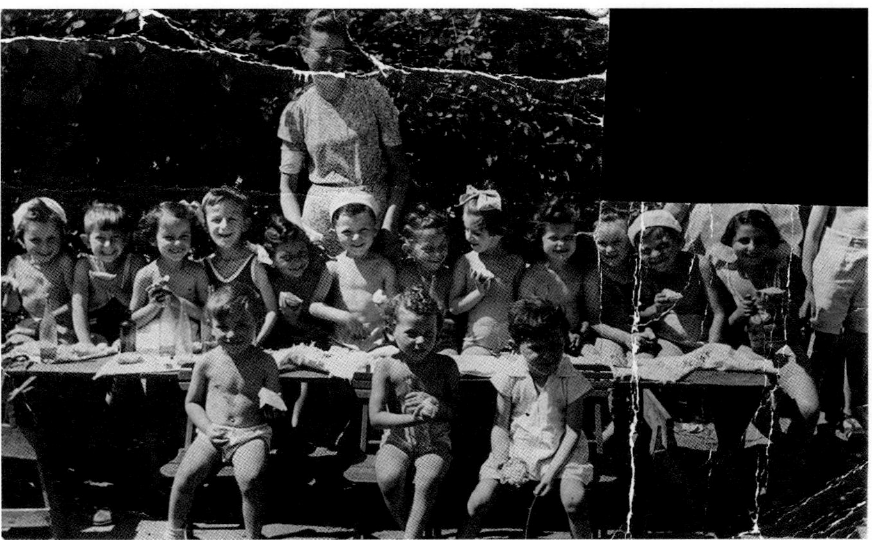

FIGURE 3.7. Jewish preschoolers in the kindergarten established by Ita Rozencwajg in the Warsaw ghetto. (United States Holocaust Memorial Museum, courtesy of Ita Rozencwajg Dimant)

of an epidemic and requisitioned all school buildings. Subsequently, when the Warsaw Jewish ghetto was established and sealed off in November 1940, the Germans initially authorized Jewish vocational training schools but not primary or secondary ones. Only in September 1941, nearly a year later and two years after the German occupation, was the ghetto's *Judenrat* permitted to open elementary schools for the youngest children—in all likelihood as a means to free their mothers for forced labor. But officially sanctioned Jewish secondary schooling was never restored, and the briefly permitted elementary schooling ceased to exist in July 1942, three months before the first mass deportation of the ghetto population to the killing center of Treblinka.[15]

In Lithuania in 1941, occupying German authorities quickly established ghettos in Vilna (Vilnius) and Kovno (Kaunas), both cities with sizeable Jewish populations.[16] As in Warsaw and Lódź, Jewish schools officially sanctioned by Nazi authorities existed in these cities on an on-again, off-again basis. When the Kovno Jewish ghetto was set up and sealed off in July 1941, all schools were initially ordered to remain closed. Toward the end of that year, however, a kindergarten was set up and, on the initiative of some teachers, ghetto authorities agreed to reopen two primary schools—schools that were closed down again a few months later, in the winter of 1942, ostensibly because of the immense cold and a shortage of firewood to heat the classrooms. They were briefly reauthorized to open in the spring of that same year but then in the summer were ordered to shut again and to cease functioning. Only vocational training schools maintained their sanctioned existence.[17]

Vilna, the largest of the Lithuanian cities and home to the renowned Yiddish Institute for Higher Learning (YIVO), had had a very strong tradition of secular and religious schooling for Jewish children and young adults in the prewar years. Astonishingly, even after the Jewish ghetto was established and tens of thousands inhabitants whom the Nazis and their henchmen considered "incapacitated or unfit for productive labor" were deported and killed, schooling and schools remained alive here until the ghetto was liquidated at the end of 1943. This was due less to Nazi officials' outright authorization of such education than to a kind of *laissez-faire* attitude about it on their part. More here, perhaps, than in other places under their control, Nazi civil authorities granted greater autonomy to their appointed *Judenrat*—and especially to its dominant figure, the Jewish police commander Jacob Gens—to administer and oversee various ghetto departments, including housing, health, labor, and schooling. Consequently, after the initial deportations in late 1941 and the ensuing difficult winter, over two thousand children and adolescents (out of a total ghetto population of some twenty thousand people) received primary and secondary schooling throughout 1942 and early 1943—classes that even included courses at the gymnasium level.[18]

Certainly, for Nazi authorities—especially for officials connected to the Reich Propaganda Ministry under Josef Göbbels—permitting a very limited number of Jewish children some access to education for a brief period enhanced the enormous lie on which the machinery of genocidal death rested: that ghettos and work camps were merely transit stations to relocation rather than to extermination. But even when officially mandated closings and interdictions against schools and classes were in effect—which in the case of nonvocational education meant during most of the war years— Jewish teachers and adults in the ghettos set up clandestine schools and, wherever and whenever possible, held makeshift, often secret, classes. A report on schooling in the Warsaw ghetto, written in 1942 for the secret *Oyneg Shabes* historical ghetto archive, noted: "We cannot give the number of clandestine classes, or of children attending them, and nobody can estimate the figure even reasonably accurately, since it has expanded without check. It is however thought on the basis of statistics kept by the particular schools . . . that 20 percent of children attend clandestine classes, and as many again are being taught privately."[19]

Since approximately forty-eight thousand school-age children were in the Warsaw ghetto when the school study was compiled in January 1942, about ninety-six hundred pupils were in concealed classes, and approximately the same number were being taught at home or elsewhere.[20] Already two years earlier, in July 1940, Miriam Wattenberg (Mary Berg), then a teenager in Warsaw, had noted in her diary:

> *Twice a week . . . courses are given at our home, which is a relatively safe spot because of my mother's American citizenship. We study all the regular subjects, and have even organized a chemistry*

*and physics laboratory using glasses and pots from our kitchen
instead of test tubes and retorts. Special attention is paid to the
study of foreign languages, chiefly English and Hebrew. Our discussions of Polish literature have a particularly passionate character.*

But she also wrote: "There are now a great number of illegal schools, and
they are multiplying every day. People are studying in attics and cellars, and
every subject is included in the curriculum, even Latin and Greek. Two such
schools were discovered by the Germans some time in June. Later we heard
that the teachers were shot on the spot, and that the pupils had been sent to
a concentration camp near Lublin."[21]

Ghetto inmates' efforts to teach children, even if only minimally, and to
provide them with at least some of the daily routine of schooling, reflected
an impulse to render a sense of routine to extraordinary circumstances.[22]
"Lessons were conducted in a different place every day, in the houses of
teachers and pupils," Nehama Eckheizer-Fahn indicated about her schooling
in the Warsaw ghetto; "They were conducted clandestinely, in small groups,
by the light of a single candle, each evening somewhere else. . . . It was not
an escape from the dreadful reality but an expression of opposition to the
iniquity and the desecration of cherished values."[23]

In ghettos throughout German-annexed and -occupied Poland, teachers
and adults associated with soup kitchens, day care centers, orphanages, and
so-called children's corners in residential structures used these spaces with
a double purpose in mind: to provide nourishment to thousands of children, many of them destitute, and to disguise the school classes they were
covertly holding there. "The lessons were at night in a broom closet," Ruth
Klüger writes, in her memoir *Still Alive*, about the clandestine school class
she attended during her two-year confinement in the Terezín ghetto starting
in September 1942. "Since we weren't allowed to study, studying became a
forbidden, desirable fruit."[24]

Time and again, as documents and survivor testimonies tell us, these
secret classes also became momentary havens from the otherwise envel-
oping deprivation and gloom. "With beating hearts we conducted lessons
[while] simultaneously on the alert for the barking voices of the SS, who frequently raided Jewish homes," wrote N. Korn, a teacher in the Lublin ghetto.

"In such a case all incriminating traces immediately disappeared. . . . The pupils began to play and the teacher became a customer. In a tailor's house he began to try on clothes and in a shoemaker's house—shoes."[25]

"These lessons were our joy, our forgetting," recorded Pola Rotszyld, who both taught younger children and attended clandestine gymnasium classes in the Warsaw ghetto: "Outside, the storm of war raged, you could hear the groans of those dying from starvation . . . , and somewhere in the corner of a room in Pawia Street or Nowolipki Street eight girls aged thirteen to fifteen were sitting at a table, with a male or female teacher, absorbed in learning, forgetting about God's world, even about the fact that they were a little hungry, or perhaps more than a little."[26]

"The teachers," Miriam Wattenberg added in her diary, "put their whole heart and soul into teaching, and all the pupils study with exemplary diligence. There are no bad pupils. The illegal character of the teaching, the danger that threatens every minute, fills us all with a strange earnestness. The old distance between teachers and pupils has vanished. We feel like comrades-in-arms responsible to each other."[27]

Indeed, within sealed ghetto walls intended to exclude Jews from the mainstream of social belonging and to isolate them as subordinate and different—and, astoundingly, even in some of the concentration and extermination camps—teachers became primary agents of cultural and social resistance. Their numbers included long-experienced educators and talented youth leaders and instructors—Stella Rein in Łódź, Shmuel Rozental in Kovno, Leo Baeck in Terezín, Janus Korcak in Warsaw, Fredy Hirsch in Terezín and Birkenau, and Hannah Lévy-Hass in Bergen Belsen. Many of the teachers, however, were resolute and tenacious nonprofessional pedagogues: parents, caretakers, older students, and young adults who have remained unidentified by name and personally unacknowledged in the historical record. Without textbooks, notebooks, or material resources of any kind to aid them or their students, these dedicated amateurs taught basic reading, writing, and arithmetic skills to their youngest pupils and a range of higher-level subjects to the more advanced ones. Recalling her experience in one such advanced class in the Warsaw ghetto, Janina Bauman noted that her teachers would sometimes even help "translate Horace from the Latin or toil over the theorems of Pythagoras."[28]

Teachers and children made radical sacrifices to continue schooling. "It was not easy to write without any kind of book," Hanna Lévy-Hass writes about her experience in the Bergen Belsen concentration and death camp,

> *and I have to write subjects down on dozens and dozens little pieces of paper. . . . [The children] get pencils and paper in whatever way they can, selling their bread ration or doing some other kind of deal, or simply stealing from each other. . . . I distinctly feel that our "school" has become indispensable and that it's the only way to revive and maintain any freshness in their souls. The vast majority of the children evince a strong desire to study, to make up for lost time; it is with cries of joy and "hooray!" that they welcome my calls to gather together. The most resourceful among them then fight to get a free corner in the barracks where we can have a class. They all settle in and I see adorable children's faces around me, on which I read both cheerfulness and concentration.*[29]

THE NAZI GAZE

In viewing photos of Jewish victims of persecution taken during National Socialist rule, it is important to bear in mind that, as the photo published in *Der Stürmer* derisively labeled "Satan's Brood" suggests, most of the images that have survived were originally made by perpetrators to further Nazi aims. They were produced by Nazi officials and by professional *Propaganda Kompanien* (PK), photographers in militarized units subservient to the directives of the Reich Propaganda Ministry in Berlin. Many of these perpetrator images were specifically taken to stir up anti-Jewish hatred by staging Jews as "subhuman" and "degenerate" and to document, meticulously, the annihilation of Jewish communities as well as the killing of individuals. Thus photographs taken of *Einsatzgruppen* operations in the killing fields—frontal or side images of undressed victims walking to the sites of their execution or facing their executioners—clearly illustrate photography's implication in the death machine. Shot before they are shot, these victims are subject to a genocidal Nazi gaze that shatters a visual field in which looks are exchanged and photography is collaborative or consensual.[30] In the words of Frances

Guerin, the PK photographers taking these images "shared the positionality, the perspective, even the identity of those high-level Nazis who wrote and disseminated the racist concepts of Jews, Slavs, and other enemies to be destroyed."[31]

Some photographs taken in Jewish ghettos by German photographers are structured by a similarly totalizing Nazi gaze. The images contained in the *Stroop Report*, for example, a set of fifty-three images and text sent by SS general Jürgen Stroop to Heinrich Himmler detailing the Warsaw ghetto's destruction in 1943, are a case in point. One need only think of the exclamation point in the report's title, "The Jewish Quarter of Warsaw Is No More!," as a sign of how the perpetrator's gaze is connected to the perpetrator's deed, and how we, as viewers, inevitably become implicated by the very act of looking at these images.[32]

By far the largest number of photographs of Jews in the Nazi-established ghettos, however, were taken not by professional PK photographers but by amateur *Wehrmacht* soldiers and a few sanctioned German civilians engaged in so-called ghetto tourism. Intended as souvenirs for viewing in private and family albums, they, like all souvenir photos, offered "indisputable evidence that the trip was made, . . . the program was carried out, . . . the fun was had," core features of souvenir photography in Susan Sontag's insightful definition of the genre.[33]

Certainly, some ghetto tourists did visibly display sympathy for the emaciated and wretched subjects that they photographed in their ghetto internment—sympathy discernable, for example, in the Warsaw ghetto photos taken (and subsequently published) by Joe J. Heydecker, a photo lab technician with one of the militarized *Propaganda Kompanien* units, and by Willy Georg, a radio operator and former professional photographer.[34] And yet most ghetto tourist images archived since the end of World War II were visually shaped by the ideological objective to strip their Jewish subjects of their personhood and humanity.[35] Indeed, for a number of ghetto photographers, the hoped-for "conversion of experience into souvenir pictures" was augmented by a sinister ethnographic purpose. Capturing images of Jews and details of Jewish existence in photographs; accruing pictures of beings that Nazi ideology presented as *subhuman*; displaying these photos in oftentimes beautifully scripted and annotated albums and in slide shows:

all these activities reflected a desire to produce, archive, and flaunt a type of photographic *tableau vivant*—a sealed, motionless, frozen-in-time, two-dimensional visual staging of an inferior species on the eve of its extinction.

Functionally, this ethnographic desire was analogous to the motivation behind the so-called Museum of an Extinct Race—the Hitler-approved space in Prague's Josefov (Jewish Quarter) in which hundreds of thousands Jewish artifacts were to be displayed after the war like trophies or archaeological remains of a vanished breed.[36] Significantly, however, small acts of resistance by the subjects, likely unperceived by the photographers and thus uncontrollable by them, are subtly embedded within the photos they took. Perpetrator photos register details that, when closely viewed and judiciously decoded, permit us to penetrate and look beyond a sealed Nazi frame. They exhibit their subjects' individual glances exchanged among themselves or with the photographer, looks that traverse the images and restore the visual field's heterogeneity. Through a haptic reading that supplements the contemporary historical details they contain—their *studium*, in Roland Barthes's terminology—they enable us to consider a realm of affect and sensation that enhances and amplifies our conventional historical understanding of the times.

Three surviving school photos from the Lódź ghetto illuminate this point.

Two of them, titled *Getto Schulausspeisung* ("Ghetto school feeding," fig. I.2 and plate 9) and *Schuljugend* ("School youths," fig. 3.8) by their photographer and seemingly taken only moments apart, show children outside a building that may have been their school, waiting, according to one of the labels, to receive food.

The third, identified as *Getto Litzmannstadt* [Lódź] *Sattlerei* ("Lódź Ghetto saddlery," fig. 3.9), was photographed indoors in what appears to be a large vocational class instructing students to fabricate leather products for the German war effort. The three are part of a trove of over six hundred transparent color slides taken over four years (from 1940 to 1944) by a German civil servant, Walter Genewein, chief accountant of the Lódź ghetto, member of the Nazi party, and skilled amateur photographer privileged with access to a high-grade camera and to extremely difficult to acquire IG Farben/Agfa color stock and processing.[37] Although the slides are not precisely dated, Genewein's labeling and numbering, and what we know about the

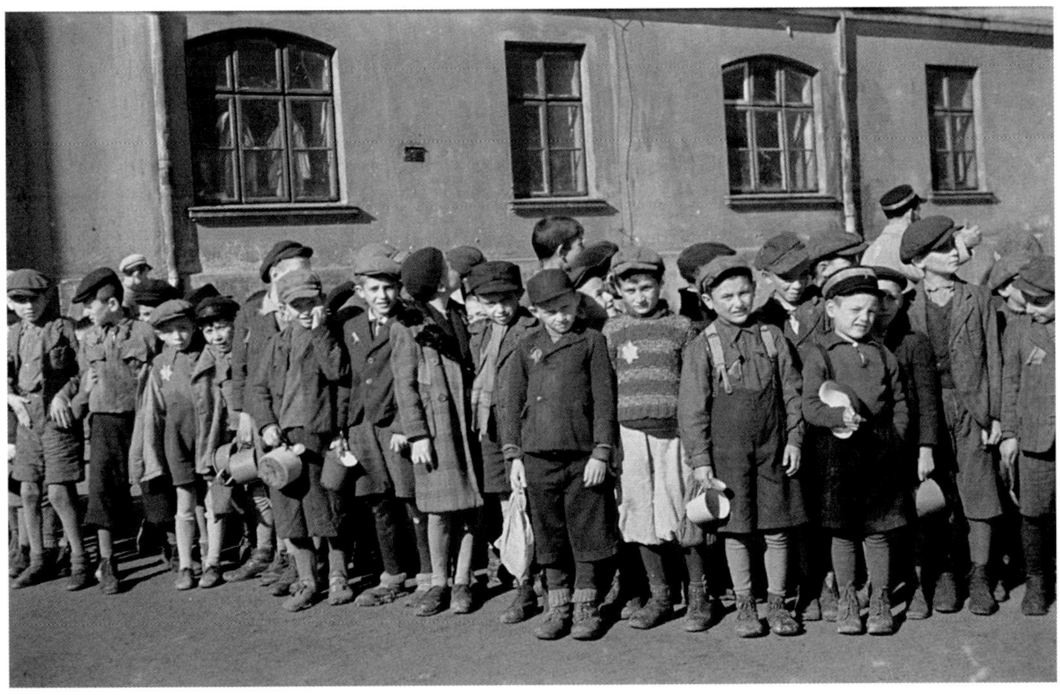

FIGURE 3.8. *Schuljugend*, ca.1941. Photo by Walter Genewein. (Mis)titled by USHMM: "Ghetto school children holding small pails and cups wait in line outside the ghetto soup kitchen." See also plate 10. (United States Holocaust Memorial Museum, courtesy of Robert Abrams, 1940–44)

chronology of Lódź ghetto events, suggest that the three images were taken at least a year apart, the first two perhaps in late spring or early summer 1941 and the third sometime in the latter part of June 1942.[38]

A quick look at these images—the first two of young boys in somewhat jumbled lineups, squinting into the sun and seemingly bewildered by the photographer, and the third, of older children largely intent on their work— might lead a viewer to consider them as projecting what Nazis advertised as their "benign" rule over Jews, a kind of normalcy and continuity of Jewish existence in designated ghettos and labor camps. Seen in this cursory manner, these photos do function as German ghetto authorities like Genewein and Reich propaganda officials in Berlin most probably would have wanted: to demonstrate the achievements of Nazi-German ghetto planning and

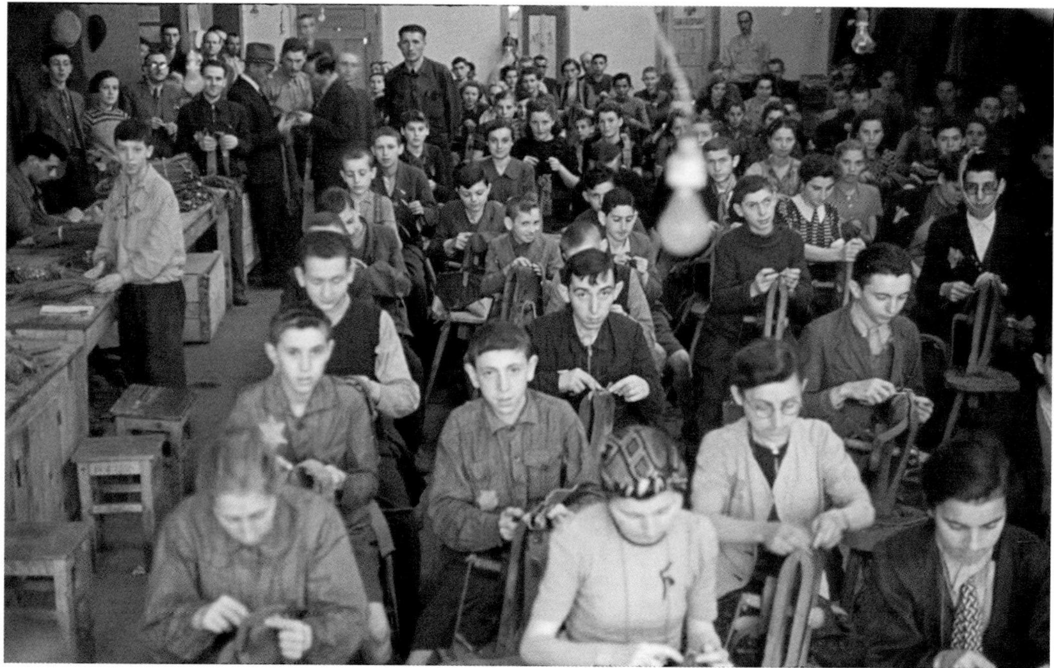

FIGURE 3.9. *Getto Litzmannstadt Sattlerei* (Saddlery), ca. 1942–43. Photo by Walter Genewein. See also plate 11. (Jewish Museum Frankfurt)

administration, and to mislead and conceal both what was actually going on and what was being planned.

A closer, more contextual look at the photographs, however, reveals both Genewein's ethnographic project and this ghetto's darker story. The photos' divergence from the genre is telling. As we have argued, a central aim of class photography is to make each child visible individually even while enfolding them into a class collective. Genewein's group images, like other photographs taken by those who assert their social dominance over subjects staged as "other," have a different objective. As many, if not most, of the children's faces remain hidden from view, Genewein makes it clear that he is interested in the social type and not the individual.

The smiles on some of the children's faces in the two photos in front of the school building (figs. I.2 and 3.9; plates 9 and 10) are, in such a viewing, shadowed not only by the "Jew Star" that all Jews were forced to display, and

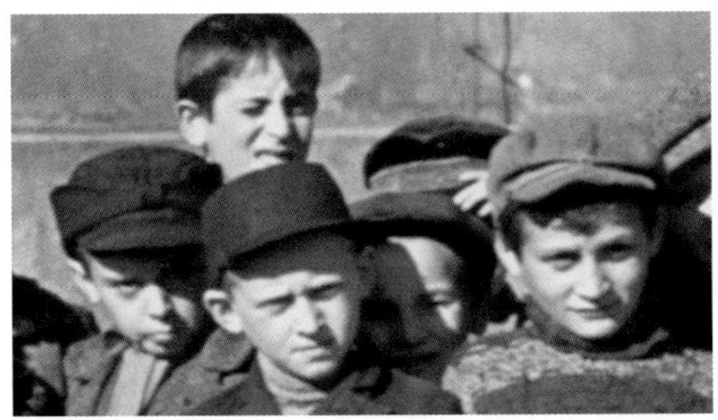

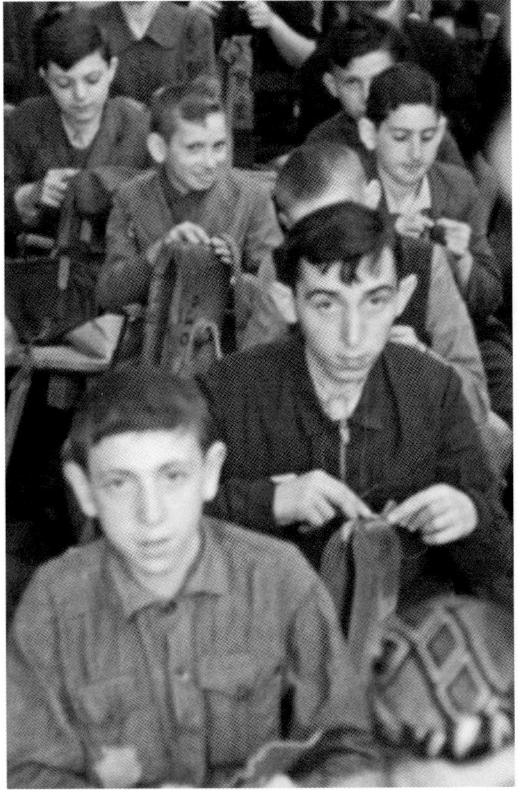

FIGURE 3.10. The boys stare back.

not only by the children's gaunt, impoverished appearance, but also by our knowledge that Nazis shut down all officially sanctioned ghetto schools in Lódź, other than specialized vocational ones, in October 1941, not very long after these photos were taken.[39] And beyond this, we are overwhelmed by our recognition that most of the children depicted in these photos were slated to be killed not long after being photographed. It is difficult to restore the future embedded in the school photography genre to photos such as these, and thus difficult even to see them within the frames of this genre.

Can we detect the order in which these outdoor photos were taken? Zooming in on the boys' faces, we might surmise that the photo with the ghetto police officer wearing a black gold-banded cap in the background (*Getto Schulausspeisung*, fig. 3.8) was the first one snapped. The children's seemingly disoriented perspective, the various directions—front, sideways, backward—in which their heads and eyes are turned, and the handful of seemingly puzzled stares at Walter Genewein, the Nazi photographer and authority figure behind the camera, indicate that the photo was taken unexpectedly.

But the three boys in the front row in the two photos—the one in the red-striped sweater and the two standing to his right (fig. 3.10, top)—*stare back* directly and unsmilingly at the photographer (and, by extension, at us as viewers of his photos), and in doing so they take an artful command of the experience of being photographed. In seemingly refusing to obey what may have been

Genewein's efforts to order and group them and their schoolmates into a lineup of smiling and compliant Jewish ghetto children, and to objectify them for display and propaganda, the three boys willfully withhold acquiescence and sternly subvert the monolithic power of the Nazi photographer's organizing gaze. Ironically, in framing the image around the boy whose red-striped sweater attracts the viewer's eye, Genewein also frames it around one of the less compliant children.

The photographer's control is further undermined by a scene that seems to be going on in the background, to the right of the policeman who turns to address it, also drawing some of the boys' attention away from the camera. The other image of the children, perhaps taken a few moments later, displays a more orderly assemblage that faces forward. The resistant boy in the striped sweater is no longer at the center, and thus the image corresponds more closely to a conventional class photo. Or is the order reversed, and the children turn back to look at the policeman *after* having lined up in more orderly fashion?

Genewein's third Lódź ghetto class photo, *Getto Litzmannstadt Sattlerei* (fig. 3.9), made some months later in a vocational classroom, further underscores the link between perpetrator photography and the Nazi killing machine. By the time it was taken in mid-1942 (in the aftermath of the Wannsee Conference to coordinate implementation of the Final Solution),[40] the Nazis had set in motion mass deportations from Lódź to nearby Chelmno. In Chelmo, by the end of May of that year, over 55,000 Lódź deportees were asphyxiated in gas vans. Children under ten, old folks, the infirm and incapacitated—persons least able to perform the skilled and unskilled forced labor that the Nazis demanded to feed their war machine—were the most vulnerable and most likely to be selected for deportation and, as rumors circulating within the ghetto correctly speculated, selected for death.[41]

"*Unser einziger Weg ist Arbeit*" ("Our only course is work"), declared the Lódź Jewish Council head, Chaim Rumkowski, in the aftermath of these mass transports.[42] His directive, and the ongoing deportations and killing of those considered unable to do the hard work Nazis required (including, no doubt, many of the children in the first two photos), make the vocational class picture especially heartrending. Within it, in the young apprentice leatherworkers' faces and eyes, we can discern apprehension and dread, most certainly intensified by the intimidating presence of Genewein—a high-ranking Nazi ghetto official—in a class where laboring ability and competence were being scrutinized and judged. Some of the craft students gaze at Genewein and his camera (fig. 3.10, bottom)—and by extension at us, the viewers—and offer a small, perhaps hesitant, ingratiating smile. Others look down and focus intently on their work, hoping, perhaps, that their apparent dedication might bring them the nod of recognition and approval that would earn them an extension of life.

Genewein's astounding trove of images has elicited an extensive discussion about his project in particular and ghetto photography more generally. In his beautiful book *Spectral Evidence,* Ulrich Baer discusses Genewein's photographs in the context of a haunting film about Genewein and his ghetto photographs, *Fotoamator* by Dariusz Jablonski. Jablonski animates Genewein's images and also the lives of their murdered subjects, and he supplements them with present views of Lódź and eloquent accounts by a ghetto survivor. Through Jablonski's animation, Baer attempts to "rescue" the images from the photographer's "perspective and incontestable authority."[43] He enjoins viewers to consider and take responsibility not only for the Jewish subjects' lived reality but also for the future they were envisioning and stubbornly hoping for as they faced Genewein's camera. Contextualizing these images both in the ghetto's timeline and among Genewein's images, we have responded similarly, allowing ourselves to be addressed by the children in the photos, granting them their own present as well as their imagined future. Attempting to insert them into liquid time, we have tried to unsettle the inevitability of their outcome, without minimizing the ways in which their imagined future was being eradicated by the Nazi killing machine.[44]

CLANDESTINE IMAGES

It is essential to highlight that in Lódź, as in other ghettos, professional Jewish photographers also took many Nazi-approved pictures of ghetto Jewish life, including class photos. The photos of young students with Lódź Jewish Council head Chaim Rumkowski and with some of their teachers, which we discussed earlier, enable us to see how these photographers and Council members used photography to document ghetto activities and their political position, as well as to influence their captors (figs. 3.6, 3.12, and possibly 3.11).

But Jewish photographers also took hundreds of covert photos of ghetto existence. Georg Kadish in Kovno and Mendel Grossman and Henryk Rozencwaig Ross in Łódź have, over the course of time, become three of the best known of these. All were employed as official photographers and dark-room technicians by the Jewish Councils in their respective ghettos and, in this capacity, took, developed, and printed hundreds of sanctioned photos. Each one of them, however, also secretly managed to stash film stock and to pilfer cameras from their places of work. Using this equipment they photographed ghetto activities, including clandestine schooling, surreptitiously—

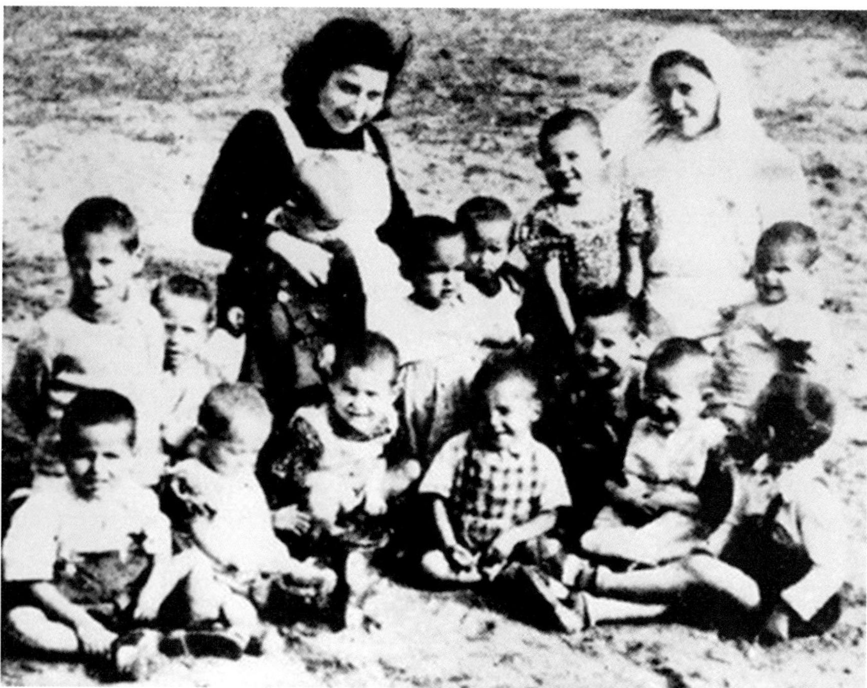

FIGURE 3.11. Preschool children with their teachers in the Kovno ghetto, December 1941. According to the caption provided by the USHMM Photo Archives: "Approximately 10,000 children and youth below the age of 20 moved into the Kovno ghetto in August, 1941. Within a few months almost half of them (4,400) had perished in the 'Great Action' of October 28, 1941. After the Germans issued a decree in July 1942 making pregnancy illegal and punishable by death, few children were born in the ghetto. During the fall of 1941 the community organized schools for children, but on August 25, 1942 educational instruction was formally banned." (United States Holocaust Memorial Museum)

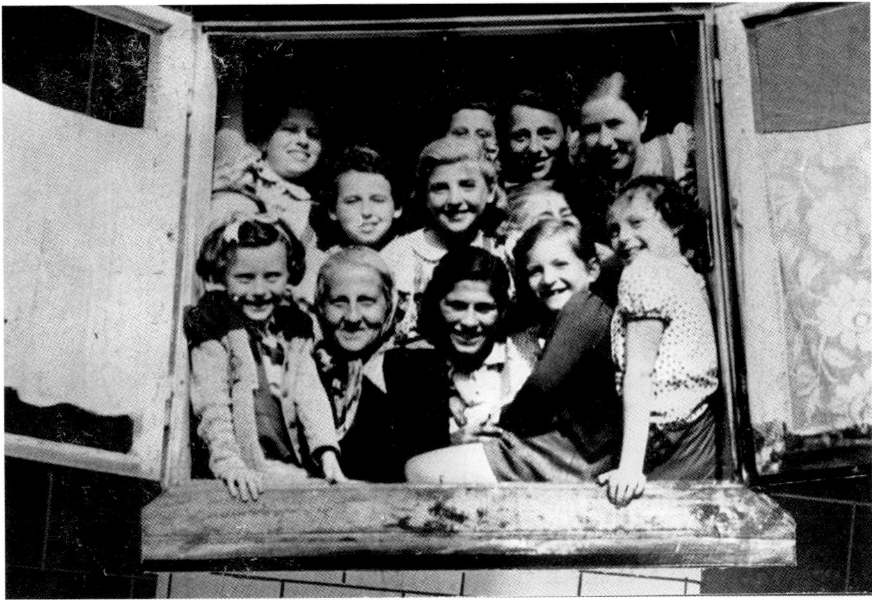

FIGURE 3.12. Teacher Stella Rein and students, Łódz ghetto, ca. 1942. Photo by Mendel Grossman. (United States Holocaust Memorial Museum, courtesy of Ari Ben Menachem)

sometimes through cracks in doors or buttonholes in their coats. Over a three-year period in the Kovno ghetto, Kadish took, developed negatives, and then buried more than one thousand of his secret photos, images he retrieved in 1945 after surviving the war.[45] Grossman and Ross hid and buried more than ten thousand negatives in barrels and crates beneath the ground and in the walls of their homes.

In taking, amassing, and deliberately concealing this visual evidentiary archive of images, these three photographers knowingly performed acts of civil resistance that, if discovered, would have resulted in their certain death. The numbers of images they took and the cache that survived is an extraordinary testament to their bravery and ingenuity. Equally astonishing as their contribution, however, is the fact that many other clandestine ghetto photographs have also emerged, taken by anonymous photographers who in all likelihood would have had much more restrictive access to cameras and film stock. Most of these unnamed and thus unacknowledged photographers probably belonged to communist, labor Zionist, or other underground

organizations. The surviving negatives and prints tend to lack precise identification or labeling. Their dates and provenance have thus been difficult to
determine with certainty. Taken to insure that a visual record of a population
targeted for destruction be left behind for possible future viewing, they document day-to-day life in the ghettos as it was lived, in *its present*. In examin-
ing these photos in *our* present, we must keep this goal in mind and resist the
compulsion to backshadow, that is, to read them only through our historical
knowledge about the dire fate that awaited most of the Jews in the images—
especially the children—soon after the photographs were made. Instead,
by scrutinizing and attempting to read them from the perspective of *their*
present, we can share Michael André Bernstein's insightful realization "that
the present contains the seeds of diverse and mutually exclusive futures."[46]

The ideological and memorial work of school photos, as well as the contradictions that structure them, help explain known and unknown photographers' extraordinary efforts to document clandestine ghetto school classes
and the teachers and pupils who created them. One photo of children from
a clandestine school in the Mielec ghetto, for example (fig. 3.13), shows children lined up outdoors, squinting into the sun, not unlike the Genewein

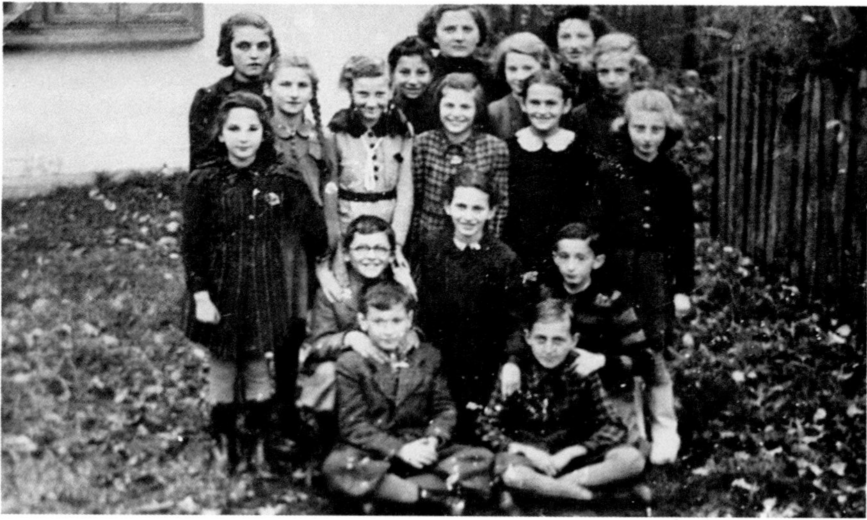

FIGURE 3.13. Group portrait of pupils attending a clandestine school in the Mielec
ghetto, 1941. (United States Holocaust Memorial Museum, courtesy of Irene Geminder
Eber)

images of the "*Getto Schulausspeisung.*" But here all the children are visible and recognizable; they smile and hold each other, displaying their affiliation and their recognition of and collaboration with the photographer. They exhibit the joy of learning, the desire to be part of a school group, and the ability to forget that they were "more than a little" hungry, as the memoirs proclaim.

Other clandestine images violate many school photo conventions. Their unconventional angles and poses and their dependence on natural lighting betray their furtive character and the haste with which they were taken, thus conveying the risks their makers undertook. We see these risks in Henryk Ross's picture of a kindergarten class in the Lódź ghetto and in a photo taken by an unknown photographer of a class in the Kovno ghetto.

In Ross's dimly lit picture (fig. 3.14) of the kindergarten group sitting on a bare floor, the photographer placed himself and his camera at the children's level, close to the ground. The children are not posing: some are paying attention while others seem distracted. Shadowy and blurred, this surely

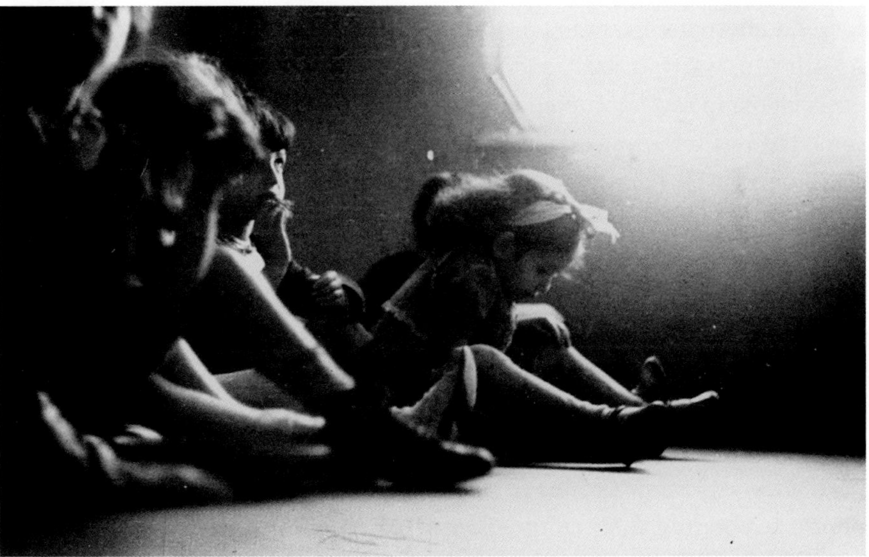

FIGURE 3.14. Young children sitting on bare floor in a clandestine Lódz ghetto kindergarten, ca. 1940–42. Photo by Henryk Rozencwaig Ross. (United States Holocaust Memorial Museum, courtesy of Beit Lohamei Haghetaot [Ghetto Fighters House Museum])

is not a traditional school photo touting an institution or confirming grade participation. It captures a moment of intimacy with the children marked by a reluctance to organize them for the camera gaze.

In the photo from Kovno (fig. 3.15), taken in a small and seemingly make-shift classroom, the children are sitting at a table or desk, intently concentrating on their work. None look at the photographer. The teacher, Shmuel Rozental, is at the head of the table with pen or pencil in hand. The tight space and inadequate natural lighting from above underscore the school's clandestine character.

As photos taken by an underground resistance, these are also propaganda images, but here the photographer stays close to the children and refrains from dominating the scene. In treating the children with such seriousness, and in showing their earnest concentration, the Kovno image, like all ghetto photos of instruction, attests to the life-affirming role that schooling came to play in moments of hopelessness and despair, and to the lengths to which adults went to ensure that children could continue to learn. (See also figure I.4.)

In photographing children in clandestine schools and in hiding, educators and photographers were recording their own courage and will to survive. As radical as war and Nazi genocidal practices were in rupturing the textures of social life in Nazi-occupied Europe, so were victims and bystanders determined to restitch some qualities of that life through small acts of repair. In response to utter dehumanization, photographers embraced schoolchildren in a group identity and in an affirmation of continuity made all the more precious in the context of the violent destruction to which they were subject.

IMAGINED FUTURES

As acts of defiance, some ghetto images profoundly challenge the common understanding of ghetto life. Two photos from Warsaw and Bedzin (figs. 3.16–3.17) show groups of girls, along with some boys in the second photo, celebrating their completion of school exams and their graduation by sunbathing and being photographed. In both images, the young people are smiling at the photographer, eager to display their accomplishment and their pleasure. They are closely grouped, and nothing in these images betrays the hardships of schooling under these circumstances, nor the dangers they

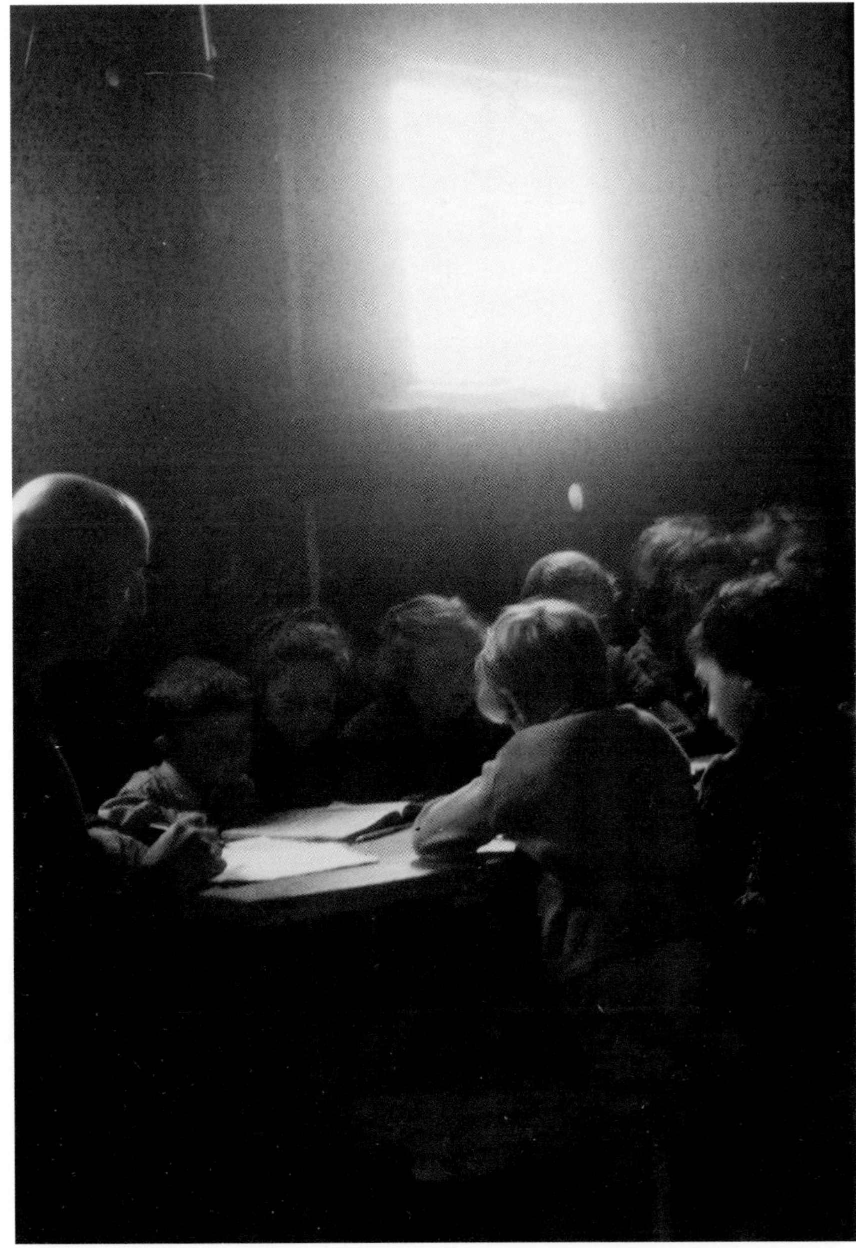

FIGURE 3.15. Clandestine school in the Kovno ghetto organized by the communist underground. Teacher Schmuel Rozental. Unknown photographer, possibly David Chaim Ratner. (Lithuanian Central State Archive)

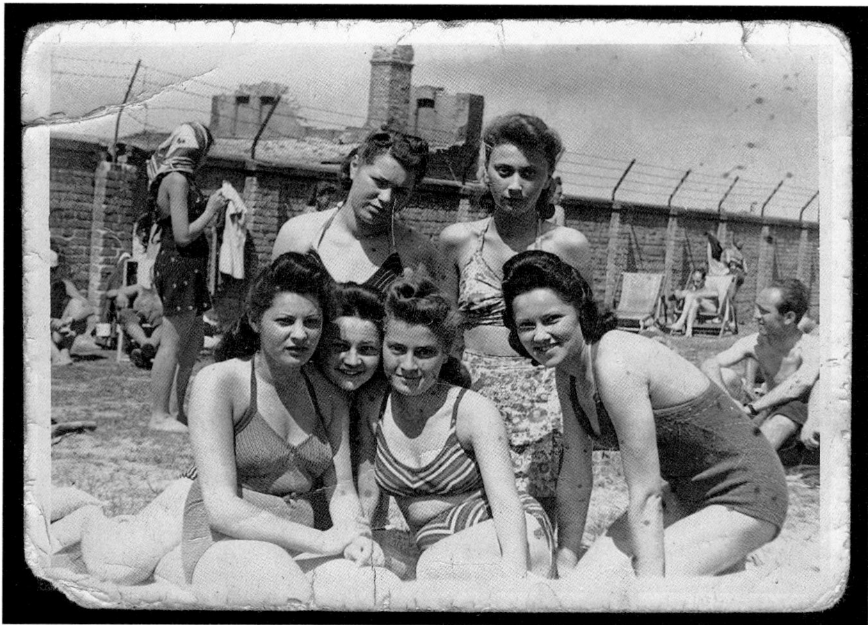

FIGURE 3.16. "Six young women sunbathing in the Warsaw ghetto on the day they finished their high school matriculation exams, 1942." The young women continued their education in an underground ghetto school. (United States Holocaust Memorial Museum, courtesy of Eugenia Tabaczynska Shrut [*front row, second from left*])

and their community are facing. Clearly, the performance of daily practice can itself give courage and pleasure, but here, celebrating a milestone, the anticipation of a future is made visible and palpable. When these photos were donated to the United States Holocaust Memorial Museum, they were meant to evoke that anticipated future, visually and affectively.

Some of the ghetto and camp teachers, new or longer-term adherents of Zionism, did reject the possibility of Jewish survival and acceptance without the supporting existence of a Jewish homeland. Persecuted as Jews in what came to be disparaged as "their diasporic existence," they envisaged and sought a brighter alternative future to the dark one imperiling them. The classes and subjects they taught reflected this belief: Jewish and Near Eastern history, modern Hebrew, Jewish literature, the ethical tenets of Jewish culture—subjects, skills, and values that would both prepare them and help them realize the creation of a Jewish Zion. Principally, however, while envel-

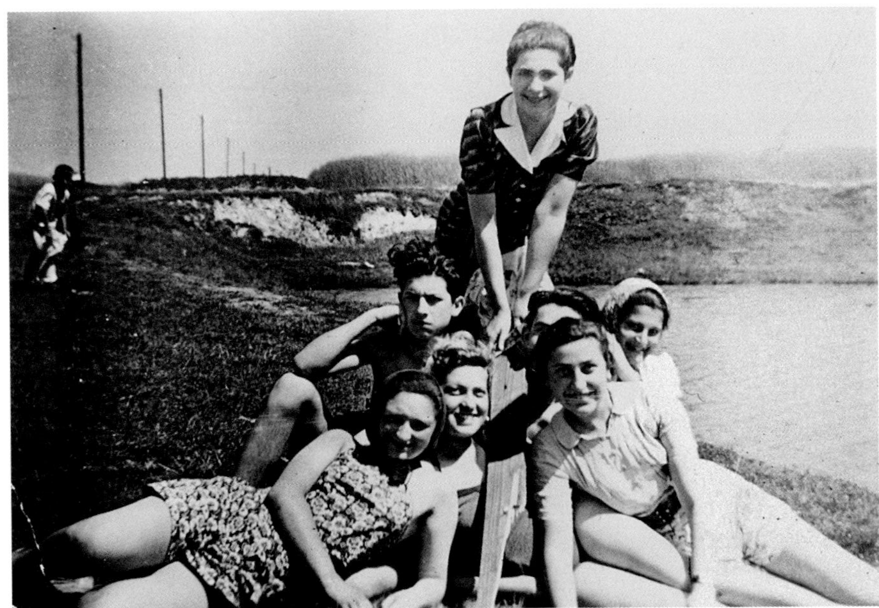

FIGURE 3.17. Bedzin ghetto: Teenagers sunbathing, celebrating their high school graduation. "All had been students at the Furstenberg Gymnasium, and they continued their studies clandestinely after the school was forced to close." (United States Holocaust Memorial Museum, courtesy of Eugenia Pinski [*front row left*])

oped by utter dehumanization and threatened with annihilation, ghetto and camp teachers repeatedly invoked personal as well as social and cultural memory to recall and transmit knowledge and values associated with a liberal humanism and cosmopolitanism that the Nazis were determined to obliterate. As Helen Fagin, who survived the Radomsko and Warsaw ghettos, writes: "I conducted a clandestine school [in the Warsaw ghetto] offering Jewish children a chance at the essential education denied them by their captors. But I soon came to feel that teaching these young sensitive souls Latin and mathematics was cheating them of something much more essential—what they needed wasn't dry information but hope, the kind that comes from being transported into a dream-world of possibility."[47] Ruth Klüger echoes this sentiment as she recalls a lecture she heard in Terezín. "Rabbi Leo Baeck talked to us in the attic of L414. . . . This rabbi offered us our heritage like a gift: the Bible in the spirit of the Enlightenment. One could have both the old myth and the new science: life was going to be a wonder and a joy."[48] Refusing to give up hope that Nazi Germany would eventually be defeated, the teachers taught subjects and imagined futures—if not for themselves, then for their pupils—that transmitted their own humanistic education and upbringing. Among these teachers undoubtedly were those who wished to believe, and wanted their students to believe, that despite the everyday evidence to the contrary, a world would again come into being in which Jews would be accepted and integrated.

HIDDEN CHILDREN

One set of wartime school photos—the photographs of hidden Jewish children in Izieu, France—are some of the best-known images taken of Jewish children during Nazi rule. Paradoxically, these hidden children were photographed even as they tried to elude the lethal gaze that positioned them as undesirable, as dispensable fodder for the Nazi killing machine. Their pictures were taken when collaborationist Vichy officials had expelled Jews from schooling, and when the children's parents had already been arrested, deported, or gone into hiding in different locations. These images and their multiple afterlives throw additional light on the historical, memorial, and also legal function of school pictures in liquid time.[49]

The history of Jewish children in France during the Holocaust differs from that in other parts of Nazi-occupied Europe. Despite French collaboration with the Nazi regime, sixty thousand of the seventy-two thousand Jewish children living in France in 1939 survived the war. Many of them went into hiding and thus survived without their parents. They hid with non-Jewish families, on farms, and in religious and secular institutions.

The numerous children's homes and schools that worked to rescue Jewish children throughout the occupation, and to continue educating them in a French curriculum, had in fact been founded long before World War II by a charitable organization, the Oeuvre de Secours aux Enfants (OSE).[50] By 1943, after Nazis occupied the southern zone of France, these institutions were potentially easy targets for discovery, and the OSE, fearing that its hidden Jewish boarding school children would be exposed, considered shutting them down. The tactic they decided upon instead, however, was to try to pass the schools off as Christian institutions, disguising them administratively so they would not appear to be under OSE control, and to make every effort to find the children temporary homes with Christian families. Ultimately, they hoped to smuggle the children across borders, out of occupied French territory altogether. Between 1943 and 1944, while the school functioned as a rescue home, 105 children went through Izieu.

Quite possibly, it was Izieu's hilly remoteness, its protection by the nearby Belley subprefecture, and the local population's hospitality that led the staff to believe that this particular rescue home, to which teacher Sabine Slatine had brought children from various transit camps in 1943, remained relatively safe—despite the raids and arrests that had forced many similar institutions in the broader region to shut down. The Gestapo's lethal raid on April 6, 1944, in which forty-four children from the Izieu home were seized and deported to Drancy and then to Auschwitz, was thus unexpected.

All but one of the Izieu group photos made during the war were taken by a non-Jewish assistant instructor, Paulette Pallarès, who had brought her camera to the home during the summer of 1943. A neighbor took the remaining photo in 1944. Paulette Pallarès's camera, and the amateur group pictures she took with it, produced a poignant and rare record of nearly all the institution's children and teachers who were eventually murdered in Auschwitz.

The best-known of these photos (fig. 3.18) loosely conforms to class photo conventions. The children smile and face forward, most of them looking intently at someone standing to the left of the camera. The danger to which the children are subject, the efforts of the townspeople and international agencies hiding them, the worries they might have about their parents and their own future—all these remain outside the frame. In the picture itself, they seem happy and closely knit as a group, and the moment itself seems ordinary, normal. The image's conventionality disguises and renders invisible the extraordinary circumstance in which this picture and others from the same home were taken.

This image was widely circulated in 1987 during the trial of Klaus Barbie, the Gestapo chief in Lyon responsible for carrying out the Izieu raid after a still-unidentified informant revealed the boarding school's composition to authorities.[51] It was Barbie's order to deport the children, and the quick release of one non-Jewish child during the raid, that enabled charges of genocide and crimes against humanity to be brought against him. But in order to function as an effective evidentiary and memorial medium for such a crime, the original image from Izieu had to be cropped, its message consolidated.

The cropping (fig. 3.19) unifies what looks like an image of a small group of younger and older people posing jointly outdoors, folding it more effectively into the genre of the class photo and its fixed, single-point perspective. Here, only five children—older ones—and one teacher are visible; the other children, some quite young, sitting on the floor and squinting into the sun, have been cropped out. Certainly, this is not a professional photo, and this mixed-age assemblage is not one cohort. The larger group's glances (fig. 3.18) are disparate—while some children are looking straight ahead at the camera, others look at someone standing to its left, and one or two look in a different direction altogether. Two children on the extreme right thumb their noses in a manner quite uncharacteristic of class photos. This larger image opens up a multiplicity of looks, gestures, and affects that in their turn point to the het-

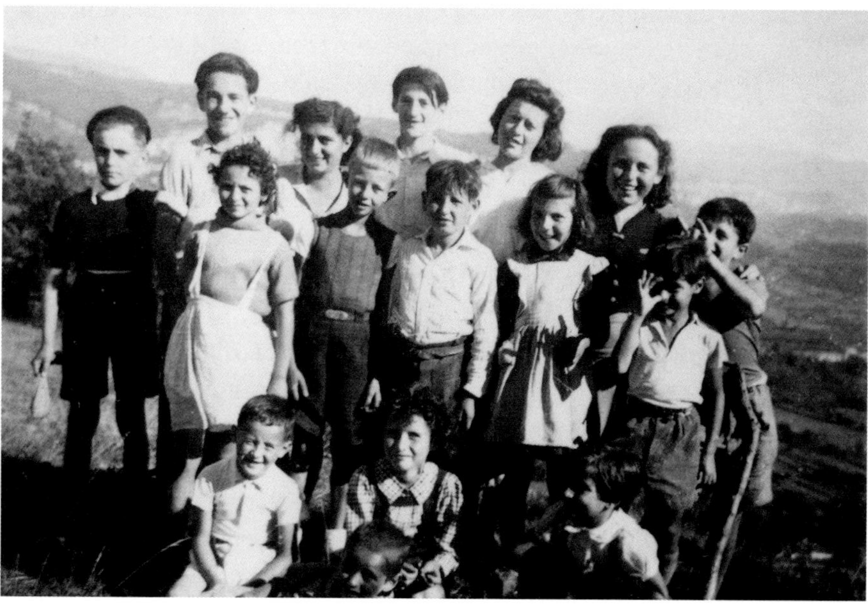

FIGURE 3.18. Children and teachers at Izieu, summer 1943. (Maison d'Izieu, mémorial des enfants juifs eterminés)

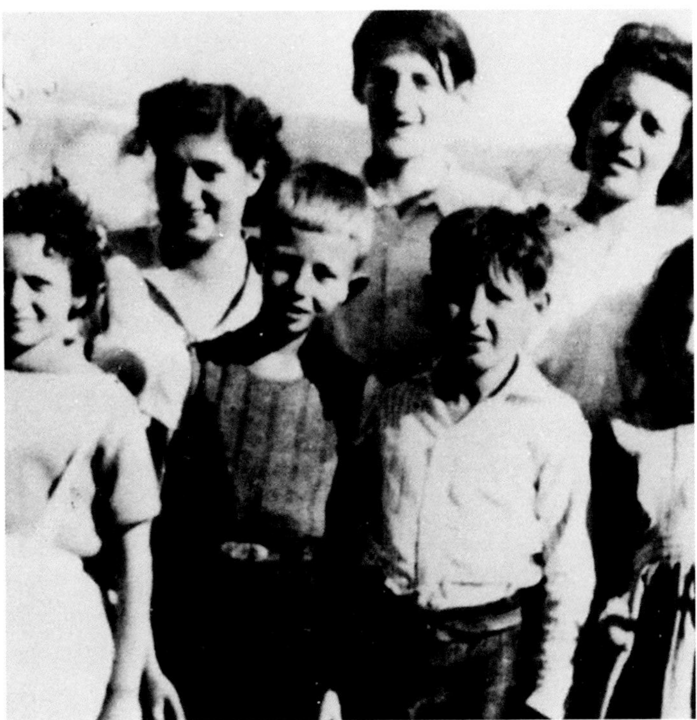

FIGURE 3.19. Cropped closeup of the summer 1943 photo of children and teachers at Izieu, published in 1989 during the trial of Klaus Barbie, who arrested the children and teachers and deported them to Auschwitz, where they were murdered.

erogeneous and contradictory knowledge it can convey. But it also shows the group's comfort and cohesiveness and the easy rapport they share with the photographer. Other Izieu photos, taken by Paulette Pallarès, display some of the same qualities: informal groupings and setup, poor lighting—random snapshots by an amateur who seems not to be in a position of authority over the children. The looks traversing the camera gaze can only begin to suggest the differences among these children who are from different backgrounds, speak different languages, and have different relationships to the dangers that surround them. Thus, we might wonder about the uniform smiles that the smaller group of Izieu children display in the cropped image. The ideologically unifying medium of the school picture could have elicited, if not coerced, these expressions on the faces of these boys and girls who were being saved. But what, in such circumstances, does it mean to *save* a child? What is the image's relationship to the liquid temporality of its own future?

In the museum now housed in the Izieu schoolrooms, Paulette Pallarès's photographs are supplemented by diaries and letters the children wrote; only some of the latter reached their destination. These qualify the smiles we see in the photographs. A few days before the raid, for example, eleven-year-old Liliane Gerenstein, whose parents had already been deported, wrote a letter addressed to God: "I ask you only one thing: MAKE MY PARENTS COME BACK, MY POOR PARENTS, PROTECT THEM (more than myself) SO THAT I CAN SEE THEM AS SOON AS POSSIBLE . . ."[52]

The children and young adults in the Izieu photo did not live to look back at the image from the vantage point of adulthood: their lives were cut short. Its *New York Times Magazine* cover reproduction in relation to an article about the Barbie trial, however, prompted artist Lorie Novak to use it as the basis for her composite 1987 projection *Past Lives (for the children of Izieu)* (fig. 3.20). The projection's title signals retrospection and evolution, the inscription of this group picture into a public memorial and historical context and into liquid time. Novak's projection and superimposition restores some of the messiness and multivalence, some of the affective registers, that were cropped out of the 1987 image.

Marking the moment of the Barbie trial but through a personal, affective, and artistic act of engagement, Novak projected the *New York Times* image onto the wall of a room, superimposing onto it two other images—that of herself as a small child held in her mother's arms, projected on the left wall, and that of Ethel Rosenberg's face, on the right. *Past Lives* connects the group picture to two individual familial images, of a mother and child, and of a public figure, a mother who, like the children in the group picture, was killed by the state.

Past Lives enacts the tensions and paradoxes already present in the multiple images from wartime Izieu. The corner wall and its straight lines enclose the figures like a photographic frame, yet the children's faces exceed the limits of those lines. Gone is the apparent freedom of the outdoor assemblage:

FIGURE 3.20. Lorie Novak, *Past Lives (for the children of Izieu)*, 1987. See also plate 12. (Courtesy of the artist)

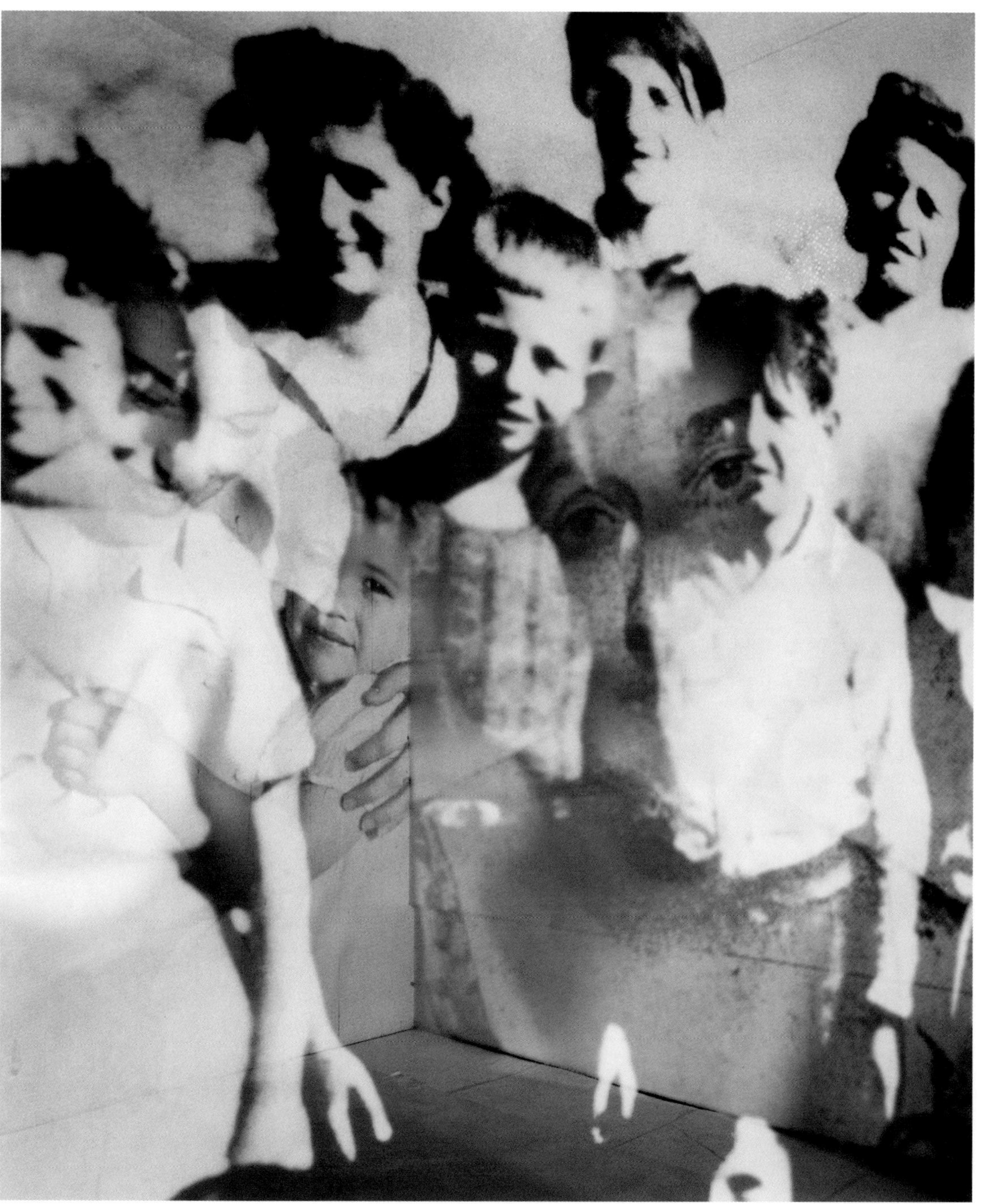

these children are trapped in a room, enclosed in the nightmare of the little girl whose mother, like Ethel Rosenberg, cannot shield her from the vulnerability and danger those other children faced.

In *Postmemory*, a 2012 reworking of the original Izieu school photo (fig. 3.21), Novak has brought the children back outdoors, allowing them to float eerily in a luminous forest setting.[53] Now, however, the original image is utterly disaggregated and no longer recognizable. Faces float separately as though they had escaped from a photo album that, incongruously, is held by two hands that hover over the forest floor. The album is a family album, open to a page that has a mother, father, and child on one side and a woman alone on the facing page. All are outdoors, in freedom, though an open door behind the single woman points to a dark domestic interior, invisible to our eyes. The faces float out of and above the family album, no longer affixed with photo corners as the two main images are. They coexist with one another but they refuse to cohere in the same space or on the same plane, blending into the natural background instead.

When the Izieu image circulated during the Barbie trial and appeared on the cover of the *New York Times Magazine* forty-three years after the genocidal murder of its subjects, it served as incontrovertible evidence of their past existence. It aided in their memorialization, and it helped indict Klaus Barbie for their murder. But Novak's projections and installations show us more than the photos on which they are based. They bring out some of the contradictory forms of knowledge the original images carried, the mixture of hope and hopelessness, the choiceless choices of parents and teachers, the combination of protection and exposure hidden children faced in wartime Europe. When Novak disaggregates the school picture on which this image is based, she separates the children from each other, evoking the school group's dissolution in catastrophic times, as well as the division and isolation that times of extremity can impose on group members who are forcibly disconnected from one other. Gone is the sense of commonality and integration that school pictures perform. And gone, as well, is the sense of a future to be shared, the lies and deceptions that lured Holocaust victims into holding on to education and modernity as a lifeline. The Izieu children are known, individually; their fate can be traced and their destruction documented. The faces in Novak's projection have lost these firm indexical and

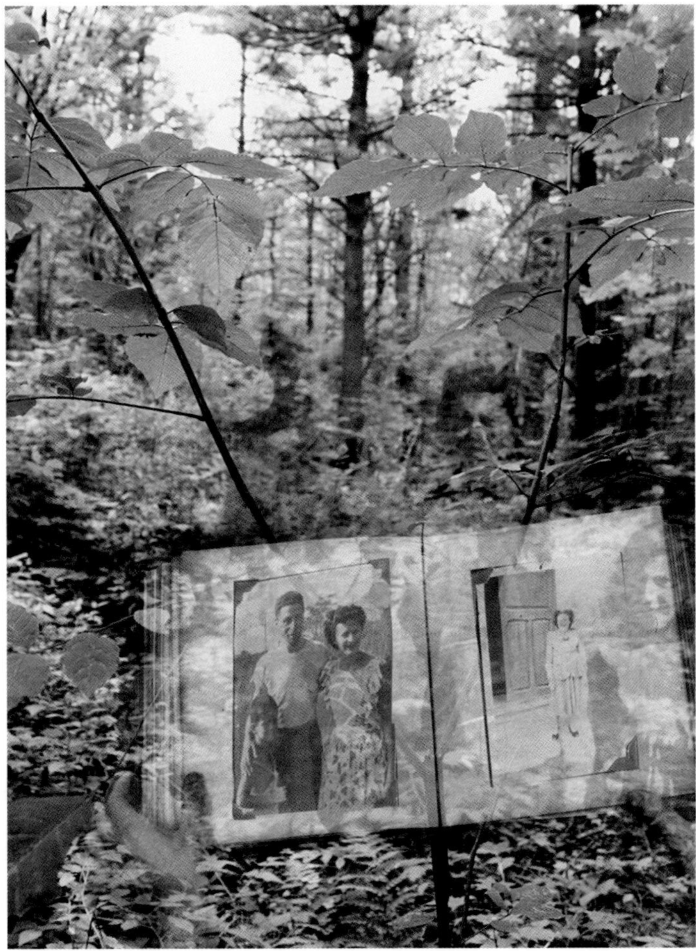

FIGURE 3.21. Lorie Novak, *Postmemory,* 2012. See also plate 13. (Courtesy of the artist)

historical connections, standing in for countless nameless and anonymous victims who could not be saved by going to school. They remind us of the many anonymous faces floating in the school pictures that survive in private and public archives throughout the world, hard to find, waiting to be identified, documented, adopted, and re-placed into history and memory. Novak undertook such an act of adoption in her artwork, but she takes the children's faces out of history, projecting them into a present that cannot repair the losses of the past.

In her *Postmemory* the ghosts of past lives—schoolchildren, teachers, individuals, and family groupings—have become part of the present landscape. Hovering in the greenery, they are intruders in the domestic as well as the natural and public spaces of the post-generation. They may gesture back to the past, reminding us of its presence in our lives, but they do not signal any form of continuity with it, nor do they illuminate it. The past remains opaque, distant, yet also part of our surroundings' very material textures. The dense woods over which the faces float continue to be replenished in the bright sunshine; the trees persist in reaching upward, indifferent witnesses to the layered histories that are projected onto them but will never be integrated within them. As the faces float up out of the archive, disappearing back into the trees that were the very source of the album into which they are affixed, they perform the entire process of assimilation *as disappearance.* We live among these heterogeneous projections of separate worlds, unsure of how to respond to their multiple, ultimately unreadable demands.

And yet between the green leaves of Novak's image, as between the pages of the photo album the artist's hands hold, the Izieu children's faces peer out at us, stubbornly affirming their ghostly presence. We cannot forget them.

ARCHIVES OF POSSIBILITY

School photos are particularly effective memorial objects in the aftermath of persecution, incarceration, and destruction. Because they show individuals in group settings, they can serve as a confirmation of presence, collective belonging, and intergroup cohabitation in a cohort of age-mates through schooling and beyond. But they are more than mnemonic aids helping identify particular classmates, especially in an aftermath affected by shifting political circumstances—and by oppression, war, or genocide. As archival documents carrying incontrovertible evidence of past existence and previous acceptance, and especially as documents that are broadly disseminated and held in multiple archives—analog and now also digital—they can also serve as powerful emotive and political vehicles to combat forgetting, and to mark the exclusion or eradication of members from the group—or of the group itself.

By putting together ghetto photos taken by perpetrators and by officially sanctioned and clandestine photographers, and by connecting them to photographs of hidden children, of children in US concentration camps, of Indian children in boarding schools, and of children in European-run colonial schools, we go beyond the limitations of specialized photo archives devoted to specific histories. Considering all of these different images under the generic category of school photos, we create what we would like to think of as an archive of possibility—an archive that enables us to learn not only about carceral life but also about photography as a technology of subjugation, of memorialization, and of resistance. Read specifically as *school photos*, the images of incarcerated children learning together attest to the value of dailiness and continuity in times of extremity. They affirm the importance of being part of a collective, however vulnerable, however threatened.

To be sure, the present of confinement is made more bearable by ordinary, daily communal activity. And yet as school photos, these images also, stubbornly, envision a future in which children can profit from their education as citizens. School photos are the products of an institutional gaze that certifies these qualities, makes them official—continuity, collectivity, citizenship, the future. As *school photos*, then, these images of incarceration can show us how that institutional gaze functions and how, at times of war and genocide, it fails. But they can do more—they can reveal improbable acts of individual and collective resistance at such moments of failure. They can memorialize teachers and students who, though abandoned and brutalized by state institutions, live on in these images. And they can affirm a horizon of freedom that persists even amid catastrophe.

WITNESSING FOR THE WITNESS

Contemporary artists engaging with Holocaust photography face ambiguities and confusions surrounding their sources, collections, and categorizations. Novak bases her *Past Lives* and *Postmemory* on an image taken by a friendly bystander. Yet more often than not, due no doubt to their ubiquity, images taken by perpetrators and shaped by an exterminationist Nazi gaze are the ones that, paradoxically, become the basis of art projects memorializing the victims.[54] Neutralizing this gaze is one of the objects of Mirta Kupferminc's *Mendel Grossman, The Witness* (fig. 3.22), a recent work made in response to Walter Genewein's color slides from the Lódz ghetto.

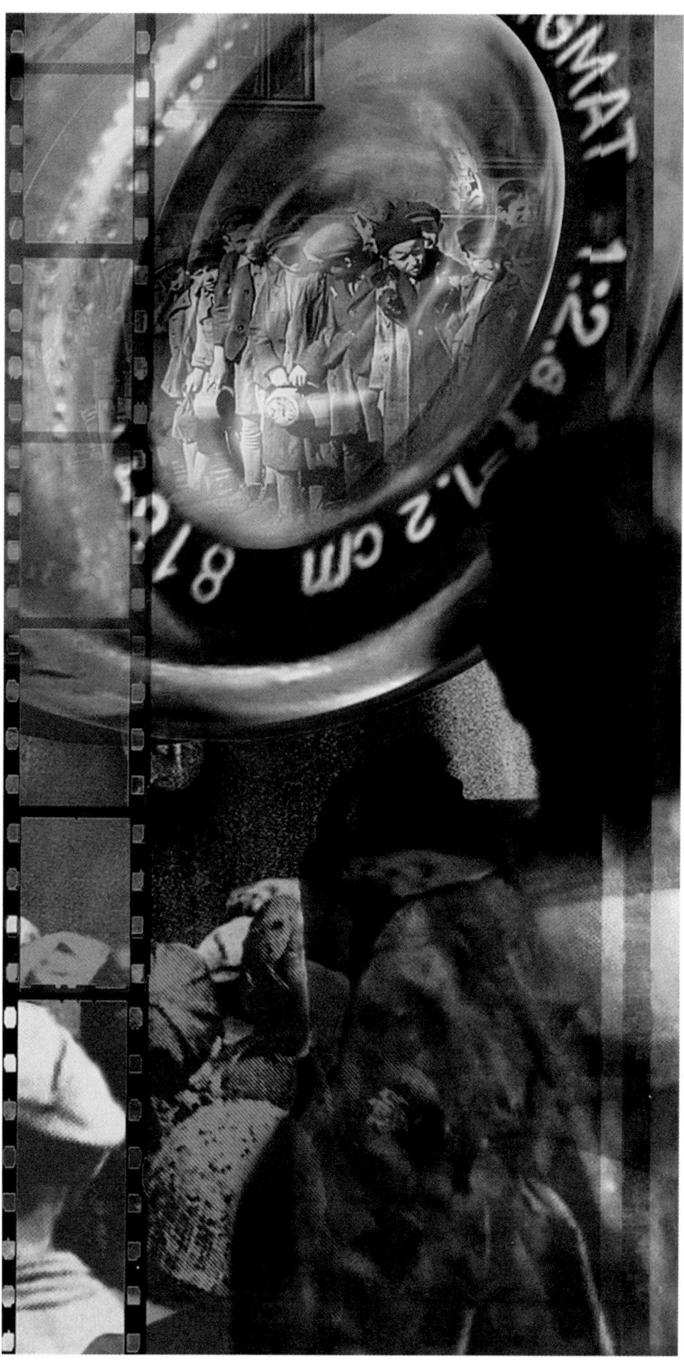

FIGURE 3.22. Mirta Kupferminc, *Mendel Grossman, The Witness*, 2019. Inkjet print and drawing on cotton paper. See also plate 14. (Courtesy of the artist)

What do the children see when they look into Genewein's camera lens, Kupferminc wonders. Aligning herself with them, and thereby animating their presence and their experience of the photographic event, she creates an alternate photographic event. She reverses the image and grants the children a point of view, all the while refraining from animating Genewein himself. The photographer is represented by his cold static lens, situated above the children, focused on capturing their image. But in the lens his look is also returned. We see the children but, more than that, in a fleeting, barely visible reflection, we also see another photographer, one Kupferminc places into this scene: Mendel Grossman. Even as Genewein is ethnographically recording the ghetto and casting the children as objects of his exploration, Grossman is staging his own images, clandestinely offering a fuller, expanded and reframed, visual record. In that record, Kupferminc imagines, he stands behind the children. He photographs the photographer Genewein. He scrutinizes his gaze and its effects, all the while remaining unseen and thus also free. By way of Grossman's lens, the children can look back at Genewein, making *him* the object of *their* gaze.

On the surface of her layered work, Kupferminc graphically inscribes, in her own handwriting, the story of Grossman's subversive work in the ghetto. She writes that "the texture of the graphic handwriting produces a veil that paradoxically, unveils Mendel's hidden way of taking the photos. While writing, I felt like a scribe who copies by hand a millenary text on the scrolls of a Torah."[55] Writing her text on the projection of a shadow, Kupferminc touches Grossman from a great distance and, by way of her direct touch, brings him closer to us. Though the work is digitally produced through the possibilities offered by Photoshop, she brings back the contingencies, haptic qualities, and "liquid intelligence" of the analog.

Kupferminc describes her work as a tribute to photography. She pays homage to photography's potential, one Grossman realized in the images he took clandestinely and buried. Here he gave us another view, one not ruled by the Nazi visual field. It is to that view, and to its resistant force, that Kupferminc bears witness, disabling the power of the Nazi gaze.[56] She thus practices a "disobedient gaze" that reframes the ghetto images, granting them a renewed life and purpose in liquid time.

¡Vivos se los llevaron
Vivos los queremos!

(They were taken alive,
we want them back alive!)

AYOTZINAPA FAMILIES

4

The "Disobedient Gaze"

How can we best remember children who were persecuted by the state and expelled by institutions that had been educating them for future citizenship? What commemorative strategies can do justice to young lives threatened and cut short, and to hopes and aspirations brutally crushed? In recent years, a global public memory culture has attempted to respond to these difficult questions. Moving memorial projects employing school photos have become common, especially in Western Europe. Efforts to recall individual names and lost lives, and attempts to recover stories and to perform small acts of repair—these have come to be expected memorial features in institutional memory culture.

It has also become clear that present-day students need to be reminded of the histories—sometimes nefarious—of the schools they currently attend. Throughout Europe, many such implicated educational institutions have installed memorial plaques that identify students and teachers who were expelled and deported to ghettos and death camps during the iniquitous Nazi years. Some schools, like the one in the former children's home in Izieu, France, have been modified into memorial museums displaying commemorative objects, photographs, letters, and other writings. In large part, these projects of remembrance have been motivated by earnest reverence for the students and teachers who suffered, and by the desire to apply the lessons of the past to the present.

Complementing institutional responses such as these, moreover, contemporary states have also developed encompassing national acknowledgments of responsibility for past injuries and suffering, as well as various efforts to seek "truth and reconciliation." Along these lines, both the Australian and Canadian parliaments apologized to indigenous populations within their borders for wrongs committed in the past—the Australians, in 2008, to the Aborigines and especially to the tens of thousands of children of the Stolen Generations, and the Canadians, in 2008 and again in 2018, for the forced removal of indigenous children to boarding schools. Critics have argued that these kinds of apologies, made without accompanying compensation, remain merely symbolic. But even if so, and if efforts at regret and national reconciliation are as yet incomplete, they do constitute pedagogies of memory and repair that address the ill use of schooling and the harms inflicted on children. As such, they acknowledge and bring to public attention histories that would otherwise have remained dark scars in the workings of contemporary civil society.

To be sure, creative works by postmemorial artists we have discussed in this book display a much sharper, more disruptive, and irreverent approach to commemorating past crimes. Their interventions are devoted not as much to memory and repair as to revelation and critique. Intent on exposing the connections and complicities in state-sponsored violence, they look at educational institutions and institutional images and refract them through what, borrowing Gabrielle Moser's term, we have been referring to as a "disobedient gaze."

It is such a "disobedient gaze" that artist Carrie Mae Weems applied to Frances Benjamin Johnston's photographs taken at the Hampton Normal and Agricultural Institute at the very end of the nineteenth century. Her installation's irreverence may perhaps account for the decision by officials of Hampton University, the late twentieth-century iteration of Hampton Institute, not to display her *Hampton Project* (figs. 2.24 and 4.1; plates 6 and 7) in the university's museum—this despite the fact that the project was conceived in collaboration with then-enrolled students. The university museum issued a considered explanation of its decision, which was based on two principal objections. One concerned Weems's use of past students' names, which, the museum feared, appropriated distinct individual lives for

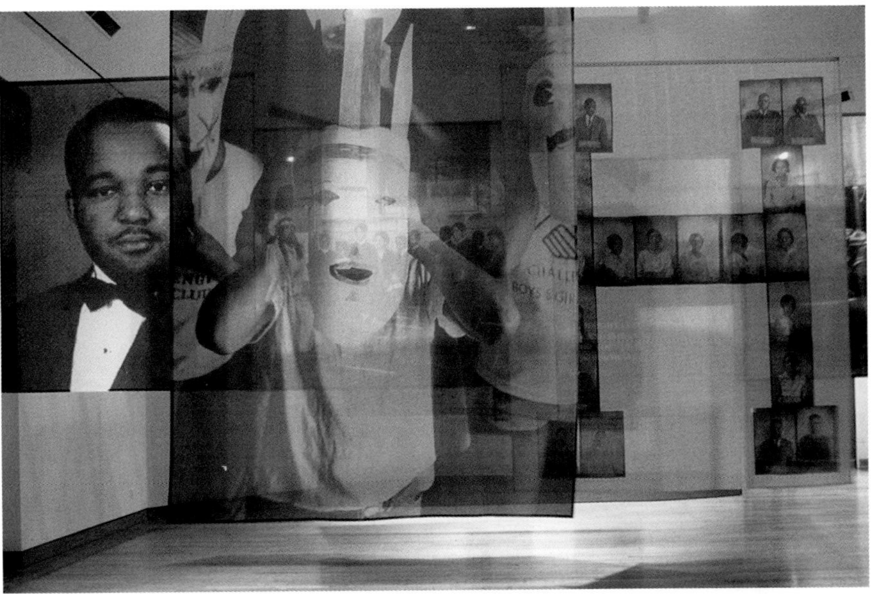

FIGURE 4.1. Carrie Mae Weems, *The Hampton Project*. Installation view. Williamstown, MA: Williams College Museum of Art, March 4–October 22, 2000. Photo credit: Arthur Evans. (Photo courtesy of the Williams College Museum of Art)

a symbolic artistic statement about the group fate of African American and American Indian students more generally. The second noted that Weems's installation was based on her judgment that "education is conformity"—an opinion incompatible with the university's belief that education, certainly *their* education, could also serve as a tool for potential rebellion and liberation.[1] As such, to show Weems's work at its museum would require the university to relinquish control over its own institutional narrative—a step it seems to have been unwilling to take.

Hampton's response, sadly, misses Weems's artistic and political intervention. Ironically, the "disobedient gaze" of her *Hampton Project* supports the suggestion that education *can* become a tool for rebellion and liberation. Filtering Johnston's images through multiple diaphanous screens and projections, and immersing them in the sounds of subversive voices, opens a space of disobedience inside the original images and contests their apparent conformity. Weems enables us to reclaim the students from the images' anonymity and uniformity, to imagine them outside of Johnston's static setup and tight frames. In her direct second-person address and her biting words, the artist animates their quiet, obedient faces and gestures. She provokes us to grant that they recognized the contradictions structuring their boarding-school education and the tensions underlying the assimilationist process in which they were engaged. As Weems says, "I'm interested in the tangled web of history, in the rough edges, and the bumpy surface, the mess just beneath the veneer of order."[2] Uncovering the mess of history, it seems, may not serve contemporary institutional needs.

LESSONS OF DARKNESS

The anti-institutional disobedience that shapes Weems's commemoration of the past and its erasures enables us to return to Christian Boltanski's work and to view his installations in a different frame (figs. I.5 and 4.2; plates 1 and 2). In the light of Weems's disruptions, Boltanski's works appear not only as "lessons of darkness" (as he titled them) but also as pedagogies of political anger.

Many of the images in the *Lessons of Darkness* installations derive from one specific source: a class photograph (fig. 4.3) taken in 1932—a year before Hitler came to power and six years before Germany annexed Austria—at Vienna's Chajes Jüdisches Realgymnasium. Founded in 1919, this Realgymnasium was the only state-accredited Jewish high school in the city, one that prided itself on offering "outstanding high school instruction, connected to Jewish knowledge (*Wissen*) and Jewish rearing (*Erziehung*)."[3]

Why does Boltanski use this particular picture? He found the photo of the school's senior graduating class and their teacher, Professor Kestenbaum (an instructor in religion and Hebrew), in *Die Mazzesinsel*, an illustrated history of Vienna's largely Jewish Second District from 1918 to 1938, edited by Austrian Jewish filmmaker Ruth Beckermann.[4] As a class photo, this image is appealing for its unusual qualities. While students in its first two rows pose and smile conventionally, three students in its top row, out of the teacher's sight, clown by striking amusing poses—parodies, perhaps, of theatrical or silent film melodrama—that, intended or not, undermine the disciplined group conformity that school photos generally seek to display.

As the students act out, their teacher remains serious, almost dour, in the middle of the front row, perhaps signaling his inability to control the disobe-

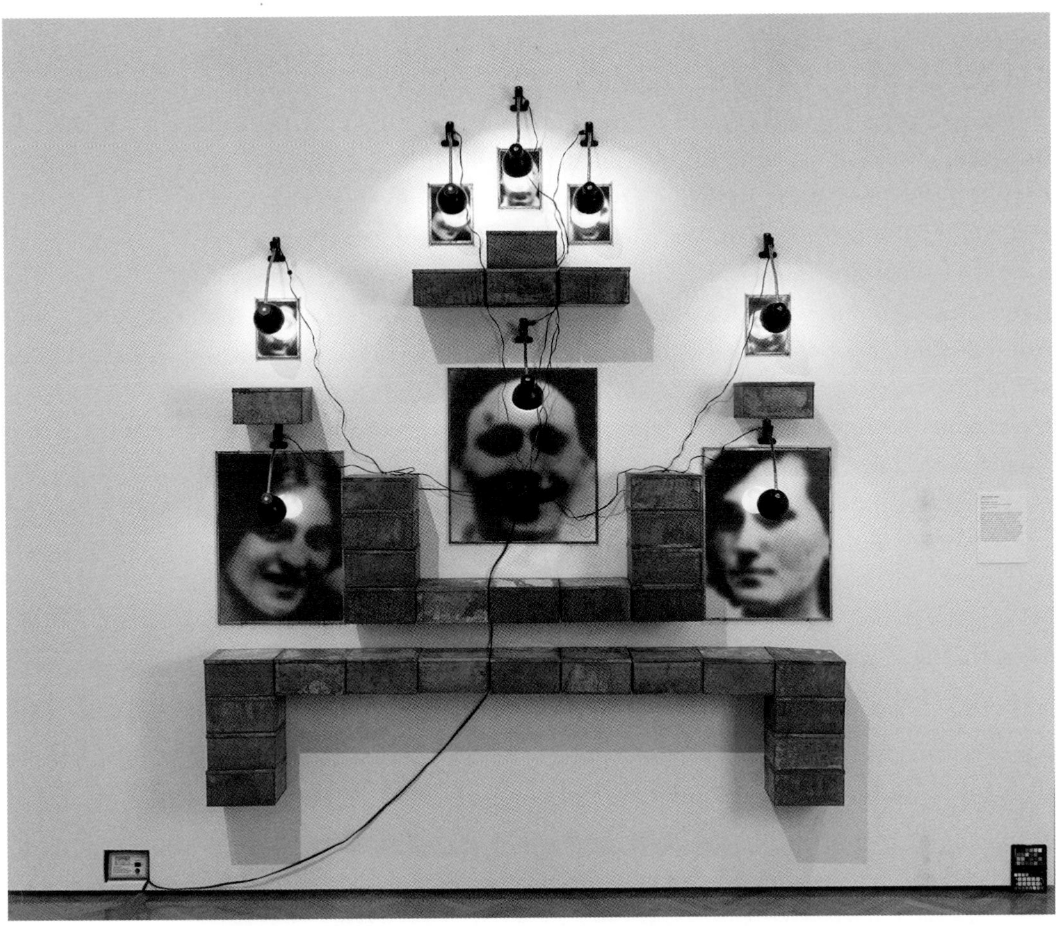

dience behind him. Quite possibly, their spoofing attitude also reflects the low esteem that many European Jewish students from secular homes felt for religious and Hebrew instruction—and for the teachers of these subjects—in the interwar years.[5]

Yet it may have been precisely this irreverent attitude that insured the photo's survival and notoriety in Boltanski's multiple installations.[6] We could argue that in selecting this particular image, Boltanski contests the limits of his own strategy for anonymity and generalization—an approach in which ghostly faces serve as stand-in icons for genocidal annihilation. In choosing a school photo showing clowning faces that remain memorable, he gestures toward reclaiming identifiable people with personal stories—toward a distinguishable individuality that Carrie Mae Weems's Hampton installation also projects. The overly enlarged and blurred faces in his *Lycée Chases*—unlike in some of his other installations—do, in fact, distinguish themselves by different facial expressions. Irony, humor, mockery—these are some of the marks of individuality that persist even in the most spectral aesthetic projections. They provide an affective trigger for the viewer who, in the aftermath of genocidal destruction, can return to a "before" to recognize a persistent, individual aliveness that defies the will to murder and erase.

By preserving this tenacious particularity, however muted, Boltanski adopts a "disobedient gaze" in relation to the archives of destruction, one that moves his works out of an anonymously elegiac memory culture. The smiling and ironic gestures and expressions on these young faces, expressions that endure even through multiple ghostly enlargements, provide an

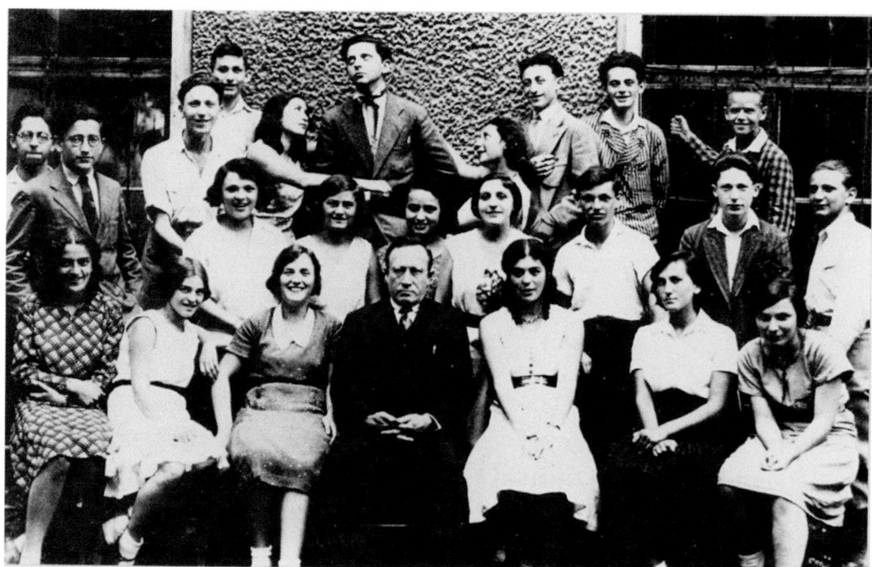

FIGURE 4.3. *Chajes Gymnasium* class with their Hebrew teacher, Vienna, 1932. (Courtesy of the Leo Baeck Institute, New York)

entry point for our own "disobedient gaze" as viewers. Recognizing that these images were cropped from school photos, and from the community they forge, reveals the poignant irony inherent in Boltanski's installations. We could argue that in abstracting individual faces from the collectivity of class photographs, the artist levels powerful accusations against regimes that would expose children to persecution rather than protection—states that would, on the one hand, appear to incorporate children into nationality and citizenship through schooling and ideological inculcation but, on the other hand, target a group among them (unspecified but, by implication, Jewish) for deportation and murder.

HOLDING MEMORY

Mourning and melancholy, nostalgia and protectiveness of children, anger and outrage: the range of affective responses school photos elicit in the memories and postmemories of state-sponsored violence and murder emerge even more clearly when we view Carrie Mae Weems's and Christian Boltanski's installations alongside those of Argentinian artist Marcelo Brodsky. When we turn to how Brodsky uses class photos, we are struck by the different memorial registers in which these three artists participate, and by the different ways in which they invoke or contest the tension between anonymity and individuality inherent in class pictures. Although they all use images or notions of a time "before" to mark catastrophic loss caused by war, racism, and persecution, these artists' memorial creations follow quite divergent chronologies. Both Boltanski's *Lessons of Darkness* and Weems's *Hampton Project* are defined by their temporal belatedness: they engage *inherited* and not personal or participant memory, although Weems creates her work in an environment in which the legacies of slavery, racism, and segregated schooling continue to fuel crucial social inequities. Brodsky, on the other hand, began working on what is known as Argentina's "Dirty War" and its victims, the *desaparecidos* (the disappeared), almost immediately after returning in the late 1980s from political exile in Barcelona. He helped create a resistant local memory culture just a few years after the end of the military dictatorship that had lasted from 1976 to 1983, during which his brother and many of his contemporaries were victims of political disappearance, torture, and murder.[7]

Brodsky's best-known work, *La Clase* (fig. 4.4), part of his *Buena Memoria* (Good Memory) installation, originates in his own school picture, the photo of the first-year students, sixth division, of the Colegio Nacional Buenos Aires.[8] In using portraits of individuals and groups in his memorial work, Brodsky is responding to the specific temporal, psychic, and political legacy of an aesthetics inspired by forced disappearance. Specifically, it both echoes and supplements an influential photographic iconography defining local memory practices, pioneered by the protest actions of the Madres de la Plaza de Mayo (the Mothers of the Plaza de Mayo) in Buenos Aires, who used photographs of their disappeared children. Notably, as early as the mid-1970s, the mothers began to use official identification photos—required of all citizens in Argentina—as evidence of their children's existence and as an insistent demand for their reappearance. Magnified copies of these ID photos became instruments of proof—a way both to bring to visual attention the military government's abductions and to impede its agents' systematic efforts to erase records and images of its victims, thereby denying their very existence. Exceeding their institutional functions, the ID photos in these circumstances also became archives of attachment and loss. In their weekly protests (which are still ongoing), the Madres made it a practice to circle around the Plaza de Mayo, a focal site of Argentine political life, with large, blown-up copies of ID photos of the *desaparecidos* strapped to their bodies.

These same official photos have also been carried as powerful reminders and "placeholders" for the *desaparecidos* in demonstrations by the HIJOS, the organization of the children of the disappeared—both by children born before their parents' abductions and raised by grandparents or other relatives and by those born in prisons or concentration camps and given away for adoption by military families.[9] Regular features in memory museums and memorials, these photos have been invoked as (symbolic) instruments of detection and recognition in the attempt to reunify families brutally separated.

Marcelo Brodsky works within the context and influence of this genealogical memory structure, but instead of a vertical, familial chain of transmission, Brodsky offers a lateral, affiliative web of mourning and resistance. In its original iteration, Brodsky's class photograph is quite conventional. The depicted children are lined up in four rows, facing forward and smiling; some

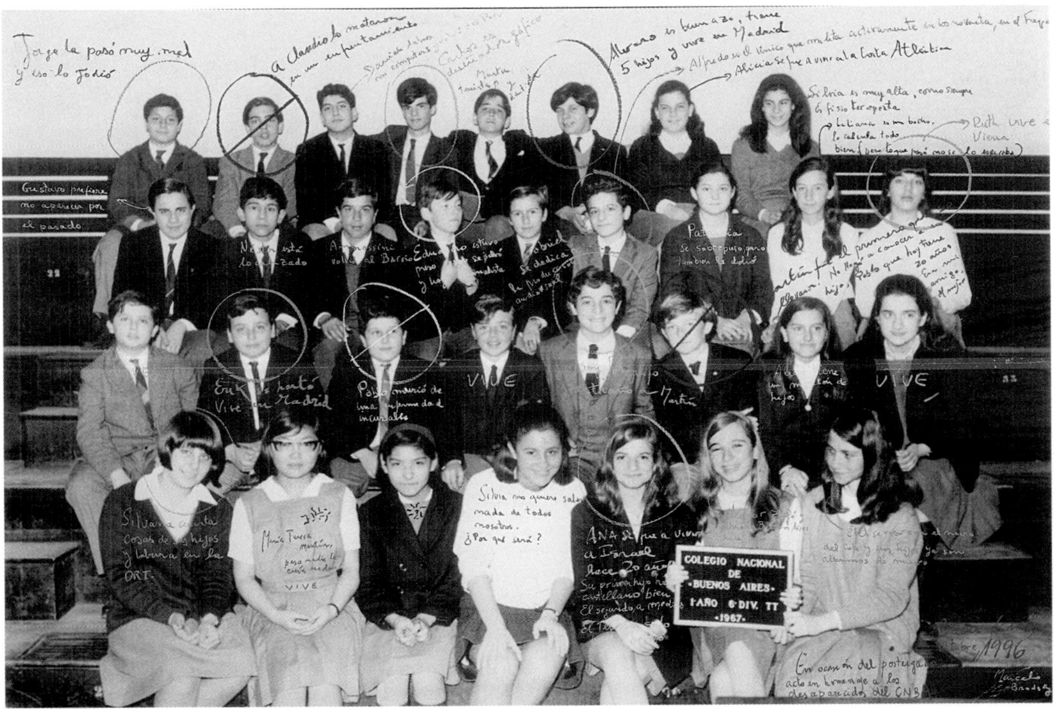

FIGURE 4.4. Marcelo Brodsky, *La Clase* (The Class). 1997. See also plate 15. (Courtesy of the artist)

are looking off to the side. Two girls in the front row together hold up a sign with the school's name, the class, and the year, 1967. There is a great deal of individual variation in dress and expression—no school uniforms, no standardization of appearance—and although the setting is institutional, the mood of the picture is, within the confines of the genre, quite informal.

In *La Clase*, the picture is intact but blown up to huge proportions (Brodsky labels it a "gigantograph"). The artist has inscribed the children's bodies with brief comments written in a variety of colors on the photo's skin. The text is simple, abbreviated, but it points to divergent aftermaths: "Carlos is a graphic designer"; "Claudio was killed fighting the military in December 1975"; "Silvia does not want to know anything about us. Why would that be?" One inscription, in yellow ink, simply reads "ALIVE." Disturbingly, some faces are simply circled and others, the disappeared and killed, are circled and crossed out. The mark of erasure on the photographic print's skin-like surface recalls the institutional violence of selecting individuals out of the social body with the intent to annihilate them and their memory. The bureaucratic circles and cross-outs etched into the print's skin, erasing individuals from the group, transmit that cold, institutional violence, puncturing us as viewers. But they transmit defiance and the determination to call public attention to classmates' murders as well.

In the gallery and museum installations of *Buena Memoria*, and in the catalogs that were published in conjunction with them, Brodsky placed individual portraits of class members, now as adults, next to or holding the original class photo in their hands. Accompanying these individual photos are longer captions describing the classmates' adult lives as well as images cropped from the 1967 class picture. This multilayered installation emphasizes both rupture caused by war and persecution and, obversely, continuity between past and present for those who survived in Buenos Aires or returned there from exile. School photos that can be widely disseminated among students and their extended families provide a form of evidence that is uniquely immune to destruction by state-supported perpetrators. The classmates who were disappeared continue to live in their age-mates' memories: the class photo certifies their continued presence and reminds us of lives that were violently interrupted.

Like in the weekly demonstrations in which the Madres carry images of disappeared daughters and sons strapped to their bodies, the adults in Brodsky's installation carry the memory of their own school community prior to the disappearances. The gesture in which they grasp their class photo, literally holding memory in their arms and close to their bodies, transforms the photo into a powerful testimonial object—a testimony to remembrance. Their touch elicits a haptic, embodied look from the installation's spectators, transforming us into engaged retrospective witnesses. It is that move from personal and collective grief into the political that converts mourning into anger, defiance, and resistance. But the gaze Brodsky cultivates, even in its anti-institutional disobedience, is affirmative and caring, embodied and touching. It remembers and reanimates the dead, reinvoking them in the time of their schooling and bringing back the futures they were imagining. Brodsky envisions a political pedagogy of loss that exposes a crime the state worked hard to erase. Mariana Graciano usefully characterizes Brodsky's intervention as a distinctly *political* gesture of what she terms "tenderness," mobilized in the fight against the cold logic of political murder.[10]

In its first installation in 1996, *Buena Memoria* was addressed to a very specific audience, the then current students of the Colegio Nacional Buenos Aires, where the original class photo was taken. Titled *Puente de la memoria* ("Memory Bridge"), it was installed in the Colegio's hallways as part of a ceremony to commemorate the school's disappeared students. Brodsky took photos of current students reflected in the glass of his gigantogram as they looked at the faces behind it. And he questioned many of them about their responses to the work. "I think when one sees a picture of any of the kids, one cannot deny that it might be one of one's own classmates," Andrés, one of the current students, commented to the artist. Another, Federico, noted: "When I saw the picture of those students posing for their picture, I immediately identified with them."[11] The students are responding in an identificatory mode congruent with widespread post-catastrophic public memory politics and aesthetics. Yet we wonder if the installation is not also provoking a deeper engagement that is difficult to articulate in an interview.

The 1967 class photo has certainly permitted Brodsky to remember the disappeared, to keep them in vision, and to keep open the space they have left in the lives of those who survived them. But beyond the group photo, in an additional move toward this political and memorial intent, Brodsky has also drawn on other, more personal and familial documents, gesturing to both familial and lateral affiliations. In the *Buena Memoria* catalogs, *La Clase* is supplemented by family photos, specifically including Marcelo's brother Fernando, who was captured and murdered by the military. And it also features the photo of his best school friend, Martín Bercovich, kidnapped on May 13, 1976, and "still missing."

In the installation, we find a torn page from Brodsky's own lined school notebook with its binder holes on the right. A blurred photo showing a boy in a checkered shirt, holding a camera, is pasted onto the page. Next to the image, we read in a slanted child's handwriting, "Martín takes a picture of me with his Kodak Fiesta that is just like mine. Chascomús [lagoon] in the background." Missing from this installation, however, is the adult picture of Martín. "Martín was the best friend I have ever had," Brodsky writes. "I still dream of him often, and it has been twenty years since they [the military] took him." By including a snapshot *by* Martín, one in which he points the camera at Brodsky as a boy, the artist shows Martín as a subject and creator of images, not just as the object of institutional framing. The snapshot, the handwriting, and the torn-out notebook page all embody, animate, and contextualize the class photo and, with it, Martín's memory. This personal picture and the child's handwriting next to it serve to contrast with, and thus to define, the institutional frame that stubbornly clings to school pictures, even when they are reconfigured and reanimated in divergent historical and aesthetic contexts—a frame Brodsky both invokes and disobediently contests.

Weems, Boltanski, and Brodsky, although representing different memorial cultures, use school pictures as vehicles of political anger and resistance. What happens, they seem to ask, *after* individuals and groups have been displaced, excluded, erased, transformed, killed off by others within the same nation-state and its institutions? In such an aftermath, it is sometimes in the interest of state authorities and of citizens (especially, perhaps, in the interest of ex-perpetrators and their descendants) to try to prevent the past from surfacing to disturb their drive to return to normalcy and reconciliation. Using school pictures—the very objects originally intended to certify belonging and socialization—these artists disobediently interrupt this move toward revisionary histories. They disturb the present, and in so doing, they slow and impede the eradication of a troubling past.

VISUAL ACTION

In 2014 Marcelo Brodsky returned to *La Clase*, reactivating it in response to a new political crime. His "visual action" responded directly to the forced disappearance of forty-three students from the Raúl Isidro Rural Teachers College in Ayotzinapa, Mexico, with a call for worldwide solidarity.

The students from Ayotzinapa were on their way to a protest commemoration of the 1968 massacre of three hundred students in Mexico City's Tlatelolco neighborhood. They boarded a bus to the capital in Iguala but were immediately taken by the police. They were handed over to a local criminal organization, but then their traces were lost and remain so to this

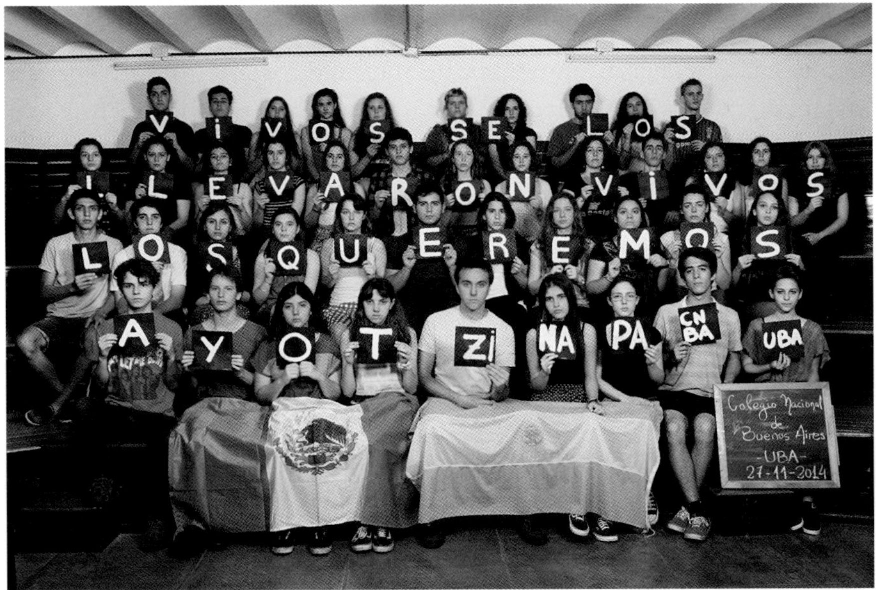

FIGURE 4.5. Marcelo Brodsky, *Ayotzinapa Visual Action*, 2014 onward. See also plate 16. (Courtesy of the artist)

day. The precise circumstances of their disappearance are still hotly contested, but the police, the army, and the government were all implicated. Why, amid myriad similar acts of disappearance and political murder in Mexico and elsewhere in Latin America, has the case of the 43 Ayotzinapa students attracted such immediate and sustained protest, as well as international attention? Why has *their* case, in particular, come to serve as a rallying point for a society fighting against rampant violence, corruption, and impunity in Mexico and elsewhere?

The powerful use of photography in protest actions against the disappearances helps explain this phenomenon.[12] Immediately after the disappearance, enlarged individual photos of the young people were being held up around the country as rallying cries for their reappearance. As Diana Taylor writes, "the grieving mothers, the chants (or *consignas*) demanding justice, and the use of photo IDs are the recognizable traumatic memes that made the tragedy immediately register with a public now only too familiar with disappearance."[13]

As in Argentina during the Dirty War, young people and students suspected to be subversive, unruly, and left-leaning have long been targets of suspicion and state-sponsored violence in Mexico and elsewhere.[14] This connection to Argentina's political disappearances provoked Marcelo Brodsky to mobilize the strategies he had used in *Buena Memoria* toward an international solidarity action on behalf of the Ayotzinapa students.

In supplementing these familial memes of loss and political demand with the tropes emerging from schooling's lateral affiliations, Brodsky introduces a different kind of disobedient action, activating a larger public. The action began by connecting the poor rural school in the Guerrero province of Mexico, where the 43 were studying to become teachers, with the Colegio Nacional Buenos Aires, the school where Brodsky studied and produced the *Buena Memoria* installation. Students from Buenos Aires reached out to the families of the 43, posing together in an image that recalls *La Clase*'s composition (fig. 4.5). The visual action that emerged from this first gesture was as simple as its effects were far-reaching. Brodsky invited students from across the globe to send in similar school class photos to mark their solidarity with the 43. Specifically, they were to hold signs that would spell out commemorative phrases or demands for justice: "Somos Todos Ayotzinapa" (We Are All Ayotzinapa), "Verdad, Justicia" (Truth, Justice), "43 Razones Para Decir Basta" (43 Reasons to Say Enough), "¡Vivos se los llevaron, Vivos los queremos!" (They were taken alive, we want them back alive!), and more. Images poured in from places as far flung as Tokyo, Montevideo, New York, Rome, London, Berlin, and New Brunswick, Canada. Younger and older classes and schools are represented, elementary schools and high schools, urban schools and rural ones, private and public ones.

As a collective project, the visual action allows participating students to assume agency in their self-representation. Working together with classmates to spell out meaningful messages, they also collaborate with agemates across the globe to create a movement. Together they redirect the class photo's institutional gaze, reframing it for their own purposes. They relearn its lessons as they practice a shared civil gaze that recognizes injustice and calls for redress. They mobilize and utilize photography's collaborative potential, thus reconceiving the genre of the school picture and its ties to specific state-accredited institutions.

The images thus produced by the students who responded to Brodsky's call join school images made elsewhere in acts of civil disobedience, as new student movements grow in our own time. Student survivors of the 2018 school shooting in Parkland, Florida, have activated the school photo to proclaim their determination to fight against gun violence. During 2019 protests, students across France have staged die-ins for the camera to contest police violence against student demonstrators. In their disobedient appropriation of the institutional genre of school photography, these images and the students who create them become agents of political action and solidarity. They undermine the power of institutions with calls for resistance and demands for accountability. In their appeals for social justice, they are able to invigorate the disruptive potential of photographic images, opening up their multiple, complex, and intersecting meanings and functions. School photos, thus reconceived, can reframe difference in liquid time.

NOTES

INTRODUCTION

1 Leo Spitzer, *Hotel Bolivia: The Culture of Memory in a Refuge from Nazism* (New York: Hill and Wang, 2000).

2 See Christina Kothemidova, "Why We Say 'Cheese': Producing the Smile in Snapshot Photography," *Critical Studies in Media Communication* 22, no. 1 (2005): 2–25. Kothemidova argues that Kodak played a key role in shaping cultural habits around photography at the time in the early twentieth century when the technology was becoming mass consumed.

3 Ernst van Alphen, *Caught by History: Holocaust Effects in Contemporary Art, Literature, and Theory* (Palo Alto, CA: Stanford University Press, 1997).

4 See, for example, readings of Boltanski's work in van Alphen, *Caught by History*, and Marianne Hirsch, *Family Frames: Photography, Narrative, and Postmemory* (Cambridge, MA: Harvard University Press, 1997).

5 See chapter 4 of this book.

6 Roland Barthes, *Camera Lucida: Reflections on Photography*, trans. Richard Howard (New York: Hill and Wang, 1981), 96.

7 Jeff Wall, "Photography and Liquid Intelligence" (1989), in *Jeff Wall: Selected Essays and Interviews* (New York: Museum of Modern Art, 2007), 109–11.

8 See the useful discussion of Wall's essay in Gabrielle Moser, "Developing Historical Negatives: The Colonial Photographic Archive as Optical Unconscious," in *Photography and the Optical Unconscious*, ed. Shawn Michelle Smith and Sharon Sliwinski (Durham, NC: Duke University Press, 2017), 229–63.

9 Barthes, *Camera Lucida*, 78, 76.

10 Barthes, *Camera Lucida*, 88. See the discussion of Barthes's reflections on photographic reference in Hirsch, *Family Frames*, 4–6, 8, 20.

11 For rich insights into such a future-oriented reading of the past, see Reinhart Koselleck, *Futures Past: On the Semantics of Historical Time*, trans. Keith Tribe (New York: Columbia University Press, 2004).

12 Katherine Bond Stockton, *The Queer Child, or Growing Sideways in the Twentieth Century* (Durham, NC: Duke University Press, 2009).

13 Wall, "Photography," 111.

14 See the caveat against such "backshadowing" in Michael André Bernstein, *Foregone Conclusions: Against Apocalyptic History* (Berkeley: University of California Press, 1994), 32.

15 See especially Marianne Hirsch, *The Generation of Postmemory: Writing and
Visual Culture after the Holocaust* (New York: Columbia University Press, 2012),
and Marianne Hirsch and Leo Spitzer, *Ghosts of Home: The Afterlife of Czernowitz in Jewish Memory* (Berkeley: University of California Press, 2010).

16 Robert Jay Lifton, *Death in Life: Survivors of Hiroshima* (Chapel Hill: University
of North Carolina Press, 1991).

17 See, for example, the online Museum of Family History, www.museumoffamily
history.com/.

18 See the press release, United Nations High Commissioner for Refugees, "Mil-
lions of Refugee Children Going without Schooling, UNHCR Report Shows,"
August 29, 2018, www.unhcr.org/news/press/2018/8/5b862f424.

19 See F. Brinley Bruton and Lawahez Jabari, "UNRWA Funding Cut Could Close
Palestinian Schools within Weeks," NBC News, September 3–4, 2018, www.
nbcnews.com/news/world/unrwa-funding-cut-could-close-palestinian-schools
-within-weeks-n905956. See also Orly Noy, "Demolishing Palestinian Schools 'a
Quiet Population Transfer,'" +972 *Magazine*, January 24, 2018, https://972mag
.com/demolishing-palestinian-schools-a-quiet-population-transfer/132662/.

20 Dana Goldstein and Manny Fernandez, "In a Migrant Shelter Classroom, 'It's
Always Like the First Day of School,'" *New York Times*, July 6, 2019, www.
nytimes.com/2018/07/06/us/immigrants-shelters-schools-border.html.

21 See Geoffrey Batchen, "Vernacular Photographies," *History of Photography* 24,
no. 3 (Autumn 2000): 262–71.

22 For a recent critical discussion of the field of "vernacular photography," and for
Geoffrey Batchen's own reconsideration of his earlier intervention, see the symposium, October 19–20, 2018, www.walthercollection.com/en/new-york/events
/symposium, and Tina Campt, Marianne Hirsch, Gil Hochberg, and Brian Wallis,
eds. *Imagining Everyday Life: Engagements with Vernacular Photography* (Göttingen: Steidl Verlag, 2019).

23 Our preference for discussing school photos as "everyday" rather than "vernacular" is also due the troubling etymology of the term *vernacular* and its
association with slavery. This early seventeenth-century term, from the Latin
vernaculus (domestic, native), comes via the Latin *verna* (home-born slave). It is

most frequently used in reference to language, distinguishing the local language of everyday use from literary or liturgical languages valued by dominant institutions. In the context of our discussion of photography's uses to further the goals of social hierarchy, colonialism, persecution, and genocide, it seems prudent to eschew a term emerging from just such hierarchical distinctions. See Patricia Hayes's incisive critique of the term and its usage, especially in the African context, in "Photographs at the Edge of History: Genre, Time, and Conquest in Southern Africa," in Campt et al., *Imagining Everyday Life.*

24 Ariella Azoulay, *The Civil Contract of Photography* (New York: Zone Books, 2008), 14.

25 For an eloquent reflection on this challenge, see Saidiya Hartman, "Venus in Two Acts," *small axe* 26 (2008): 1–14.

26 Ariella Azoulay, *Civil Imagination: A Political Ontology of Photography*, trans. Louise Bethlehem (New York: Verso Books, 2015), 25.

27 Moser, "Developing Historical Negatives"; Ann Laura Stoler, *Along the Archival Grain: Epistemic Anxieties and Colonial Common Sense* (Princeton: Princeton University Press, 2009), 22.

28 For a history of this Jewish community, see Hirsch and Spitzer, *Ghosts of Home.*

29 See, for example, Marianne Hirsch, *Family Frames*, and her edited volume *The Familial Gaze* (Hanover, NH: University Press of New England, 1999); Julia Hirsch, *Family Photographs: Content, Meaning, and Effect* (New York: Oxford University Press, 1981); Jo Spence and Patricia Holland, *Family Snaps: The Meanings of Domestic Photography* (London: Virago, 1991); Deborah Willis, *Picturing Us: African American Identity in Photography* (New York: The New Press, 1996); Gillian Rose, *Doing Family Photography* (London: Routledge, 2016). See also Lorie Novak's digital collection *Collected Visions*, http://cvisions.cat.nyu.edu/.

30 For comparative examinations of ideological functions served by schools see Lawrence Stone, ed., *Schooling and Society: Studies in the History of Education* (Baltimore: Johns Hopkins Press, 1976); Mary Jo Maynes, *Schooling in Western Europe: A Social History* (Albany: SUNY Ideological Press, 1985), 33–83, and *Schooling for the People: Comparative Local Studies of Schooling History in France and Germany, 1750–1850* (New York: Holmes and Meier, 1985); and Leo Spitzer, *Lives In Between: Assimilation and Marginality in Austria, Brazil, and West Africa, 1780–1945* (New York: Hill and Wang, 1999).

31 For the classic formulation of the concept of ideological interpellation and the role of "ideological state apparatuses" (educational institutions, family, the law, the media, and the arts) in constituting individuals as subjects within the state, see Louis Althusser, "Ideology and Ideological State Apparatuses (Notes towards

an Investigation)," in *Lenin and Philosophy and Other Essays*, trans. Ben Brewster (New York: Monthly Review Press, 1971), 143–82. For the institutional role of photography and its specific uses in the rationalization of labor in the United States in the last decades of the nineteenth century and the early twentieth century, see Elspeth H. Brown, *The Corporate Eye: Photography and the Rationalization of American Commercial Culture* (Baltimore: Johns Hopkins University Press, 2005), esp. 1–64.

32 The term *hidden curriculum* was coined by Philip W. Jackson, ed., *Life in Classrooms* (New York: Holt, Rinehart, and Winston, 1968), 33, but the notion of a hidden curriculum was explored by many educators before and after Jackson, including John Dewey, Paulo Freire, John Holt, Ivan Illich, Neil Postman, Paul Goodman, Roland Meighan, Henry Giroux, bell hooks, and Jonathan Kozol.

33 Allan Sekula, "The Body and the Archive," *October* 39 (Winter 1986): 10.

34 Muniz discusses his method in the film *Wasteland*, dir. Lucy Walker, 99 mins (London: Almega Projects, 2009).

35 See Barthes, *Camera Lucida*, 26–28, 43–59, 94–96, 116.

36 Azoulay, *Civil Imagination*, 117.

37 Azoulay, *Civil Imagination*, 117.

38 Azoulay, *Civil Imagination*, 13.

39 Azoulay, *Civil Imagination*, 96.

40 Marjane Satrapi, *Persepolis: The Story of a Childhood* (New York: Pantheon Books, 2003), 1.

41 Aby Warburg, "Einleitung zum Mnemosyne-Atlas," excerpted in *The Treasure Chests of Mnemosyne*, ed. Uwe Fleckner (Dresden: Verlag der Kunst, 1998), 248–52.

42 Jill Bennett, *Practical Aesthetics: Events, Affects, and Art after 9/11* (London: I. B. Tauris, 2012), *passim*.

43 Janis Jenkins, "The State Construction of Affect: Political Ethos and Mental Health among Salvadoran Refugees," *Culture, Medicine, and Psychiatry* 15 (1991): 139–65, cited in Ann Laura Stoler, *Along the Archival Grain: Epistemic Anxieties and Colonial Common Sense* (Princeton: Princeton University Press, 2009), 67.

44 See Hans-Georg Gadamer, *Truth and Method*, trans. Joel Weinsheimer and Donald G. Marshall (New York: Continuum, 1975). For a discussion of Gadamer and the "increase of being" in portraiture, see Ernst van Alphen, "The Portrait's Dispersal," in *Art in Mind* (Chicago: University of Chicago Press, 2005), 21–47.

45 Tina Campt, *Listening to Images* (Durham, NC: Duke University Press, 2017), 51.

46 On haptics, see Laura Marks, *Touch: Sensuous Theory and Multisensory Media* (Minneapolis: University of Minnesota Press, 2002).

47 Discussing the archive of civil rights photography, Elizabeth Abel turns to French phenomenology to see the haptic potentials of the photograph's "skin" to describe these images' affective textures. See "Skin, Flesh, and the Affective Wrinkles of Civil Rights Photography," in *Feeling Photography*, ed. Elspeth Brown and Thy Phu (Durham, NC: Duke University Press, 2014), 101. On memory and skin, see also Marianne Hirsch, "Ce qui touche à la mémoire," *Esprit*, October 2017: 42–61.

48 Marks, *Touch*, xiii.

49 Yoko Tawada, *The Emissary*, trans. Margaret Mitsutani (New York: New Directions, 2018), 41.

CHAPTER 1: IMPERIAL FRAMES

1 "Daguerreotype," Princeton University Firestone Library, accessed July 31, 2018. http://infoshare1.princeton.edu/libraries/firestone/rbsc/mudd/online_ex/dags/dag/11AT.jpg. The College of New Jersey became Princeton University in 1896. The 1843 Class had sixty-three members. Since there are only thirty-five men (students and teachers) in this daguerreotype, it is possible that this is an image of one of the two Class of 1843 debating societies.

2 For technological developments in photography see, among others, Beaumont Newhall, *The History of Photography from 1839 to the Present* (New York: Museum of Modern Art, 2009); Naomi Rosenblum, *A World History of Photography*, 4th ed. (New York: Abbeville Press, 2007); Mary Warner Marien, *Photography: A Cultural History*, 4th ed. (London: Laurence King, 2015); Grant B. Romer and Brian Wallis, eds., *Young America: The Daguerreotypes of Southworth & Hawes* (New York: International Center of Photography, 2005).

3 Frederick Douglass, "Pictures and Progress" [1865], cited in Maurice O. Wallace and Shawn Michelle Smith, "Introduction: Pictures and Progress," in *Pictures and Progress: Early Photography and the Making of African American Identity*, ed. Maurice O. Wallace and Shawn Michelle Smith (Durham, NC: Duke University Press, 2012), 6.

4 Laura Wexler, "'A More Perfect Likeness:' Frederick Douglass and the Image of the Nation," in Wallace and Smith, *Pictures and Progress*, 18–40.

5 Walter Benjamin, "The Work of Art in the Age of Mechanical Reproduction," in *Illuminations*, trans. Harry Zohn (New York: Schocken, 1969), 226.

6 Benjamin, "The Work of Art," 237. See also Hirsch, *Family Frames*, chap. 4, "Unconscious Optics"; and Smith and Sliwinski, *Photography and the Optical Unconscious*.

7 See George M. Fredrickson, *White Supremacy: A Comparative Study in*

American and South African History (New York: Oxford University Press, 1981), especially the first chapter, and Spitzer, *Lives In Between,* 19–39.

8 George S. Wilson, "How Shall the American Savage Be Civilized," *Atlantic Monthly,* 50 (November 1882): 604.

9 Richard H. Pratt, "The Advantages of Mingling Indians with Whites," quoted in David Wallace Adams, *Education for Extinction: American Indians and the Boarding School Experience, 1875–1928* (Lawrence: University Press of Kansas, 1995), 52.

10 Coco Fusco, "Racial Times, Racial Marks, Racial Metaphors," in *Only Skin Deep: Changing Visions of the American Self,* ed. Coco Fusco and Brian Wallis (New York: Harry Abrams, 2003), 60.

11 Sara Blair, "About Time: Historical Reading, Historicity, and the Photograph," *PMLA* 125, no. 1 (Winter 2010): 166, 162.

12 The class photo appears in a small collection on the website's folder dedicated to pre-1945 photographs, an assemblage donated by Arthur Rindner, a distant relative of Adolf Blond's, who became the custodian of these orphaned family pictures. See Arthur Rindner, "My Connection to Czernowitz: Documents and Photographs from Clari Blond-Morgan," in "Early 20th Century Photos from Clari Blond-Morgan by Way of Arthur Rindner," n.d., The czernowitz.ehpes.com Website, accessed July 31, 2018. http://czernowitz.ehpes.com/photos/photosplash .html.

13 Karl Emil Franzos, *Aus Halb-Asien* (Leipzig: Duncker & Humblot, 1876), 186.

14 See Spitzer, *Lives In Between,* chaps. 1 and 3. Also see Jacob Katz, *Out of the Ghetto: The Social Background of Jewish Emancipation, 1770–1870* (Syracuse, NY: Syracuse University Press, 1998).

15 See Maynes, *Schooling in Western Europe.*

16 Maynes, *Schooling in Western Europe,* 36.

17 Maynes, *Schooling in Western Europe,* 45.

18 For a comparative overview of this discussion, see Spitzer, *Lives In Between,* especially chaps. 1–4.

19 Hirsch and Spitzer, *Ghosts of Home,* 25–35.

20 Golda Tencer-Szurmeij and Anna Bikont, eds., *And I Still See Their Faces: Images of Polish Jews* (Warsaw: Shalom Foundation, 1998), 148.

21 Tencer-Szurmeij and Bikont, *And I Still See Their Faces,* 139.

22 See A. D. Bensusan, *Silver Images: History of Photography in Africa* (Cape Town: Howard Timmons, 1966).

23 Vera Viditz-Ward, "Photography in Sierra Leone, 1850–1918," in *Africa* 57, no. 4 (1987): 512–13.

24 Freetown was founded in 1787 by the British philanthropic Sierra Leone Company. It became the capital of the British Crown Colony of Sierra Leone in 1808. See Leo Spitzer, *The Creoles of Sierra Leone: Responses to Colonialism, 1870–1945* (Madison: University of Wisconsin Press, 1974), and *Lives In Between*.

25 See Spitzer, *The Creoles of Sierra Leone.*

26 "Instructions of the Sierra Leone Company Directors," in the Sierra Leone Collection, Fourah Bay College Library, Freetown.

27 See Spitzer, *The Creoles of Sierra Leone*, 51–62; Philip D. Curtin, "'The White Man's Grave': Image and Reality, 1780–1850," *Journal of British Studies* 1 (1961): 94–110; Leo Spitzer, "The Mosquito and Segregation in Sierra Leone," *Canadian Journal of African Studies* 2, no.1 (Spring 1968): 49–61.

28 On "quiet" in the photography of race, see Campt, *Listening to Images*, and Kevin Quashie, *The Sovereignty of Quiet: Beyond Resistance in Black Culture* (New Brunswick, NJ: Rutgers University Press, 2012).

29 This photograph was probably taken in the 1870s—following Britain's annexation of Sotho lands—and not in 1863, as identified in the South African archives. See Janet K. H. Hodgson, "A History of Zonnebloem College, 1858–1870: A Study of Church and Society" (MA thesis, University of Cape Town, 1975), 461–62. See also Janet K. H. Hodgson and Theresa Edlmann, *Zonnebloem College and the Genesis of an African Intelligentsia, 1857–1933* (Cape Town: African Lives, 2018).

30 "Visitation Charge of the Lord Bishop of Cape Town, delivered at St. George's Cathedral, 16.1.1861," quoted in Hodgson, "A History of Zonnebloem College," 359–60.

31 Hodgson, "A History of Zonnebloem College," 620.

32 Bishop Robert Gray, Church Chronicle for the Diocese of Grahamstown (February 1887), 9, no. 2:39f, quoted in Hodgson, "A History of Zonnebloem College," 178.

CHAPTER 2: FRAMING DIFFERENCE

1 See Carolyn J. Marr, "Assimilation through Education," in Hibulb Cultural Center, *Between Two Worlds: Experiences at the Tulalip Indian Boarding School*, accessed July 31, 2018. www.hibulbculturalcenter.org/assets/pdf/Between-Two-Worlds.pdf.

2 See Carolyn J. Marr, "Assimilation through Education: Indian Boarding Schools in the Pacific Northwest," University of Washington Digital Collections, American Indians of the Pacific Northwest Collection, n.d., https://content.lib.washington.edu/aipnw/marr.html, accessed July 31, 2018.

3 See Adams, *Education for Extinction*, 21–24, 100–112; Donal Lindsey, *Indians at Hampton Institute, 1877–1923* (Urbana: University of Illinois Press, 1995); Hayes Peter Mauro, *The Art of Americanization at the Carlisle Indian School* (Albuquerque: University of New Mexico Press, 2011); Linda F. Witmer, *The Indian Industrial School: Carlisle, Pennsylvania, 1879–1918* (Carlisle: Cumberland County Historical Society, 1879–1918); and James D. Anderson, *The Education of Blacks in the South, 1860–1935* (Chapel Hill: University of North Carolina Press, 1988). Additional studies of the US boarding school experience include Michael C. Coleman, *American Indian Children at School, 1850–1930* (Jackson: University Press of Mississippi, 1993); and Genevieve Bell, "Telling Stories Out of School: Remembering the Carlisle Indian Industrial School, 1879–1918" (PhD dissertation, Stanford University, 1998).

4 Margaret L. Archuleta, Brenda J. Child, and K. Tsianina Lomawaima, eds., *Away from Home: American Indian Boarding School Experiences, 1879–2000* (Phoenix: Heard Museum, 2000), 24–29; Clifford E. Trafzer, Jean A. Keller, and Lorene Sisquoc, eds., *Boarding School Blues: Revisiting American Indian Educational Experiences* (Lincoln: University of Nebraska Press, 2006), 72–77.

5 Guy Quoetone interview, quoted in Clyde Ellis, "We Had a Lot of Fun, but Of Course, That Wasn't the School Part: Life at the Rainy Mountain Boarding School, 1893–1920," in Trafzer, Keller, and Sisquoc, *Boarding School Blues*, 72–73.

6 Zitkala-Ša, *American Indian Stories* (Washington, DC: Hayworth Publishing House, 1921; reprint, Lincoln: University of Nebraska Press, 1985), 54–56.

7 Richard H. Pratt, "The Advantages of Mingling Indians with Whites," *Proceedings of the National Conference of Charities and Correction* (1892), 46, and *Proceedings and Addresses of the National Education Association* (1895), 761–62.

8 Archuleta, Child, and Lomawaima, *Away from Home*, 26–27; Trafzer, Keller, and Sisquoc, *Boarding School Blues*, 15–17.

9 Indeed, name changing of subordinated subjects was a widespread requirement of transformative assimilationism throughout the nineteenth and twentieth centuries. See Spitzer, *The Creoles of Sierra Leone*, 116–17, 119–20, 132; and Leo Spitzer, "A Name Given, a Name Taken: Camouflaging, Resistance, and Diasporic Social Identity," in *Comparative Studies of South Asia, Africa, and the Middle East* 30, no. 1 (2010), 21–31.

10 Brenda J. Child, *Boarding School Seasons: American Indian Families, 1900–1940* (Lincoln: University of Nebraska Press, 1998), 29.

11 Quoted in Eve Ball, with Nora Henn and Lynda A. Sánchez, *Indeh: An Apache Odyssey* (Norman: University of Oklahoma Press, 1988), 130. Also see Margaret D. Jacobs, "Indian Boarding Schools in Comparative Perspective: The Removal

of Indigenous Children in the United States and Australia, 1880–1940," in Trafzer, Keller, and Sisquoc, *Boarding School Blues*, 217–18.

12 J. D. C. Atkins, *Annual Report of the Commissioner of Indian Affairs*, xxiii, quoted in Coleman, *American Indian Children at School*, 105.

13 Francis La Flesche, *The Middle Five: Indian Schoolboys of the Omaha Tribe* (1900; reprint: Lincoln: University of Nebraska Press, 1963), xvii.

14 Child, *Boarding School Seasons*, 28.

15 Simon Ortiz, quoted in Jacobs, "Indian Boarding Schools in Comparative Perspective," 216.

16 Trafzer, Keller, and Sisquoc, *Boarding School Blues*, 20; Archuleta, Child, and Lomawaima, *Away from Home*, 38–41.

17 Quoted in K. Tsianina Lomowaima, *They Called It Prairie Light: The Story of Chilocco Indian School* (Lincoln: University of Nebraska Press, 1994), 42.

18 Louise Erdrich, "Indian Boarding School: The Runaways," in *Original Fire: Selected and New Poems* (New York: Harper Collins, 2003), 19–20.

19 Erdrich, "Indian Boarding School: The Runaways," 19.

20 In addition to the works identified in the preceding notes for this chapter, see Eric Margolis, "Class Pictures: Representations of Race, Gender, and Ability in a Century of School Photography," *Visual Sociology* 14 (1999): 7–38; Eric Margolis, "Looking at Discipline, Looking at Labour: Photographic Representations of Indian Boarding Schools," *Visual Studies* 19, no. 1 (2004): 72–96; Jacqueline Fear-Segal, "Facing the Binary: Native American Students in the Camera Lens," and Kate Palmer Albers and Jordan Bear, "Photography's Time Zones," both in *Before-and-After Photography: Histories and Contexts*, ed. Jordan Bear and Kate Palmer Albers (London: Bloomsbury Academic Press, 2017). For Canadian residential schools, see Robert Carney, "Aboriginal Residential Schools Before Confederation: The Early Experience," *Historical Studies: Canadian Catholic Historical Association* 61 (1995), 13–40; J. R. Miller, *Shingwauk's Vision: A History of Native Residential Schools* (Toronto: University of Toronto Press, 1996); John S. Milloy, *A National Crime: The Canadian Government and the Residential School System, 1879 to 1986* (Winnipeg: University of Manitoba Press, 1999); Suzanne Fournier and Ernie Crey, *Stolen from Our Embrace* (Vancouver: Douglas & McIntyre, 1997); and Truth and Reconciliation Commission of Canada, *They Came for the Children: Canada, Aboriginal Peoples, and the Residential Schools* (Winnipeg: Truth and Reconciliation Commission, 2012) and *Canada's Residential Schools: The Final Report of the Truth and Reconciliation Commission of Canada* (Winnipeg: Truth and Reconciliation Commission, 2015).

21 For example, see *The Hampton Album: 44 Photographs by Frances B. Johnston*

from an Album of Hampton Institute, with an introduction and note on the photographer by Lincoln Kirstein (New York: Museum of Modern Art, 1966) and Mauro, *The Art of Americanization.*

22 In addition to Carlisle, major off-reservation boarding schools intended to acculturate Native American children to the dominant culture were founded in Albuquerque, New Mexico; Phoenix, Arizona; Mt. Pleasant, Michigan; Chemawa, Oregon; Flandreau, South Dakota; and Lawrence, Kansas. By the early twentieth century, there were three types of schools for Indian children: off-reservation boarding, missionary (including boarding missionary schools), and on-reservation (run by the Bureau of Indian Affairs).

23 Anderson, *The Education of Blacks in the South*, 34.

24 The Hampton Indian program, which between 1883 and 1902 annually enrolled approximately 120 Indians belonging to some sixty-five tribes, lasted almost half a century. For the best account of its history, see Lindsey, *Indians at Hampton Institute.*

25 Lindsey, *Indians at Hampton Institute*, 12. Also see Henry E. Fritz, *The Movement for Indian Assimilation, 1860–1890* (Philadelphia: University of Pennsylvania Press, 2017), and Frederick E. Hoxie, *A Final Promise: The Campaign to Assimilate the Indians, 1880–1920* (Lincoln: University of Nebraska Press, 1984).

26 Wilson, "How Shall the American Savage Be Civilized?," 604.

27 For a rich discussion of this curriculum, see Margolis, "Looking at Discipline."

28 See Anderson, *The Education of Blacks in the South*, 27.

29 In great part these photos were made by professional photographers hired by institutions or for commercial purposes and by photographers working on government documentation projects. For many years, an ongoing photographic project documented Indian boarding schools that received federal financing. Two immense virtual archives—at the Library of Congress American Memory site and at the National Archives and Records Administration—contain a very large number of these photos. See Margolis, "Class Pictures."

30 By "blanket Indians" he meant Native Americans wearing traditional clothing, which often included blankets as covering.

31 Quoted in Mauro, *The Art of Americanization*, 55. Pratt sent photos in stereographic format for 3-D viewing and what were known as "Boudoir" size Cabinet Card photos (about 8½ × 5¼ inches and thus larger than the 6½ × 4¼ inches standard card-mounted photos) to President and Mrs. Hayes, Hayes administration officials, congressmen, Christian reformers, and others who might support his conviction that Indians could be "Americanized" through education.

32 Margolis, "Looking at Discipline," 79. Margolis credits John Tagg, *The Burden of*

Representation: Essays on Photographies and Histories (Amherst: University of Massachusetts Press, 1988), 82–85.

33 Fear-Segal, "Facing the Binary," 157.

34 Fear-Segal, "Facing the Binary," 157.

35 Samuel C. Armstrong to Richard H. Pratt, August 26 and September 2, 1878, Pratt Papers, Yale University, quoted in Lindsey, *Indians at Hampton Institute*, 35.

36 Renato Rosaldo, *Culture and Truth: The Remaking of Social Analysis* (Boston: Beacon Press, 1993), 69.

37 Fear-Segal, "Facing the Binary," 156.

38 Albers and Bear, "Photography's Time Zones," 5.

39 Albers and Baer note that this inability reflects a critical shortcoming in "common assumptions about photographic indexicality, for the referent that can be said to have caused the photograph to exist leaves no direct trace in the representation itself." "Photography's Time Zones," 2–3.

40 See *The Hampton Album*, 54, and Thomas Calloway, "The Negro Exhibit," in *U.S. Commission to the Paris Exposition. Report of the Commissioner-General for the United States to the International Universal Exposition, Paris, 1900*, vol. 2 (Washington, DC: Government Printing Office, 1901).

41 Quoted in David Levering Lewis, "A Small Nation of People: W. E. B. Du Bois and Black Americans at the Turn of the Twentieth Century," in Library of Congress, with essays by David Levering Lewis and Deborah Willis, *A Small Nation of People: W. E. B. Du Bois and African American Portraits of Progress* (New York: Amistad, 2003), 24–49.

42 Shawn Michelle Smith, *American Archives: Gender, Race, and Class in Visual Culture* (Princeton: Princeton University Press, 1999), 157–76.

43 Laura Wexler, *Tender Violence: Domestic Visions in an Age of U.S. Imperialism* (Chapel Hill: University of North Carolina Press, 2000), 150.

44 Wexler, *Tender Violence*, 137.

45 Wexler borrows the title of her book *Tender Violence* from the rhetoric of Charles Armstrong.

46 Fear-Segal, "Facing the Binary," 168.

47 Anne McClintock uses the notion of "panoptical time" and "anachronistic space" to mark the distant view of the imperial frame constituting the "primitive" "other" of modernity. See *Imperial Leather: Race, Gender, and Sexuality in the Colonial Context* (New York: Routledge, 1995), 36–42, 122–23.

48 Roy Harvey Pearce, *The Savages of America: The Study of the Indian and the Idea of Civilization* (Baltimore: Johns Hopkins University Press, 1965), 191–92.

49 Henry Wadsworth Longfellow, *The Song of Hiawatha* (Raleigh, NC: Generic NL Freebook Publisher, n.d.), eBook Collection, EBSCOhost, accessed July 31, 2018.

50 See K. Tsianina Lomawaima on Estelle Reel in Archuleta, Child, and Lomawaima, *Away from Home*, 31–32. Reel's curricular plan, published as *Uniform Course of Study for the Indian Schools of the United States*, was distributed to all Indian schools in 1901 and was also employed in Puerto Rico and the Philippines, colonial jurisdictions newly acquired by the United States in the Spanish-American War.

51 See Wexler, *Tender Violence*, 167–71, and Lincoln Kirstein's introduction to *The Hampton Album*, 11.

52 Campt, *Listening to Images*, 9.

53 Campt, *Listening to Images*, 9.

54 Paul Laurence Dunbar, "We Wear the Mask," in *The Complete Poems of Paul Laurence Dunbar.* (New York: Dodd, Mead and Company, 1922), 71.

55 For a groundbreaking examination of the colonial imposition of Euro-American time structures on native peoples and resistances to this, see Mark Rifkin, *Beyond Settler Time: Temporal Sovereignty and Indigenous Self-Determination* (Durham, NC: Duke University Press, 2017).

56 Quoted in Coleman, *American Indian Children at School*, 86.

57 Jim Francis Thorpe (1887–1953), at Carlisle 1904–1913, with interruptions, was a member of the Sac and Fox Nation. He was the first Native American to win Olympic gold medals for the United States, winning two in 1912 for the pentathlon and decathlon. He was also a two-time All-American winner at Carlisle.

58 Rifkin, *Beyond Settler Time.*

59 Lomawaima, *They Called It Prairie Light*, 96.

60 Cited in Trafzer, Keller, and Sisquoc, *Boarding School Blues*, 59.

61 Cited in Ellis, "'We Had a Lot of Fun,'" 92.

62 For a discussion of another such collection, equally remarkable, see Nicole Strathman, "Student Snapshots: An Alternative Approach to the Visual History of American Indian Boarding Schools," *Humanities* 4, no. 4 (205), 726–47.

63 See Jean Barman, Yvonne Hébert, and Don McCaskill, eds., *Indian Education in Canada*, vol. 1: *The Legacy* (Vancouver: University of British Columbia Press, 2007).

64 *Honouring: Project of Heart/Speaking to Memory*, Comox Valley Art Gallery, Courtney, BC, 2018.

65 Bessie Brown and Pam Brown, "Beverley Brown Collection," Communication to the Museum of Anthropology at University of British Columbia (Feb. 6, 2019).

We are grateful to the Brown family for sharing these remarkable images and to Katie Ferrante for generously arranging publication permissions.

66 bell hooks, "The Oppositional Gaze," in *Black Looks: Race and Representation* (Boston: South End Press, 1992), 115–32.

67 bell hooks, "In Our Glory: Photography and Black Life," in *Art on My Mind: Visual Politics* (New York: The New Press, 1995), 57, 59.

68 Deborah Willis and Barbara Krauthamer, *Envisioning Emancipation: Black Americans and the End of Slavery* (Philadelphia: Temple University Press, 2013), 133–36, 159.

69 See Audrey Thomas McCluskey, "Ringing Up a School: Mary McLeod Bethune's Impact on Daytona," *Florida Historical Quarterly* 73, no. 2 (October 1994), 200–217.

70 Sara Catalina, "In the Segregated Twentieth Century, Schoolchildren Embodied Black Uplift," What It Means to Be American: A National Conversation Hosted by the Smithsonian and Arizona State University (website), September 1, 2016, www.whatitmeanstobeamerican.org/artifacts /in-the-segregated-20th-century-schoolchildren-embodied-black-uplift.

71 The camps, run by the War Relocation Authority (WRA), were located at Tule Lake and Manzanar (California), Minidoka (Idaho), Topaz (Utah), Poston and Gila River (Arizona), Heart Mountain (Wyoming), Amache (Granada, Colorado), and Rohwer and Jerome (Arkansas).

72 W. H. Anderson, "The Question of Japanese Americans," *Los Angeles Times*, February 2, 1942, quoted in Linda Gordon and Gary Y. Okihiro, eds., *Impounded: Dorothea Lange and the Censored Images of Japanese American Internment* (New York: W. W. Norton, 2006), 53.

73 Jasmine Alinder, *Moving Images: Photography and the Japanese American Incarceration* (Urbana: University of Illinois Press, 2009), 1.

74 Alinder, *Moving Images*, 15, 12.

75 Contemporary Japanese Americans use the term *incarceration* instead of the euphemistic and inaccurate *internment* used by US government officials at the time. *Internment* is a term legally reserved for noncitizens or nonresidents— "enemy aliens." See Roger Daniels, "Words Do Matter: A Note on Inappropriate Terminology and the Incarceration of Japanese Americans," in *Nikkei in the Pacific Northwest: Japanese Americans and Japanese Canadians in the Twentieth Century*, ed. Louis Fiset and Gail M. Nomura (Seattle: University of Washington Press, 2005), 190.

76 Alinder, *Moving Images*, 77.

77 Linda Gordon, "Dorothea Lange Photographs the Japanese American Internment," in Gordon and Okihiro, *Impounded*, 11.

78 Gordon, "Dorothea Lange Photographs," 17.

79 Linda Gordon, *Dorothea Lange: A Life Beyond Limits* (New York: W. W. Norton, 2009), 319.

80 Gordon, *Dorothea Lange*, 319.

81 See Gordon and Okihiro, *Impounded*; Gordon, *Dorothea Lange*; and Lane Ryo Hirabashi with Kenichiro Shimada, *Japanese American Resettlement through the Lens: Hikaru Carl Iwasaki and the WRA's Photographic Section, 1943–45* (Denver: University Press of Colorado, 2009).

82 Lane Ryo Hirabayashi, "Government Photograph of the WRA Camps and Resettlement," *Denso Encyclopedia*, n.d., http://encyclopedia.densho.org/Government_photography_of_the_WRA_Camps_and_Resettlement.

83 Alinder, *Moving Images*, explains the ambiguous formal and informal arrangements made with photographers; see, for example, 86.

84 For some of these critiques, see Elena Tajima Creef, *Imagining Japanese America: The Visual Construction of Citizenship, Nation, and the Body* (New York: NYU Press, 2004); Hirabayashi with Shimada, *Japanese American Resettlement*; Nancy Matsumoto, "Reclaiming Photographs of WWII Japanese American Resettlement," Discover Nikkei: Japanese Migrants and Their Descendants (website), November 16, 2009, www.discovernikkei.org/en/journal/2009/11/16/reclaiming-photographs/.

85 Alinder, *Moving Images*, 19.

86 Diane Yotsuda Honda, ed., *Our World: Manzanar, California, 1944* (Logan, UT: Herff Jones Yearbook Company, 1998). See Alinder, *Moving Images*, 93–102, for a detailed discussion of these yearbooks.

87 This work was originally published by Columbia University Press, but a new edition, with an introduction by Christine Hong, has been issued. See Miné Okubo, *Citizen 13660* (Seattle: University of Washington Press, 2014).

88 Okubo, *Citizen 13660*, xxxvi.

89 Christine Hong, "Introduction," in Okubo, *Citizen 13660*, vii–xxiv.

90 Okubo, *Citizen 13660*, 92.

91 Okubo, *Citizen 13660*, 207.

92 Leigh Raiford, *Imprisoned in a Luminous Glare: Photography in the African American Freedom Struggle* (Chapel Hill: University of North Carolina Press, 2013), 27.

93 Azoulay, *The Civil Contract of Photography*, 97.

94 Katherine Fogg and Denise Ramzy, "Interview: Carrie Mae Weems," in *Carrie*

Mae Weems: The Hampton Project, ed. Vivian Patterson (New York: Aperture and Williams College Museum of Art, 2000), 79.

95 Quoted in "Picturing Change: The Impact of Ledger Drawings on Native American Art," notes for an exhibition at the Hood Museum of Art, Dartmouth College, December 11, 2004–May 15, 2005, accessible on line at http://tfaoi.com/aa/5aa9of.htm (accessed May 12, 2019).

96 "Picturing Change: The Impact of Ledger Drawings on Native American Art."

97 "Picturing Change: The Impact of Ledger Drawings on Native American Art."

CHAPTER 3: EXCLUSIONARY FRAMES

1 By the start of the twenty-first century, the website was devoted to Jewish historical and genealogical research in Czernowitz, which had become a sizeable cosmopolitan city within the Austrian-Habsburg realm. See the Czernowitz website, http://czernowitz.ehpes.com, accessed July 31, 2018.

2 Their appellation was technically incorrect. In the Bukowina, following the Austro-Habsburg classification, lyceums were schools for women that offered a secondary education. Gymnasia, until well into the twentieth century, provided secondary education to men as preparation for admission to university.

3 See Bianca Rosenthal, untitled post, October 29, 2012, http://czernowitz.ehpes.com/czernowitz12/testfile2012-3/0180.html, accessed July 31, 2018.

4 For a detailed discussion of Romanian anti-Semitic discrimination in schools and the use of quotas to limit or deny admission to courses of study and institutions of higher learning, see Hirsch and Spitzer, *Ghosts of Home*, esp. 69–70, 72–81.

5 Museum of Family History, www.museumoffamilyhistory.com; Tencer-Szurmeij and Bikont, *And I Still See Their Faces.*

6 Peter Gay, *My German Question: Growing Up in Nazi Berlin* (New Haven, CT: Yale University Press, 1998), 50.

7 Linda Coetzee, Myra Osrin, and Millie Pimstone, eds., *Seeking Refuge: German Jewish Immigration to the Cape in the 1930s* (Cape Town: Cape Town Holocaust Centre, 2003).

8 Ruth Klüger, *Still Alive: A Holocaust Girlhood Remembered* (New York: Feminist Press at the City University of New York, 2001), 41.

9 Frantz Fanon, *Black Skin, White Masks*, trans. Richard Philcox (New York: Grove Press, 2008), 92.

10 Deborah Dwórk, *Children with a Star: Jewish Youth in Nazi Europe* (New Haven, CT: Yale University Press, 1991), xxxiii and 274n27. In Poland the survival rate for Jewish children was less than 0.5 percent. In other words, more than 99.5

percent of Jewish children in Poland died, whether from murder, starvation, disease, or some other war-related cause.

11   Nechama Tec, "Jewish Children: Between Protectors and Murderers," Occasional Papers (Washington, DC: United States Holocaust Memorial Museum, Center for Advanced Holocaust Studies, April 2005).

12   Among the best of numerous general histories of the Holocaust, see Deborah Dwórk and Robert Jan van Pelt, *Holocaust: A History* (New York: W. W. Norton, 2002), and Saul Friedländer, *Nazi Germany and the Jews*, Vol. 1: *The Years of Persecution, 1933–1939* (New York: HarperCollins, 1997) and Vol. 2: *The Years of Extermination, 1939–1945* (New York: HarperCollins, 2007).

13   Two months after the German Wehrmacht occupied the industrial city of Lódz ("the Manchester of Poland") in September 1939, they annexed it into the Reichsgau Warthegau, an administrative division of the Reich, and renamed it Litzmannstadt, after Karl Litzmann, the German general who had captured it in the First World War.

14   Isaiah Trunk, *Lódz Ghetto: A History* (Bloomington: Indiana University Press, 2006), 54–55; Lucjan Dobroszycki, ed., *Chronicle of the Lódz Ghetto* (New Haven, CT: Yale University Press, 1984), xliv–xlv; Andrea Löw, *Juden im Getto Litzmannstadt* (Göttingen: Wallstein Verlag, 2010), 194–96; and Patricia Heberer, *Children during the Holocaust* (Lanham, MD: AltaMira Press, 2011), 115. Rumkowski, supported by funding from the American Joint Distribution Committee, had previously established a Jewish orphanage near Lódz and had been its director during the entire period between the two world wars.

15   Adam Czerniakow, *The Warsaw Diary of Adam Czerniakow* (Chicago: Ivan R. Dee, 1999), 277; Barbara Engelking and Jacek Leociak, *The Warsaw Ghetto: A Guide to the Perished City* (New Haven, CT: Yale University Press, 2009), 343–44; and Dwórk and van Pelt, *Holocaust*, 220.

16   In the late 1930s Vilna had a population of over two hundred thousand and a Jewish population of over fifty thousand.

17   Dwórk and van Pelt, *Holocaust*, 222, and Avraham Tory, *Surviving the Holocaust: The Kovno Ghetto Diary* (Cambridge, MA: Harvard University Press, 1991). See entries for April 21, 1942 (78), May 25, 1942 (90), July 6, 1942 (104), and note to entry for August 1942 (126).

18   See, for example, Yad Vashem: The World Holocaust Remembrance Center, "Vilna during the Holocaust: Daily Life in the Vilna Ghetto: Children in the Ghetto," n.d. www.yadvashem.org/yv/en/exhibitions/vilna/during/children.asp, accessed July 31, 2018.

19   Warsaw: Archive of the Jewish Historical Institute (AJHIW), Ring I, 47: Szkol-

nictwo [Schooling]. The Oyneg Shabes archive, buried before the destruction of the ghetto in 1943 but largely recovered after the war, was organized by historian Emanuel Ringelblum. It was intended to document the reality of ghetto life under Nazi occupation. For a comprehensive account see Samuel D. Kassow, *Who Will Write Our History: Emanuel Ringelblum, the Warsaw Ghetto, and the Oyneg Shabes Archive* (Bloomington: Indiana University Press, 2007).

20 Engelking and Leociak, *The Warsaw Ghetto*, 47–51.

21 See Mary Berg [Miriam Wattenberg], *The Diary of Mary Berg: Growing Up in the Warsaw Ghetto* (Oxford: Oneworld Publications, 2007), 22. In 1944, because Miriam's mother was a US-born citizen, the Wattenbergs were rescued from the ghetto and able to emigrate to the United States. Miriam managed to safeguard and bring with her twelve small spiral notebooks—writings that were published soon after, in 1945, under the pseudonym Mary Berg to protect relatives still living under German control, as *Warsaw Ghetto: A Diary*.

22 We are indebted to the pioneering research on the schooling of Jewish children in German-occupied Europe by Lisa Anne Plante in "'We Didn't Miss a Day': A History in Narratives of Schooling Efforts for Jewish Children and Youths in German-Occupied Europe" (PhD dissertation, University of Tennessee, Knoxville, 2000).

23 Nehama Eckheizer-Fahn, quoted in Abraham Lewin, *A Cup of Tears: A Diary of the Warsaw Ghetto*, ed. Antony Polonsky, trans. Christopher Hutton (Oxford: Basil Blackwell, 1988), 11.

24 Ruth Klüger, *Still Alive*, 84.

25 N. Korn, quoted in Lisa Anne Plante, "Transformation and Resistance: Schooling Efforts for Jewish Children and Youth in Hiding, Ghettos, and Camps," in *Children and the Holocaust: Symposium Presentation of the Center for Advanced Holocaust Studies* (Washington, DC: US Holocaust Memorial Museum, 2004), 44. The Lublin ghetto was set up in the Generalgouvernement in 1941 and liquidated a year later when tens of thousands of its inhabitants were deported and killed in Belzec and Majdanek.

26 Pola Rotszyld. Yad Vashem Archive O3/438. Also see Engelking and Leociak, *The Warsaw Ghetto*, 348.

27 Berg, *The Diary of Mary Berg*, 23.

28 Janina Bauman, quoted in Engelking and Leociak, *The Warsaw Ghetto*, 346.

29 Hanna Lévy-Hass, *Diary of Bergen-Belsen*, trans. Sophie Hand (Chicago: Haymarket Books, 2009), 81.

30 For a discussion of Nazi photography and, especially, the controversy about the Wehrmacht exhibit that contained many of these images, see Omer Bartov,

Atina Grossmann, and Molly Nolan, eds., *Crimes of War: Guilt and Denial in the Twentieth Century* (New York: W. W. Norton, 2002).

31 Frances Guerin, *Through Amateur Eyes* (Minneapolis: University of Minnesota Press, 2012), xiii. On the Nazi gaze, see Hirsch, *The Generation of Postmemory*, esp. chaps. 4 and 5.

32 Guerin, *Through Amateur Eyes*, 139.

33 Susan Sontag, *On Photography* (New York: Farrar, Straus & Giroux, 1977), 10.

34 See Joe J. Heydecker, *The Warsaw Ghetto: A Photographic Record, 1941–1944* (London: St. Martins, 1991); Rafael Scharf and Willy Georg, *In the Warsaw Ghetto: Summer 1941* (New York: Aperture, 1993); and Janina Struk, *Photographing the Holocaust* (London: I. B. Taurus, 2004), 77.

35 Struk, *Photographing the Holocaust*, 80–83.

36 See Rebecca Weiner, "Virtual Jewish World: Prague," Jewish Virtual Library: A Product of AICE (website), n.d. www.jewishvirtuallibrary.org/prague, accessed June 31, 2018. According to Magda Veselska, Head of Collection Management at the Jewish Museum of Prague and author of works on the wartime history of the museum, the Nazis agreed to the Prague Jewish community leadership's request in 1941 that Jewish artifacts—Torah scrolls, books, silverware, anything related to Jewish life in Bohemia and Moravia—from satellite communities whose residents were being transported to Terezín be shipped to Prague and stored in the exhibit hall of the closed-down Jewish museum and in the surrounding synagogues. But although high-ranking Nazis visited this place of storage and viewed it as a curiosity, the term "Museum of the Forgotten [or Extinct] Race" was not coined until after the war. We are grateful to Bram Presser of Melbourne, Australia, for this information and for allowing us to preview relevant pages from his novel, *The Book of Dirt* (N.p.: Text Publishing Company, 2018), which includes excerpts of his interview with Magda Veselka.

37 For an excellent examination of IG Farben/Agfa's connection with the German Ministry of Propaganda, and Genewein's privileged receipt of color stock from Agfa for his Lódź ghetto photos, see Guerin, *Through Amateur Eyes*, chap. 3: "The Privilege and Possibility of Color."

38 For a systematic, almost daily, overview of happenings in the ghetto, compiled for the Archives of the Eldest of the Jews, see Dobroszycki, *Chronicle of the Lódź Ghetto*.

39 Trunk, *Lódź Ghetto*, 55.

40 On the Wannsee conference, see Kurt Pätzold and Erika Schwarz, *Tagesordnung Judenmord: Die Wannsee-Konferenz am 20. Januar 1942* (Berlin: Metropol, 1992).

41 Löw, *Juden im Getto Litzmannstadt*, 263–91; "'Give Me Your Children': The 'Children's Actions,'" in Heberer, *Children during the Holocaust*, 121–34.

42 See Löw, *Juden im Getto Litzmannstadt*, 309–33; and Florian Freund, Bertrand Perz, and Karl Stuhlpfarrer, "Das Getto in Litzmannstadt (Lódź)," in *"Unser einziger Weg ist Arbeit": Das Getto in Lódź, 1940–1944*, ed. Hanno Loewy and Gerhard Schoenberner (Frankfurt: Löcker Verlag, 1990), 17–31.

43 Ulrich Baer, *Spectral Evidence: The Photography of Trauma* (Cambridge, MA: MIT Press, 2002), 131.

44 See Baer's discussion of the "Getto Schulauspeisung" photo's role on the cover of Dawid Sierakowiak's ghetto diary (the edition edited by Alan Adelson) (*Spectral Evidence*, 147–49). Despite the fact that this is a perpetrator image, it can serve to illustrate and memorialize the lives of children and teenagers who failed to survive. On the use of perpetrator photographs in the memorial work of victims, survivors, and their descendants, see Hirsch, *The Generation of Postmemory*, chap. 4.

45 Struk, *Photographing the Holocaust*, 84.

46 Bernstein, *Foregone Conclusions*, 32.

47 Cited in Meghan Cox Gurdon, "The Miraculous Power of Reading Aloud," *LitHub* (January 17, 2019).

48 Klüger, *Still Alive*, 85.

49 The best reproductions of the photos taken of the Izieu school's hidden children appear in *La Colonie des Enfants d'Izieu, 1943–1944* (Paris: Fondation pour la Mémoire de la Shoah, 2012). Also see Serge Klarsfeld, *The Children of Izieu: A Human Tragedy* (New York: Harry N. Abrams, 1984), and Pierre-Jérôme Biscarat, *Les enfants d'Izieu, 6 avril 1944: Un crime contre l'humanité* (Grenoble: Éditions le Dauphiné Libéré, 2003).

50 Katy Hazan, with the participation of Serge Klarsfeld, *Le sauvetage des enfants juifs pendant l'Occupation dans les maisons de l'OSE 1938–1944* (Paris: Somogy, 2008).

51 For Barbie's background, his wartime role as Gestapo chief in Lyon, and the events surrounding his "escape" to Bolivia, deportation to France, and trial, see the brilliant documentary film *Hotel Terminus: The Life and Times of Klaus Barbie*, directed by Marcel Ophuls (1988; Paris: Icarus Films, 2010), DVD.

52 Serge Klarsfeld, ed., *Mémorial de la déportation des enfants juifs en France* (Paris: Arthème Fayard, 2001).

53 Novak made the cover image for Hirsch, *The Generation of Postmemory*. Both of Novak's images are discussed in the book; see 25, 156–60.

54 See Hirsch, *The Generation of Postmemory*, chaps. 4 and 5.

55 Email communication, May 8, 2019.

56 We are grateful to Mirta Kupferminc for her generous elucidation of this image. Email and Skype conversations, Winter 2018/19.

CHAPTER 4: THE "DISOBEDIENT GAZE"

1 Jeanne Zeidler, "A View from the Hampton University Museum," in Patterson, *Carrie Mae Weems*, 77.

2 Fogg and Ramzy, "Interview: Carrie Mae Weems," 78.

3 School advertisement.

4 Ruth Beckermann, ed., *Die Mazzesinsel: Juden in der Wiener Leopoldstadt 1918–1938* (Vienna: Löcker Verlag, 1984).

5 See Marsha L. Rozenblit, *The Jews of Vienna, 1867–1914* (Albany: State University of New York Press, 1983), 122–23.

6 Brett Ashley Kaplan tells the story of adult survivor Leo Glückselig, who recognized himself in one of Boltanski's installations and was shocked to find himself figured as dead. Boltanski is said to have been moved and surprised when Glückselig later contacted him. See Brett Ashley Kaplan, *Unwanted Beauty: Aesthetic Pleasure in Holocaust Representation* (Urbana: University of Illinois Press, 2007), 133. We have now met the grandson of one other boy in the photo, the artist Eduard Freudmann, and the daughter of one of the girls, the scholar Elèna Mortara.

7 For background and testimony about the Dirty War and the *desaparecidos,* see Argentine National Commission on the Disappeared, *Nunca Más: The Report of the Argentine Commission on the Disappeared* (New York: Farrar Straus Giroux, 1986). Also see Diana Taylor, *Disappearing Acts: Spectacles of Gender and Nationalism in Argentina's "Dirty War"* (Durham, NC: Duke University Press, 1997).

8 A detailed German/English-language "photographic essay" cataloging the *Buena Memoria* exhibit prepared for its showing in Hanover, Germany, exists as Sprengel Museum, *Marcelo Brodsky: Buena memoria/Good Memory* (Hanover: Sprengel Museum, 2003). That book is based on the Spanish/English first edition of a catalog of the original Buenos Aires installation, Marcelo Brodsky, *Buena Memoria: Good Memory* (Buenos Aires: Editorial Lamarca, 1997).

9 The term *placeholder* for these memorial photographic icons is Diana Taylor's. See her book *The Archive and the Repertoire* (Durham, NC: Duke University Press, 2003), 161–89, esp. 187.

10 Mariana Graciano, "The Political Effect of Tenderness in *Buena Memoria* by

Marcelo Brodsky," *A Contracorriente: Una revista de estudios latinoamericanos* 14, no. 3 (Spring 2017): 248–66.

11 Quoted in Brodsky, *Buena Memoria.*

12 For a detailed discussion of the memetic power of holding photographs, see Diana Taylor, "The Traumatic Meme," in *Women Mobilizing Memory*, ed. Ayşe Gül Altinay, María José Contreras, Marianne Hirsch, Jean Howard, Banu Karaca, and Alisa Solomon (New York: Columbia University Press, 2019): 113–32.

13 Taylor, "The Traumatic Meme," 114.

14 For an exploration of the Cold War legacies determining current violence in Mexico and the "misrecognition" these links introduce in the current context, see the excellent introductory essay by Andrea Noble, "Introduction: Visual Culture and Violence in Contemporary Mexico," *Journal of Latin American Cultural Studies* 24, no. 4 (2015): 417–33.

SELECTED BIBLIOGRAPHY

Abel, Elizabeth. "Skin, Flesh, and the Affective Wrinkles of Civil Rights Photography." In *Feeling Photography*, edited by Elspeth Brown and Thy Phu, 93–126. Durham, NC: Duke University Press, 2014.

Adams, David Wallace. *Education for Extinction: American Indians and the Boarding School Experience, 1875–1928*. Lawrence: University Press of Kansas, 1995.

Alinder, Jasmine. *Moving Images: Photography and the Japanese American Incarceration*. Urbana: University of Illinois Press, 2009.

Althusser, Louis. "Ideology and Ideological State Apparatuses (Notes towards an Investigation)." In *Lenin and Philosophy and Other Essays*, 143–82. Translated by Ben Brewster. New York: Monthly Review Press, 1971.

Anderson, James D. *The Education of Blacks in the South, 1860–1935*. Chapel Hill: University of North Carolina Press, 1988.

Archuleta, Margaret L., Brenda J. Child, and K. Tsianina Lomawaima, eds. *Away from Home: American Indian Boarding School Experiences, 1879–2000*. Phoenix: Heard Museum, 2000.

Azoulay, Ariella. *The Civil Contract of Photography*. New York: Zone Books, 2008.

———. *Civil Imagination: A Political Ontology of Photography*. Translated by Louise Bethlehem. New York: Verso Books, 2015.

Baer, Ulrich. *Spectral Evidence: The Photography of Trauma*. Cambridge, MA: MIT Press, 2002.

Ball, Eve, with Nora Henn and Lynda A. Sánchez. *Indeh: An Apache Odyssey*. Norman: University of Oklahoma Press, 1988.

Barman, Jean, Yvonne Hébert, and Don McCaskill, eds. *Indian Education in Canada*. Vol. 1: *The Legacy*. Vancouver: University of British Columbia Press, 2007.

Barthes, Roland. *Camera Lucida: Reflections on Photography*. Translated by Richard Howard. New York: Hill and Wang, 1981.

Bartov, Omer, Atina Grossmann, and Molly Nolan, eds. *Crimes of War: Guilt and Denial in the Twentieth Century*. New York: W. W. Norton, 2002.

Batchen, Geoffrey. "Vernacular Photographies." *History of Photography* 24, no. 3 (Autumn 2000): 262–71.

Bear, Jordan, and Kate Palmer Albers, eds. *Before-and-After Photography: Histories and Contexts.* London: Bloomsbury Academic Press, 2017.

Beckermann, Ruth, ed. *Die Mazzesinsel: Juden in der Wiener Leopoldstadt 1918–1938.* Vienna: Löcker Verlag, 1984.

Bell, Genevieve. "Telling Stories Out of School: Remembering the Carlisle Indian Industrial School, 1879–1918." PhD dissertation, Stanford University, 1998.

Benjamin, Walter. "A Little History of Photography." In *Walter Benjamin: Selected Writings.* Vol. 2, part 2: *1931–34.* Translated by Rodney Livingstone et al. Edited by Michael W. Jennings, Howard Eiland, and Gary Smith. Cambridge, MA: Belknap, 1999.

———. "The Work of Art in the Age of Mechanical Reproduction." In *Illuminations: Essays and Reflections,* 217–52. Translated by Harry Zohn. New York: Schocken, 1969.

Bennett, Jill. *Practical Aesthetics: Events, Affects, and Art after 9/11.* London: I. B. Tauris, 2012.

Bensusan, A. D. *Silver Images: History of Photography in Africa.* Cape Town: Howard Timmons, 1966.

Berg, Mary [Miriam Wattenberg]. *The Diary of Mary Berg: Growing Up in the Warsaw Ghetto.* Oxford: Oneworld Publications, 2007.

Bernstein, Michael André. *Foregone Conclusions: Against Apocalyptic History.* Berkeley: University of California Press, 1994.

Biscarat, Pierre-Jérôme. *Les enfants d'Izieu, 6 avril 1944: Un crime contre l'humanité.* Grenoble: Éditions le Dauphiné Libéré, 2003.

Blair, Sara. "About Time: Historical Reading, Historicity, and the Photograph." *PMLA* 125, no. 1 (Winter 2010): 161–71.

Brodsky, Marcelo. *Buena Memoria: Good Memory.* Buenos Aires: Editorial Lamarca, 1997.

Brown, Elspeth H. *The Corporate Eye: Photography and the Rationalization of American Commercial Culture.* Baltimore: Johns Hopkins University Press, 2005.

Brown, Elspeth H., and Thy Phu, eds. *Feeling Photography,* Durham, NC: Duke University Press, 2014.

Calloway, Thomas. "The Negro Exhibit." In *U.S. Commission to the Paris Exposition. Report of the Commissioner-General for the United States to the International Universal Exposition, Paris, 1900, vol. 2.* Washington, DC: Government Printing Office, 1901.

Campt, Tina. *Listening to Images.* Durham, NC: Duke University Press, 2017.

Carney, Robert. "Aboriginal Residential Schools before Confederation: The Early Experience." *Historical Studies: Canadian Catholic Historical Association* 61 (1995), 13–40.

Catalina, Sara. "In the Segregated 20th Century, Black Schoolchildren Embodied Black Uplift." What It Means to Be American: A National Conversation Hosted by the Smithsonian and Arizona State University (website), September 1, 2016. www.whatitmeanstobeamerican.org/artifacts/in-the-segregated-20th-century-schoolchildren-embodied-black-uplift.

Child, Brenda J. *Boarding School Seasons: American Indian Families, 1900–1940.* Lincoln: University of Nebraska Press, 1998.

Coetzee, Linda, Myra Osrin, and Millie Pimstone, eds. *Seeking Refuge: German Jewish Immigration to the Cape in the 1930s.* Cape Town: Cape Town Holocaust Centre, 2003.

Coleman, Michael C. *American Indian Children at School, 1850–1930.* Jackson: University Press of Mississippi, 1993.

Creef, Elena Tajima. *Imagining Japanese America: The Visual Construction of Citizenship, Nation, and the Body.* New York: NYU Press, 2004.

Czerniakow, Adam. *The Warsaw Diary of Adam Czerniakow.* Chicago: Ivan R. Dee, 1999.

czernowitz.ehpes.com website. http://czernowitz.ehpes.com/photos/photosplash.html, accessed July 31, 2018.

Daniels, Roger. "Words Do Matter: A Note on Inappropriate Terminology and the Incarceration of Japanese Americans." In *Nikkei in the Pacific Northwest: Japanese Americans and Japanese Canadians in the Twentieth Century,* edited by Louis Fiset and Gail M. Nomura, 190–214. Seattle: University of Washington Press, 2005.

Dobroszycki, Lucjan, ed. *Chronicle of the Łódź Ghetto.* New Haven, CT: Yale University Press, 1984.

Dunbar, Paul Laurence. "We Wear the Mask." In *The Complete Poems of Paul Laurence Dunbar,* 71. New York: Dodd, Mead and Company, 1922.

Dwórk, Deborah. *Children with a Star: Jewish Youth in Nazi Europe.* New Haven, CT: Yale University Press, 1991.

Dwórk, Deborah, and Robert Jan van Pelt. *Holocaust: A History.* New York: W. W. Norton, 2002.

Engelking, Barbara, and Jacek Leociak. *The Warsaw Ghetto: A Guide to the Perished City.* New Haven, CT: Yale University Press, 2009.

Erdrich, Louise. "Indian Boarding School: The Runaways." In *Original Fire: Selected and New Poems.* New York: HarperCollins, 2003.

Fanon, Frantz. *Black Skin, White Masks.* Translated by Richard Philcox. New York: Grove Press, 2008.

Fogg, Katherine, and Denise Ramzy. "Interview: Carrie Mae Weems." In Patterson, *Carrie Mae Weems*, 78–80.

Fournier, Suzanne, and Ernie Crey. *Stolen from Our Embrace.* Vancouver: Douglas & McIntyre, 1997.

Fredrickson, George M. *White Supremacy: A Comparative Study in American and South African History.* New York: Oxford University Press, 1981.

Freund, Florian, Bertrand Perz, and Karl Stuhlpfarrer. "Das Getto in Litzmannstadt (Lódź)." In *"Unser einziger Weg ist Arbeit": Das Getto in Lódź, 1940–1944*, edited by Hanno Loewy and Gerhard Schoenberner, 17–31. Frankfurt: Löcker Verlag, 1990.

Friedländer, Saul. *Nazi Germany and the Jews.* Vol. 1: *The Years of Persecution, 1933–1939.* New York: HarperCollins, 1997.

———. *Nazi Germany and the Jews.* Vol. 2: *The Years of Extermination, 1939–1945.* New York: HarperCollins, 2007.

Fritz, Henry E. *The Movement for Indian Assimilation, 1860–1890.* Philadelphia: University of Pennsylvania Press, 2017.

Fusco, Coco. "Racial Times, Racial Marks, Racial Metaphors." In *Only Skin Deep: Changing Visions of the American Self*, edited by Coco Fusco and Brian Wallis, 13–50. New York: Harry Abrams, 2003.

Gadamer, Hans-Georg. *Truth and Method.* Translated by Joel Weinsheimer and Donald G. Marshall. New York: Continuum, 1975.

Gay, Peter. *My German Question: Growing Up in Nazi Berlin.* New Haven, CT: Yale University Press, 1998.

Gordon, Linda. *Dorothea Lange: A Life Beyond Limits.* New York: W. W. Norton, 2009.

Gordon, Linda, and Gary Y. Okihiro, eds. *Impounded: Dorothea Lange and the Censored Images of the Japanese American Internment.* New York: W. W. Norton, 2006.

Graciano, Mariana. "The Political Effect of Tenderness in *Buena Memoria* by Marcelo Brodsky." *A Contracorriente: Una revista de estudios latinoamericanos* 14, no. 3 (Spring 2017): 248–66.

Guerin, Frances. *Through Amateur Eyes: Film and Photography in Nazi Germany.* Minneapolis: University of Minnesota Press, 2012.

Gurdon, Meghan Cox. "The Miraculous Power of Reading Aloud." *LitHub*, January 17, 2019.

The Hampton Album: 44 Photographs by Frances B. Johnston from an Album of Hampton Institute, with an introduction and note on the photographer by Lincoln Kirstein. New York: Museum of Modern Art, 1966.

Hartman, Saidiya. "Venus in Two Acts." *small axe* 26 (2008): 1–14.

Hazan, Katy, with the participation of Serge Klarsfeld. *Le sauvetage des enfants juifs pendant l'Occupation dans les maisons de l'OSE 1938–1944.* Paris: Somogy, 2008.

Heberer, Patricia. *Children during the Holocaust.* Lanham, MD: AltaMira Press, 2011.

Heydecker, Joe J. *The Warsaw Ghetto: A Photographic Record, 1941–1944.* London: St. Martins, 1991.

Hirabayashi, Lane Ryo. "Government Photography of the WRA Camps and Resettlement." *Denso Encyclopedia,* n.d. http://encyclopedia.densho.org/Government_photography_of_the_WRA_Camps_and_Resettlement.

Hirabayashi, Lane Ryo, with Kenichiro Shimada. *Japanese American Resettlement through the Lens: Hikaru Carl Iwasaki and the WRA's Photographic Section, 1943–1945.* Denver: University of Colorado Press, 2009.

Hirsch, Julia. *Family Photographs: Content, Meaning, and Effect.* New York: Oxford University Press, 1981.

Hirsch, Marianne. "Ce qui touche à la mémoire." *Esprit,* October 2017: 42–61.

———, ed. *The Familial Gaze.* Hanover, NH: University Press of New England, 1999.

———. *Family Frames: Photography, Narrative, and Postmemory.* Cambridge, MA: Harvard University Press, 1997.

———. *The Generation of Postmemory: Writing and Visual Culture after the Holocaust.* New York: Columbia University Press, 2012.

Hirsch, Marianne, and Leo Spitzer. *Ghosts of Home: The Afterlife of Czernowitz in Jewish Memory.* Berkeley: University of California Press, 2010.

Hodgson, Janet K. H. "A History of Zonnebloem College, 1858–1870: A Study of Church and Society." MA thesis, University of Cape Town, 1975.

Hodgson, Janet K. H., and Theresa Edlmann. *Zonnebloem College and the Genesis of an African Intelligentsia, 1857–1933.* Cape Town: African Lives, 2018.

Honda, Diane Yotsuda, ed. *Our World: Manzanar, California, 1944.* Logan, UT: Herff Jones Yearbook Company, 1998.

hooks, bell. "In Our Glory: Photography and Black Life." In *Art on My Mind: Visual Politics,* 54–64. New York: The New Press, 1995.

———. "The Oppositional Gaze." In *Black Looks: Race and Representation,* 115–32. Boston: South End Press, 1992.

Hoxie, Frederick E. *A Final Promise: The Campaign to Assimilate the Indians, 1880–1920.* Lincoln: University of Nebraska Press, 1984.

Imagining Everyday Life: Engagements with Vernacular Photography. Symposium, the Walther Collection, October 19–20, 2018. www.walthercollection.com/en/new-york/events/symposium.

Jackson, Philip W., ed. *Life in Classrooms.* New York: Holt, Rinehart, and Winston, 1968.

Kaplan, Brett Ashley. *Unwanted Beauty: Aesthetic Pleasure in Holocaust Representation.* Urbana: University of Illinois Press, 2007.

Kassow, Samuel D. *Who Will Write Our History?: Emanuel Ringelblum, the Warsaw Ghetto, and the Oyneg Shabes Archive*. Bloomington: University of Indiana Press, 2007.

Katz, Jacob. *Out of the Ghetto: The Social Background of Jewish Emancipation, 1770–1870*. Syracuse, NY: Syracuse University Press, 1998.

Klarsfeld, Serge. *The Children of Izieu: A Human Tragedy*. New York: Harry N. Abrams,1984.

———, ed. *Mémorial de la déportation des enfants juifs en France*. Paris: Arthème Fayard, 2001.

Klüger, Ruth. *Still Alive: A Holocaust Girlhood Remembered*. New York: Feminist Press at the City University of New York, 2001.

Koselleck, Reinhart. *Futures Past: On the Semantics of Historical Time*. Translated by Keith Tribe. New York: Columbia University Press, 2004.

Kothemidova, Christina. "Why We Say 'Cheese': Producing the Smile in Snapshot Photography." *Critical Studies in Media Communication* 22, no. 1 (2005): 2–25.

La Colonie des Enfants d'Izieu, 1943–1944. Paris: Fondation pour la Mémoire de la Shoah, 2012.

La Flesche, Francis. *The Middle Five: Indian Schoolboys of the Omaha Tribe*. 1900. Reprint, Lincoln: University of Nebraska Press, 1963.

Lévy-Hass, Hanna. *Diary of Bergen-Belsen*. Translated by Sophie Hand. Chicago: Haymarket Books, 2009.

Lewin, Abraham. *A Cup of Tears: A Diary of the Warsaw Ghetto*. Edited by Antony Polonsky, translated by Christopher Hutton. Oxford: Basil Blackwell, 1988.

Lewis, David Levering. "A Small Nation of People: W. E. B. Du Bois and Black Americans at the Turn of the Twentieth Century." In *A Small Nation of People: W. E. B. Du Bois and African American Portraits of Progress*. New York: Amistad, 2003.

Lifton, Robert Jay. *Death in Life: Survivors of Hiroshima*. Chapel Hill: University of North Carolina Press, 1991.

Lindsey, Donal. *Indians at Hampton Institute, 1877–1923*. Urbana: University of Illinois Press, 1995.

Lomowaima, K. Tsianina. *They Called It Prairie Light: The Story of Chilocco Indian School*. Lincoln: University of Nebraska Press, 1994.

Löw, Andrea. *Juden im Getto Litzmannstadt*. Göttingen: Wallstein Verlag, 2010.

Margolis, Eric. "Class Pictures: Representations of Race, Gender, and Ability in a Century of School Photography." *Visual Sociology* 14 (1999): 7–38.

———. "Looking at Discipline, Looking at Labour: Photographic Representations of Indian Boarding Schools." *Visual Studies* 19, no. 1 (2004): 72–96.

Marien, Mary Warner. *Photography: A Cultural History*, 4th ed. London: Laurence King, 2015.

Marks, Laura. *Touch: Sensuous Theory and Multisensory Media*. Minneapolis: University of Minnesota Press, 2002.

Marr, Carolyn J. "Assimilation through Education." In Hibulb Cultural Center, *Between Two Worlds: Experiences at the Tulalip Indian Boarding School*, www.hibulbculturalcenter.org/assets/pdf/Between-Two-Worlds.pdf. Accessed July 31, 2018.

———. "Assimilation through Education: Indian Boarding Schools in the Pacific Northwest." University of Washington Digital Collections, American Indians of the Pacific Northwest Collection. N.d. https://content.lib.washington.edu/aipnw/marr.html, accessed May 19, 2019.

Matsumoto, Nancy. "Reclaiming Photographs of WWII Japanese American Resettlement." Discover Nikkei: Japanese Migrants and Their Descendants (website), November 16, 2009 www.discovernikkei.org/en/journal/2009/11/16/reclaiming-photographs.

Mauro, Hayes Peter. *The Art of Americanization at the Carlisle Indian School*. Albuquerque: University of New Mexico Press, 2011.

Maynes, Mary Jo. *Schooling for the People: Comparative Local Studies of Schooling History in France and Germany, 1750–1850*. New York: Holmes and Meier, 1985.

———. *Schooling in Western Europe: A Social History*. Albany: State University of New York Press, 1985.

McClintock, Anne. *Imperial Leather: Race, Gender, and Sexuality in the Colonial Context*. New York: Routledge, 1995.

McCluskey, Audrey Thomas. "Ringing Up a School: Mary McLeod Bethune's Impact on Daytona." *Florida Historical Quarterly* 73, no. 2 (October 1994), 200–217.

Miller, J. R. *Shingwauk's Vision: A History of Native Residential Schools*. Toronto: University of Toronto Press, 1996.

Milloy, John S. *A National Crime: The Canadian Government and the Residential School System, 1879 to 1986*. Winnipeg: University of Manitoba Press, 1999.

Museum of Family History (website). http://www.museumoffamilyhistory.com/.

Newhall, Beaumont. *The History of Photography from 1839 to the Present*. New York: Museum of Modern Art, 2009.

Noble, Andrea. "Introduction: Visual Culture and Violence in Contemporary Mexico." *Journal of Latin American Cultural Studies* 24, no. 4 (2015): 417–33.

Novak, Lorie. *Collected Visions* (digital collection). http://cvisions.cat.nyu.edu.

Noy, Orly. "Demolishing Palestinian Schools 'a Quiet Population Transfer.'" +972

Magazine, January 24, 2018. https://972mag.com/demolishing-palestinian-schools
-a-quiet-population-transfer/132662/.

Okubo, Miné. *Citizen 13660*. Seattle: University of Washington Press, 2014.

Ophuls, Marcel, dir. *Hotel Terminus: The Life and Times of Klaus Barbie*. 1988; Paris:
Icarus Films, 2010. DVD.

Patterson, Vivian, ed. *Carrie Mae Weems: The Hampton Project*. New York: Aperture
and the Williams College Museum, 2000.

Pätzold, Kurt, and Erika Schwarz. *Tagesordnung Judenmord: Die Wannsee-Konferenz
am 20. Januar 1942*. Berlin: Metropol, 1992.

Pearce, Roy Harvey. *The Savages of America: The Study of the Indian and the Idea of
Civilization*. Baltimore: Johns Hopkins University Press, 1965.

Picturing Change: The Impact of Ledger Drawings on Native American Art. Exhibition at the Hood Museum of Art, Dartmouth College, December 11, 2004–May 15,
2005). https:hoodmuseum.dartmouth.edu/

Plante, Lisa Anne. "Transformation and Resistance: Schooling Efforts for Jewish Children and Youth in Hiding, Ghettos, and Camps." In *Children and the Holocaust:
Symposium Presentation of the Center for Advanced Holocaust Studies*. Washington, DC: US Holocaust Memorial Museum, 2004.

———. "'We Didn't Miss a Day': A History in Narratives of Schooling Efforts for Jewish
Children and Youths in German-Occupied Europe." Doctor of Education dissertation, University of Tennessee, Knoxville, 2000.

Pratt, Richard H. "The Advantages of Mingling Indians with Whites." *Proceedings of
the National Conference of Charities and Correction* (1892) and *Proceedings and
Addresses of the National Education Association* (1895), 761–62.

Presser, Bram. *The Book of Dirt*. Melbourne: Text Publishing Company, 2017.

Quashie, Kevin. *The Sovereignty of Quiet: Beyond Resistance in Black Culture*. New
Brunswick, NJ: Rutgers University Press, 2012.

Raiford, Leigh. *Imprisoned in a Luminous Glare: Photography in the African American Freedom Struggle*. Chapel Hill: University of North Carolina Press, 2013.

Rifkin, Mark. *Beyond Settler Time: Temporal Sovereignty and Indigenous Self-
Determination*. Durham, NC: Duke University Press, 2017.

Romer, Grant B., and Brian Wallis, eds. *Young America: The Daguerreotypes of Southworth & Hawes*. New York: International Center of Photography, 2005.

Rosaldo, Renato. *Culture and Truth: The Remaking of Social Analysis*. Boston: Beacon
Press, 1993.

Rose, Gillian. *Doing Family Photography*. London: Routledge, 2016.

Rosenblum, Naomi. *A World History of Photography*, 4th ed. New York: Abbeville
Press, 2007.

Rozenblit, Marsha L. *The Jews of Vienna, 1867–1914*. Albany: State University of New York Press, 1983.

Satrapi, Marjane. *Persepolis: The Story of a Childhood*. New York: Pantheon Books, 2003.

Scharf, Rafael, and Willy Georg. *In the Warsaw Ghetto: Summer 1941*. New York: Aperture, 1993.

Sekula, Allen. "The Body and the Archive." *October* 39 (Winter 1986): 3–64.

Smith, Shawn Michelle. *American Archives: Gender, Race, and Class in Visual Culture*. Princeton: Princeton University Press, 1999.

Smith, Shawn Michelle, and Sharon Sliwinski, eds. *Photography and the Optical Unconscious*. Durham, NC: Duke University Press, 2017.

Sontag, Susan. *On Photography*. New York: Farrar, Straus & Giroux, 1977.

Spence, Jo, and Patricia Holland. *Family Snaps: The Meanings of Domestic Photography*. London: Virago, 1991.

Spitzer, Leo. *The Creoles of Sierra Leone: Responses to Colonialism, 1870–1945*. Madison: University of Wisconsin Press, 1974.

———. *Hotel Bolivia: The Culture of Memory in a Refuge from Nazism*. New York: Hill and Wang, 2000.

———. *Lives In Between: Assimilation and Marginality in Austria, Brazil, and West Africa, 1780–1945*. Studies in Comparative World History. New York: Hill and Wang, 1999.

———. "The Mosquito and Segregation in Sierra Leone." *Canadian Journal of African Studies* 2, no.1 (Spring 1968): 49–61.

———. "A Name Given, a Name Taken: Camouflaging, Resistance, and Diasporic Social Identity." *Comparative Studies of South Asia, Africa, and the Middle East* 30, no. 1 (2010), 21–31.

Stockton, Katherine Bond. *The Queer Child, or Growing Sideways in the Twentieth Century*. Durham, NC: Duke University, 2009.

Stoler, Ann Laura. *Along the Archival Grain: Epistemic Anxieties and Colonial Common Sense*. Princeton: Princeton University Press, 2009.

Stone, Lawrence, ed. *Schooling and Society: Studies in the History of Education*. Baltimore: Johns Hopkins University Press, 1976.

Strathman, Nicole. "Student Snapshots: An Alternative Approach to the Visual History of American Indian Boarding Schools." *Humanities* 4, no. 4 (2015): 726–47.

Struk, Janina. *Photographing the Holocaust*. London: I. B. Taurus, 2004.

Tagg, John. *The Burden of Representation: Essays on Photographies and Histories*. Amherst: University of Massachusetts Press, 1988.

Taylor, Diana. *The Archive and the Repertoire.* Durham, NC: Duke University Press, 2003.

———. *Disappearing Acts: Spectacles of Gender and Nationalism in Argentina's "Dirty War."* Durham, NC: Duke University Press, 1997.

———. "The Traumatic Meme." In *Women Mobilizing Memory*, edited by Ayşe Gül Altinay, María José Contreras, Marianne Hirsch, Jean Howard, Banu Karaca, and Alisa Solomon. New York: Columbia University Press, 2019.

Tec, Nechama. "Jewish Children: Between Protectors and Murderers." Occasional Papers. Washington, DC: United States Holocaust Memorial Museum, Center for Advanced Holocaust Studies, April 2005.

Tencer-Szurmeij, Golda, and Anna Bikont, eds. *And I Still See Their Faces: Images of Polish Jews.* Warsaw: Shalom Foundation, 1998.

Tory, Avraham. *Surviving the Holocaust: The Kovno Ghetto Diary.* Cambridge, MA: Harvard University Press, 1991.

Trafzer, Clifford E., Jean A. Keller, and Lorene Sisquoc, eds. *Boarding School Blues: Revisiting American Indian Educational Experiences.* Indigenous Education Series. Lincoln: University of Nebraska Press, 2006.

Truth and Reconciliation Commission of Canada. *Canada's Residential Schools: The Final Report of the Truth and Reconciliation Commission of Canada.* Winnipeg: Truth and Reconciliation Commission, 2015.

———. *They Came for the Children: Canada, Aboriginal Peoples, and the Residential Schools.* Winnipeg: Truth and Reconciliation Commission, 2012.

"Unser einziger Weg ist Arbeit": *Das Getto in Łódź 1940–1944. Eine Ausstellung des Jüdisches Museums Frankfurt am Main.* Wien: Löcker, 1990.

van Alphen, Ernst. *Art in Mind.* Chicago: University of Chicago Press, 2005.

———. *Caught by History: Holocaust Effects in Contemporary Art, Literature, and Theory.* Palo Alto, CA: Stanford University Press, 1997.

Viditz-Ward, Vera. "Photography in Sierra Leone, 1850–1918." *Africa* 57, no. 4 (1987): 512–13.

Walker, Lucy, dir. *Wasteland.* London: Almega Projects, 2009. 99 mins. DVD.

———. "Photography and Liquid Intelligence" (1989). In *Jeff Wall: Selected Essays and Interviews*, 109–11. New York: Museum of Modern Art, 2007.

Wallace, Maurice O., and Shawn Michelle Smith, eds. *Pictures and Progress: Early Photography and the Making of African American Identity.* Durham, NC: Duke University Press, 2012.

Warburg, Aby. "Einleitung zum Mnemosyne-Atlas." Excerpted in *The Treasure Chests of Mnemosyne*, edited Uwe Fleckner, 248–52. Dresden: Verlag der Kunst, 1998.

Weiner, Rebecca. "Virtual Jewish World: Prague." *Jewish Virtual Library: A Product of AICE* (website), n.d. www.jewishvirtuallibrary.org/prague, accessed June 31, 2018.

Wexler, Laura. *Tender Violence: Domestic Visions in an Age of U.S. Imperialism.* Chapel Hill: University of North Carolina Press, 2000.

Willis, Deborah. *Picturing Us: African American Identity in Photography.* New York: The New Press, 1996.

Willis, Deborah, and Barbara Krauthamer. *Envisioning Emancipation: Black Americans and the End of Slavery.* Philadelphia: Temple University Press, 2013.

Wilson, George S. "How Shall the American Savage Be Civilized." *Atlantic Monthly* 50 (November 1882): 596–606.

Witmer, Linda F. *The Indian Industrial School: Carlisle, Pennsylvania, 1879–1918.* Carlisle: Cumberland County Historical Society, 1879–1918.

Yad Vashem: The World Holocaust Remembrance Center. "Vilna during the Holocaust: Daily Life in the Vilna Ghetto: Children in the Ghetto." n.d. www.yadvashem.org/yv/en/exhibitions/vilna/during/children.asp, accessed July 31, 2018.

Zitkala-Ša. *American Indian Stories.* Washington, DC: Hayworth, 1921. Reprint, Lincoln: University of Nebraska Press, 1985.

Hodgson, Janet, 66

Hoffmann, Leo, 126

Hoffmann Gymnasium (Lyceum), 126–28

Holocaust: Bolivia and, 5–6; Boltanski, Christian, and, 10–12; Izieu, France, and, 158–66, *160–61*; Jewish forced labor and, 136, 138; schooling during, 136–42; survival rates and, 136, 201n10; teachers and, 141–42. *See also* Jewish ghettos; Jews; Nazis

Holocaust effect, 10

Home for Working and Destitute Lads in England, 81

homosexuality, 39–41

Hong, Christine, 113

Honouring: Project of Heart / Speaking to Memory (exhibit), 96

hooks, bell, 99, 102

Hotel Bolivia (Spitzer), 5

I

ideology: education and, 49, 52–55, 60–61, 69–71, 77–78, 90, 119–20, 132, 143, 161, 177; photography and, 12, 16–21, 26–27, 31–36, 119–20, 132, 143, 161, 177. *See also* schooling

imperialism: imperialist nostalgia and, 83; photography and, 60–67; schooling and, 49–51; Sierra Leone and, 61

Imprisoned in a Luminous Glare: Photography in the African American Freedom Struggle (Raiford), 116

"Indian Boarding School: The Runaways" (Erdrich), 76

individuality, 33–36

Indoctrination #3 (Deo), 120–23, *122*

institutional gaze, 33–36, 47–48, 69–71

institutional memory culture, 171

integration, 51–53

Iranian Islamist Revolution, 34

Iwasaki, Hikaru Carl, 112

Iwata, Jack, 112

Izieu, France, 158–66, *160–61*

J

Jablonsky, Dariusz, 149

Japanese Americans, 7, 8, 104–15, 199n75

Jewish ghettos: assimilationism and, 41; Bedzin (Poland), 154–55, *157*; clandestine photography in, 149–54; ghetto tourism and, 143; Kovno (Lithuania), 7, *8*, 138, 150, 154, *155*; Lódz (Poland), 7, *8*, 134–37, 144–48, *145–47*, 153, 167–69, *plate 9*, *plate 10*, *plate 11*; Lublin (Poland), 140–41, 203n25; Mielec (Poland), 152, *152–53*; *Oyneg Shabes* and, 139; photos taken in, 7, *8*, 15, *133*; propaganda photography and, 142–49, *145–47*; schooling in, 133–36, 149–58; teachers and, 141–42; Terezín (Czechoslovakia), 140; Vilna (Lithuania), 138; Warsaw, 137, *137–41*, 143, 154–55, *156*, *157*; Zionism and, 156

Jews: *And I Still See Their Faces* (Tencer-Surmiej) and, 57–59; assimilation and, 19, 54, 56, 57, 135, 132; Austro-Habsburg Empire and, 52–57; deportation of, 127; emancipation of, 52–54, 128; forced labor and, 136, 138; Izieu, France and, 158–66, *160–61*; Museum of an Extinct Race and, 144, 204n36; Nazi propaganda and, 134–35, 142–49, *145–47*; as refugees, 3–6, *4*; religious freedom and, 54; Romania and, 127–28; school integration and, 128–32; Star of David and, 7, *7*, 133, *133–36*, *135*, 146; subordi-